The High Sheriff:
John Perry McDaniel III

Author R. L. Dodson

An Authorized Biography

The High Sheriff:
John Perry McDaniel III

Author R. L. Dodson

Editor:
Jeff LaFerney

DEEP SOUTH PUBLICATIONS

ISBN-13: 978-0998746005
ISBN-10: 0998746002
Library of Congress Control Number: 2017902860

CONTENTS

Maps of Jackson County, Florida

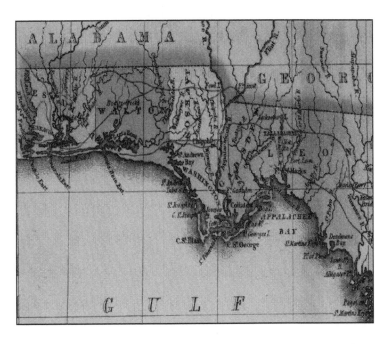

1827 Historical Map

Jackson County was created in 1822. It was named for Andrew Jackson, general in the War of 1812, first territorial governor of Florida, and seventh President of the United States of America, who served from 1829 to 1837.
Jackson County is a county located in the U.S. state of Florida. As of the July 1, 2015 United States Census Bureau, the estimated population was 48,599. Its county seat is Marianna. The county has a total area of 955 square miles, of which 918 square miles is land and 37 square miles is water. Jackson County is the only county in Florida that borders both Georgia and Alabama. The county is known for its true southern charm.

"The following are things I have tried to live by and instill in my employees:

Let no victims ghost rest until we have done our best.
Work today just like tomorrow was election day.
The job of law enforcement is to take away from the problem, not add to it.
If it is important enough for a citizen to call us, you will call the citizens back.
The sheriff's job is to be everything to everybody."

J1 ~ John P. McDaniel

Current Map of Florida

Jackson County

EPIGRAPH

"Biographies are but the clothes and buttons of the man. The biography of the man himself cannot be written."

Mark Twain

"All things are possible to him who believes." [Mark 9:23]

Bible

"Be true to your work, your word, and your friend."

Henry David Thoreau

"Success is not final; failure is not fatal: it is the courage to continue that counts."

Winston Churchill

PREFACE

His Christian name is John Perry McDaniel III, but his family and friends fondly refer to him as "Johnny Mac" or simply "Sheriff."

He is a straight-forward, honest man of reason, passion, compassion, and unwavering faith in God. When I began writing this book several years ago, I did so because I considered the events which made the McDaniel Administration a long-standing success to be of historical significance to Jackson County, Florida. I came to realize that tucked away in Johnny Mac's recollections, reminiscences, and remembrances are not only the unique and intriguing stories of his life, but a living anecdotal history of Jackson County, Florida, during some turbulent times.

No greater honor could be bestowed upon me than to author a biography for the man who paid the ultimate sacrifice while serving as sheriff of Jackson County for almost three decades.

His commitment to the people of Jackson County has remained unwaveringly vigil in the face of his own personal pain, losses, and suffering. He always served with integrity and honor. His greatest joys came in being able to help those in need.

John P. McDaniel III was elected to the office of sheriff in 1980. Mere weeks before he took office, his father was senselessly murdered by serial killers.

He retired 28 years later, on November 4, 2008, on the heels of his wife's brutal murder.

His tenure as sheriff began and ended in tragedy, but his faith in God remained uncompromised.

This book will present Johnny's multi-faceted life— from the times of his earliest childhood memories, youthful escapades, high school football rivalries, military service, marriage, children, murdered loved ones, law enforcement career, and ultimately his transition and adjustment to retirement.

The High Sheriff gives you an up-close and personal account of the life of John Perry McDaniel III.

I hope through the pages contained in this book, you will come to know and appreciate Johnny Mac as I do. He is an unforgettable character—a child, son, father, husband, friend, survivor, and the man behind the badge. He is a throwback to the days when a handshake was all that was needed to finalize a deal—a self-made, God-fearing man of courage. I am proud to call him my friend.

CHAPTER 1
Roots Run Deep

It was a mild summer day back on June 14, 1936, when Reverend Chester Pelt arrived at the Bascom, Florida, home of John Perry McDaniel. On this day, Reverend Pelt traveled dusty dirt roads to perform wedding vows for John Perry McDaniel Jr. and Marjorie Ruth Grant McDaniel. Five days after John Jr. turned twenty years old, he married his seventeen-year-old blushing young bride, Ruth. John Jr. worked for Lehigh in Marianna, building furniture. He worked hard, searching for advancement opportunities as he had big plans for their future.

Two sets of proud parents—Lessie Watford McDaniel with John Perry McDaniel and Laura Belle Davis Grant with James William Grant—lovingly blessed the union.

Ruth would have their first child, Iris Iden McDaniel, on June 3, 1937—the first of three children born of this marriage.

A cold October afternoon in 1940 would prove to be another very special day for Marjorie Ruth McDaniel. On that Wednesday afternoon at 3:00 p.m., she gave birth to a ten pound, black-haired, blue-eyed baby boy named John Perry McDaniel III.

John was born in his Granddaddy McDaniel's old house in Bascom, Florida. This was the very same white clapboard house where his momma and daddy said their "I do's" some four years earlier. When it came time for Ruth to deliver the baby, they carried her up to Grandma McDaniel's house as she was going to help the midwife with the birth.

Hattie Brinson, the midwife, was always Grandma McDaniel's helper in giving birth to babies and that sort

1

of stuff. Hattie was no Prissy from *Gone with the Wind* type lady. Mrs. Hattie knew about birthing babies. Sure enough, always in a hurry, Little Johnny came before the doctor got there.

Dr. C. H. Ryals had a place in Dellwood a few miles up the road. He came by after the birth. On October 9, 1940, Johnny came screaming into the world in the front bedroom of an old, wooden farmhouse in Bascom, Florida. Dr. Ryals cleared his throat and announced, "Well, Ruth, you got a boy. He's got two balls and a bat, so you got yourself a boy."

It cost her $8 for him to tell her she had a healthy baby boy. On October 18, 1940, at a big nine days old, Grandmother and Granddaddy Grant came and got Little Johnny and his mom and took them back home to live with Daddy. Friends and family stopped by and visited over the next few weeks, bringing gifts of diapers, blankets, rubber pants, sweaters, rattlers, gowns, socks, bibs, and booties. Grandmother Laura Belle contributed to Johnnie's financial future with his first twenty cents.

Little Johnny was taking steps by eight months and walking all over the place by the time he was nine months old. Big sis, Iris, had a real live "baby doll" to dress up and teach to talk. His first words were "Mama" and "Dadtie" followed closely by "Sistie," "Ainey," and "moo-o-cow."

CHAPTER 2

From Oakdale to Oakdale:
1943-1945

When John Perry McDaniel III was about three years old, his daddy, John Jr., left Lehigh Furniture in order to make a little more money. He went to work at the Coca-Cola plant as a mixer of the ingredients. He worked for Mr. Charlton King who owned the Coca-Cola business in Marianna, Florida.

A better job opportunity gave John Jr. the chance to move to Oakdale, Pennsylvania, which is a borough in Allegheny County, a suburb of Pittsburgh with a total area of 0.5 square miles. In the early 1940's, the population was 1,766.

He went up there and found a place for the family to live and came back and got Ruth, Iris, and John III. The family moved north from Oakdale, Florida, to Oakdale, Pennsylvania, fifteen hours or 922 miles away from family, friends, and everything John and Ruth knew as home. The McDaniels met a family in Oakdale by the name of Brud Quein. The Quein family had three boys, all older than John III, who was four-years-old, and Iris who was seven.

In December of 1944, snowfall hit 27.3 inches in Oakdale, Pennsylvania. The wind whispered as thousands and thousands of small white ice crystals fell like confetti, covering the ground in a thick blanket of white. Little John had never seen snow. The Quein brothers pulled out their box sled, taking turns pushing and riding Little John up and down the hill.

The crisp, clean, cold air was filled with squeals of laughter as the brothers spent hours speeding to the bottom of the slope and pulling John back up, and away they would go again.

3

There was a lady by the name of Madge who owned a doughnut/coffee shop in downtown Oakdale. It was a real treat on Sundays for John's daddy to take him down to Madge's shop and get doughnuts for the family. Smells of just-cooked dough, sugary confections, and fresh-brewed coffees streamed out onto the street as the tiny bells on the door of the shop gently tinkled, alerting Madge she had customers. Little John would press his face up to the doughnut display counter where it seemed hundreds of doughnuts lay warming under a lamp. It was the highlight of his life at that time; being raised in the country, he had never seen a doughnut before.

In early 1945, the McDaniel family left Oakdale, Pennsylvania, and came back to Jackson County, Florida. They settled in a house that little John's daddy, Granddaddy McDaniel, and Granddaddy Grant all built down by the Interstate near Blountstown Highway, a little community called Oakdale below a place called Magnolia. So the family returned from Oakdale, Pennsylvania, to the little community of Oakdale in Jackson County Florida.

The home sat where the westbound lane of the Interstate came through years later. If the house still remained, the Interstate would have run right over it. It was a little three-bedroom house with one bathroom, a kitchen, and a dining room. That was it. That small frame structure built by hand with lots of love was a place little John III called home.

Shortly after the family returned home to Oakdale, Little John was playing in the dirt yard when his daddy quickly picked him up and put him up on his shoulders and ran toward the field. A plane from Marianna Airbase had crashed in the field behind their home. John rode on his daddy's shoulders as he ran out to the plane.

His daddy sat him down on the ground and took an old axe to cut the canopy open and get the pilot out of the plane.

John Jr., Ruth, Iris, and Little Johnny had been home for about six months when they welcomed a new member to the family. On July 15, 1945, William Wayne McDaniel arrived in the world. Iris now had another "live baby doll," and Little Johnny was more than ready to teach his little brother everything he had learned in all of his five years of living.

CHAPTER 3
Slamming Screen Door

E arly one September Sunday morning in 1945 after
Wayne was born, Little John III's parents were
fussing in the kitchen. His brother, Wayne, was
just a baby. The arguing between John Jr. and Ruth
continued for quite a while.

The sounds of their parents' fussing woke all the
children. Little John sat on the couch with Wayne in
his lap, giving him a bottle. John's daddy walked by
the couch, looked down, and said, "I'll see ya later, boy."

Out the door he went. The screen door slammed as
John Jr. went out the door and walked across the street. A
flood of tears rolled down Little John's cheeks as he
stared after his daddy's retreating figure. Little John
continued to cry as he watched his Daddy start hitch-
hiking until he caught a ride into town and out of his life
for years to come. Little John III didn't remember seeing
his daddy again until around 1954 when he would turn
fifteen years old.

John Jr. didn't take care of the financial needs of his
children. Ruth McDaniel had to be the mother, father, and
bread winner for her three children. This meant she had
to find a job.

John III's granddaddy (his mother's father) was J.W.
Grant. J.W. lived next door to them and had a little
country store, J.W. Grant's Country Store. In early 1946,
Granddaddy Grant had bought the old grocery store from
Claude Medlock. The small block store covered with a tin
roof sat on Hwy 71 South of Marianna where the I-10 on-
ramp is today across from Ruby Tuesday's. Under the
porch entrance area sat old, wooden rockers and a bench
just to the side. You would often see patrons hanging out
front drinking RC Colas, eating moon pies, and sharing

the happenings of the day. RC Colas were a nickel, and a large moon pie was also a nickel. Growing up in the Deep South, you knew the ten-cent southern tradition well. J.W. and Laura Belle Grant would let the family have groceries on credit so they could at least eat and never go hungry.

Ruth finally got a job at Department of Labor, with the Florida State Unemployment Compensation. She would work there for the next 33 years.

On a bitterly cold winter night, shortly after John Jr. left the family, things got really tough. Their mother, Ruth, sat on the large, worn couch, crying. John III was a small child of six, his older sister Iris was nine, and Wayne was almost six months old. The three children huddled around her like little bitties, wanting to know what was going on. Little John reached up and brushed his mom's tears away, patting her on the cheek saying, "It'll be okay; it'll be okay, Momma."

Momma Ruth had her check from the State of Florida in one hand and bills from the grocery store in the other hand. She only made $120.00 a month, drawing $98.00 after tax and insurance deductions.

The grocery bill was $98.00, and she sat there crying, not knowing how they were going to make it, but they kept going and going, never giving up.

They never went hungry, never starved, and never went on welfare. The McDaniel family didn't have a television or telephone; they had nothing really and truly but each other.

There were many hard times for the McDaniel family. At one time, John III wanted to join the 4-H Club. For one of the projects, he had gotten himself a pig. He paid five dollars for him. That was going to be his project. The only way we could feed him was to let him graze down where Grandma's cows grazed.

Grandma milked cows and furnished the family with milk, cream, and butter. Little John would buy Jim Dandy hog feed in big old sacks and mix it with water and feed that hog. His 4-H Club Project was coming along really well, but that grocery bill was coming along even better.

So as it worked out, that pig got to be a pretty good-sized hog, and granddaddy had to sell it to pay the grocery bill because Little John had been charging the hog feed on the grocery bill. That was just the way of life.

Johnny's Granddaddy Grant and Grandma Grant were always there for him. Her name was Laura Bell. They basically were responsible for the children being fed and being taken care of. Momma Ruth had to work for a living. Johnny recalled, "There was nobody to take care of us young'uns so we had to take care of ourselves under the supervision of Grandma Grant and Granddaddy Grant."

Johnny worked around the old store there for a Coca-Cola and a pack of peanuts. Granddaddy Grant would let Johnny work doing things he wanted done around the old store. Grandma McDaniel and Grandma Grant would make the children's clothes. Little Johnny wore those big-collared, square shirts and pants that had been altered. Granddaddy Mac had a shoe ad, he used to fix shoes. Johnny remembered, "Granddaddy would drill a hole in the shoe and take bailing wire and tie the sole to the upper part of the shoe so the grandchildren could continue wearing those old shoes."

They didn't have clothes except hand-me-downs and homemade. Of course, everybody else was in the same shape, so nobody knew who was poor.

Grandma Grant had an old wringer type washing machine; it was in the back room of that store. The old floor would get wet and every once in a while, it would shock the pure daylights out of you. How it didn't kill them, God only knows. They would take those clothes out of the agitator. One of them would push them through the wringer, and the other one would pull them out on the other side. They would rinse the clothes, Johnny and his sister Iris.

Dallas Malloy owned the property behind them, and they would hang their clothes on those old barbed wire fences so the wind wouldn't blow them off into the pasture. Iris and Little Johnny did all the laundry. Wayne was too little to do anything.

Johnny recollected, "Grandma Grant saw to it we were fed and went to school. We caught the bus there. When we got in from school, Grandma would have us a little something left over from lunch on the table."

Grandma Grant and women from the church had a big frame they worked and quilted on. The young'uns weren't allowed in the house when they were quilting. Every now and then, Little Johnny would run through and scoot under the quilt they were making. Grandma Grant would take her quilting needle and stick him in the butt, saying "Boy, I told you to get out of here."

During those times, they didn't have grass in the yards. They used stick brooms to sweep the dirt. The property had an old, white picket fence that surrounded the house. The gate had an old weight on it to keep it closed. There was one pecan tree in the front and a huge oak tree on the side. Chinaberry trees and persimmon trees in the back yard provided much entertainment for the children to climb.

CHAPTER 4
A Child of the Depression:
Early 1940's

The 1940's-1950's was a hard time, but the McDaniel's made it through the rough times together as a family. The Depression still heavily impacted the area. New Deal programs were still in the works in the early 1940s. The thirty-bed Jackson Hospital was not completed until December of 1941 (officially opened in January of 1942 with Dr. D. A. McKinnon as Chief of Staff). Work would still continue on the airport at that time. Jackson County Sheriff W. L. Watford died in office in 1941 and was succeeded by W. Barkley Gause.

A world-changing event occurred on Sunday, December 7, 1941, when the Japanese bombed Pearl Harbor. The struggling nation sprang into action and emerged as an industrial giant. Citizens of Jackson County flooded the armed forces and initiated strong defense efforts at home.

The expanded role of aircraft in the Military turned the focus again to the Marianna Airfield which had never been completed. In April of 1942, Senator Claude Pepper announced that an air base would be constructed at the Marianna Airfield cite at a cost of more than $5 million. Jackson County residents were ecstatic.

The influx of soldiers caused problems. By mid-1943, there were numerous noise complaints regarding "Juke Joints." By early 1944, the Marianna Police Department and Sheriff Barkley Gause had arrested sixty prostitutes.

Marianna followed suit with other surrounding agencies by implementing the "Work or Fight" ordinance which permitted the arrest of "any person found idling,

11

loitering, or loafing upon the streets of the City of Marianna."

The shortage of farm labor created a problem in Jackson County. In the latter part of 1943, a new source of labor was discovered. During the harvest seasons of 1944 and 1945, approximately 500 prisoners were transported to locations throughout the county to work.

In 1943, an important change occurred regarding the role of Jackson County African Americans. The Jackson County Commission—composed of Curtis Jackson, J. B. Garrett, George Lawrence, J. K. Powell, and J. W. Grant (grandfather of John P. McDaniel III)—decided on their own initiative to prepare new jury lists for 1943 to include the names of blacks. The commission felt that the conviction of blacks by all white juries wasn't fair and could lead to reversals by the appellate courts. The *Floridan* reported that for the first time in the memory of Jackson County citizens, blacks were summoned for jury duty in the circuit court in May, 1943.

Local radio stations and newspapers filled with celebratory news when Germany surrendered in the spring and even more elation when the Japanese followed suit in the fall of 1945. Jackson County emerged from the war years with a population of 34,509.

The McDaniels were part of a loving and giving community who treated everyone equally. People didn't know who was rich and who was poor because nobody had anything.

CHAPTER 5

Big Move to Indoor Plumbing
(of a Kind):
1946-1948

Somewhere between 1946 and 1948, Momma Ruth bought the big house from John's grandmamma and granddaddy which had more room. It was a bigger house for all the young'uns. She rented out the small house that Johnny's daddy had built for them. Ruth and John Jr's divorce became final between 1947-'48. He was traveling the world. Ruth and the children had no idea where he was during that time.

They moved from the first house they had when Granddaddy sold them his old two-story house he had which was next to the store. It was a great big, old house with floors made from 1 x 6 boards. John shivered recalling. "Honest to goodness, wind would come up through the cracks of that house and freeze you to death. We had a fireplace; it was double-faced and opened with one side in the bedroom and the other to the living room. You fired it from one side and that was what was used for heat. There was a shower in the big ole bathroom. The shower was something that granddaddy had made. You turned the water on and a can was what the water came through....Water would go everywhere. If it was cold, you just took a cold shower. We didn't have hot water. As years went on, it got better."

The big house had an upstairs. Johnny's sister, Iris, lived in the attic. Off the side porch, John had a room, and his little brother, Wayne, had a bedroom next to Momma Ruth.

Momma Ruth cooked on a kerosene stove with three eyes. Johnny recalled, "The stove had an oven which wasn't worth a flip for cooking."

13

There was a sink and an icebox but no refrigerator. An icebox was a small, compact non-mechanical version of a refrigerator. Johnny reminisced about it. "A fellow named Mr. Bowden from Altha, Florida, would go to the ice house and come to your home to deliver chunks of ice. Momma Ruth would order enough to keep milk and perishable items cold. Mr. Bowden would deliver pounds of ice, chipping it up in no time at all, and place it in the top of the ice box. He was a master with that ice pick."

In the kitchen sat an old pie safe. Common pie safes were made of wood, around the same size as a large bureau, and approximately eighteen inches deep. The shelves within the storage area were often perforated. The safe normally had two hinged doors on the front. These doors, and usually the sides, were ordinarily ventilated either with tin plates with punched holes or screens. The holes in the tin were often punched to produce an image such as a simple shape or something more intricate like a church scene, eagles, stars, or even a Masonic emblem.

Johnny loved his food. "Momma Ruth would cook and put the leftovers in the pie safe." He would look inside the safe and see biscuits and bacon sitting inside. He would take out a biscuit and put his finger through it, pour fresh cane syrup inside, and eat it with a piece of bacon. That was a highlight of John III's life that continued. He still loves his biscuits, syrup, and bacon.

CHAPTER 6
Grade School at
University of Magnolia

In 1946, when Little Johnny was about six years old, he started to school at Magnolia. Locals called it University of Magnolia. It was first through eighth grade. It was located where Hope School is now, just south of I-10 off Hwy 71 in Jackson County. The old school was about three feet off the ground and sat on lime rock. It was a huge thing with classes grouped—first and second in one room, third and fourth in one room, fifth and sixth in one room. Seventh and eighth each had their own room.

Johnny recalled, "The boys' bathroom was on one side of the building and the girls' bathroom was on the other. There was an old trough that water ran in all the time. You would have to get a brick to stand on to pee."

The first-year Johnny went to school in 1946, he wasn't quite six years old. There was no lunchroom, so he had to take his lunch with him. The next year they had a lunchroom which gave children milk or juice.

The following year, they started preparing food for children on site, which was good. Momma Ruth always fixed breakfast for her children. It was lumpy oatmeal with a little bit of sugar and cream and a piece of toast cooked on that old kerosene stove. Sometimes the children would make a peanut butter sandwich, or if they had any eggs, they could make those.

Grandma Grant always had something to eat in the evenings when the children came in from school. The buses would pick the children up. They lived about a mile and a half away. Mr. Kairo Pelt would pick up children at Granddaddy's old store. There would be a pile of them. Momma Ruth's three children, Johnny's Aunt Elner's three children, and the Lanes and Brocks that lived in the area would catch the bus at the old store. Magnolia School had dirt ball courts. The hoops had no nets. Johnny played softball a little and tried shooting hoops but wasn't worth a flip at basketball.

Once while in first grade, Little John and his friend, also named Johnny, crawled up underneath that old school house and started throwing dirt. They dug holes and stirred up so much dust it filled the whole inside of the schoolhouse. The teachers stormed out and tore their tails up.

Little Johnny's first teacher was Vader Dean Peacock. He honestly believed that was the meanest woman to a little child that ever existed. Johnny was a bashful, shy child. "If you got in trouble, Mrs. Peacock would take your hand and twist your fingers down and take a ruler and pop you in the palm of your hand. She would make you stand up and hit you in the bend of your legs with a paddle. That was the discipline you got from Mrs. Peacock. I was as afraid of that woman as if she had been a bear." Johnny remembered crying many a time, scared to death of that woman. He had first and second grade with her, and was so glad to get out of her classroom.

In 1947, when Johnny was in second grade, Jackson County experienced a great flood. The Chipola, Chattahoochee, and Apalachicola Rivers all flooded their banks. A series of slow-moving tropical systems had combined with unusual weather conditions in the Midwest that year to create torrential rains across eight states. The magnitude of the disaster is difficult to assess today because at that time, modern emergency management procedures did not exist. The Chipola River, where Little Johnny fished and played, had changed from a peaceful stream to a muddy torrent of deep, fast-moving water. Railroad and highway travel between Marianna

16

and Chattahoochee was cut off by the flood, and every low-lying area in the county was inundated. The Great Flood of 1947 was the final straw in forcing the decision to construct the Jim Woodruff Dam between Chattahoochee and Sneads on the Chattahoochee River.

In third and fourth grade, Johnny had Mrs. Crutchfield. She had a little harp that had three cords. The class would sing every morning—songs like, "She'll Be Coming Around the Mountain When She Comes" and "The Star-Spangled Banner." Mrs. Crutchfield would blow the one note and say, "All right, children." The children would sing to that one note.

Johnny was never a really good student; his attention span was very shallow. Johnny left third and fourth grade and went to fifth and sixth. Mrs. Ruby Higgins was his teacher. Her husband was a sailor off in service. She didn't have any children herself and was a very strong disciplinarian.

"During the spring of the year, we would open the windows up to get some ventilation in the classroom. Back then, the schools had no form of air-conditioning. The windows didn't have any screens, and bumblebees covered the old flowers under the windows. I would lean out the window and swat at them with a book."

Mrs. Higgins had already gotten onto Johnny about doing that and caught him doing it again. She had warned him, but he kept leaning out and swatting at the bees. Mrs. Higgins snuck up behind Johnny while he was leaning out the window and pulled his britches up real tight and fired his tail up with a paddle. After that, he didn't want to swat at any more bees.

One afternoon, Johnny was walking home from school with his dog trotting along behind him when he saw movement in the bushes. Little Johnny stopped and looked real close at the small, black, furry animal easing through the edge of the woods. It was a little black kitten, and Johnny wanted it.

He ran into the woods just as the little startled animal began to run. Johnny ran as fast as he could, trying to catch the little black kitten, getting closer and closer. All of a sudden, the little kitten stopped. Right before Johnny was about to snatch it up, he noticed it had a pretty white stripe running all the way down its back. Johnny had never seen a little kitten with that type of coloring. About that time, the spray hit him—all over him. It wasn't a little black kitten after all.

Little Johnny ran home in a blur as his eyes were red and burning. Iris was hanging out clothes when Johnny came tearing up in the yard, squalling. She smelled him long before she saw him; he reeked of a nauseating sulfur smell.

Iris hosed Johnny off, and they scrubbed and scrubbed his clothes. The homemade white chunk of lye soap was no match for the skunk stench. The more Iris lathered him up, the worse he smelled. It did no good. The smell would not go away. Iris and Johnny ended up digging a big hole in the back yard and burying Little Johnny's clothes so Momma Ruth wouldn't spank his butt.

CHAPTER 7

Tom Sawyer / Huck Finn Years (in the Words of John P. McDaniel III)

"Up the road from where we lived were my Uncle Wilson and Aunt Polly. They had two children. Jimmy was born in 1937 and was the same age as my sister, Iris. He was older than me, and we grew up kind of like Tom Sawyer and Huck Finn. We did get into some kind of mischief.

"A little further up the road, where Sonny's Barbeque is now in Marianna, Florida, was a boy named Lloyd Johnson. He had a brother named Lavon and a sister named Alice Faye. Me and Lloyd and Jimmy and sometimes Lavon would play together. We would use broomsticks to make frog gigs. We gigged fish and moccasins with our homemade gigs.

"Down behind Jimmy's house lived our great-grandmother, Lucinda Pelt Davis. There was a little, wet water pond behind her house. When it dried up a little, me and Jimmy would wade out there with baseball bats and muddy it up so the fish couldn't breathe, and they would have to come to the top. We would hit the fish with the baseball bats and throw them up on the bank. Water moccasins would come up as well. We knocked them in the head and threw them up on the bank too.

"Jimmy and I used to dig fox holes. A fox hole to us was finding a soft sandy place to dig and make a tunnel. It's a wonder it didn't fall in on us.

"There was a lane filled with tall trees that ran by Jimmy's house. Down the lane lived a man named Pete Degrete. We would hear him coming and climb up in the trees and drop stuff down on his truck. He would stop and look around. We were just being mean boys. We even tried to wee wee on his truck as it went by to make him think it was raining.

19

"One time, Lloyd, Jimmy, and I went to the picture show to see *Lone Ranger and Tonto*. We watched intently as they tied the cowboys to the tree and slung the rope way off. Since I was a small-framed, asthmatic child, they tied me off to the tree and let it swing. The rope was loose enough that I just kept bumping into the tree, busting my lip all up.

"We all had bicycles. So bicycle races were the thing. We ran up to the culvert and raced down it as fast as we could. At Uncle Wilson Grant's house, there was an old cedar stump. I got a running start and jumped the culvert and came off my bike, landing right on the old stump. It nearly killed me. How we ever had children after all the mess we did, God only knows.

"Red Rider BB guns came out during this time. Me and the boys worked a little bit to save up and buy us the guns. Then the BB wars were on. We would shoot each other in the butt or wherever we could. We shot Lloyd one time right in the eye. When he got to the doctor, the BB fell out. It didn't puncture the eyeball, but was underneath the lid. He had trouble his whole life with that eye.

"Slingshots were our next adventure. My God a mighty, we shot birds and whatever moved in the trees. We stripped persimmons for ammo. If you ever hit a white house with a green persimmon, you would never get the stain off. We hit a couple of cars too and got in a lot of trouble. It was always a delight for one of us boys to talk another one into biting into a green persimmon. Just to watch their face was so much fun. It was so bitter, it would turn your mouth inside out.

"Every so often, we would save up enough money to get us a few fireworks. The cherry bombs, lord have mercy... we would put a can over one and watch it blow up.

"Granddaddy Grant fell in and became the daddy to me that I needed and made a man out of me. Uncle Wilson and several others tried to step up and help. It was quite a chore. Granddaddy took me and Jimmy... and taught us to fish. Granddaddy had a boat he kept down at Magnolia; we kept it sunk until we needed it. When we got ready to fish, we would pull it up and use turpentine cans to dip the water out. It had a 3hp Elgin engine. We would troll up and down Chipola River, diving off the front to catch soft-shell turtles. Granddaddy cleaned them and made us turtle soup.

"Huck Finn and Tom Sawyer had nothing on us. We were barefooted as yard dogs with feet so tough we could run through a sandspur bed with no shoes."

CHAPTER 8
Too Big for His Britches

Little Johnny finally got old enough to do a little work at his granddaddy's store. One of the suppliers for the store was Daffin Mercantile Company. Daffin's gave away little KutMaster knives. They had two blades and Daffin Mercantile Company on the yellow handle. Mr. Joe Hankins, the salesman for Grant's Store, gave Mr. Grant a few of the knives every Christmas to give to his grandsons; Johnny always got one of the knives.

Little Johnny would unbox the supplies that came into the store and put them on the shelves. He swept up and kept the store clean.

Around September and October of every year, it was hog killing time. It was cold enough that time of year that the meat would not spoil so quickly. The heel strings of hogs were cut and a stick run between them. They were hung up with their throats slit so they could drain out.

Johnny recalled, "They were then soaked in a big skillet of hot water before hanging them back up and shaving them. Little boys couldn't participate because you didn't want to accidentally cut the meat. Crackling was made out of the hide. The women would take a number two washtub and make sausage by running it through a grinder."

Little John's job was to build a fire in the smokehouse. He dug it out before layering it with pine tops. He put rock salt and pine tops down, and adults would layer the meat on racks and hang them up. Once there was a good bed of coals, wet wood was added so it would just smoke, never hot enough to burn. Little John liked having jobs to do and working at the store. It made him feel all grown up.

Little Johnny was up at his granddaddy's one day and the smokehouse door was open. There was ham and sausage hanging just inside the door. He thought about how good that meat would taste. Easing inside the open door, he took out his little pocket knife and cut off a bunch until he had eaten a belly full. Before eating it, he had to scrape off the mildew and rickets. His granddaddy caught him. Johnny recalled, "You talk about a child getting a spanking....Granddaddy Grant put a good one on my butt."

CHAPTER 9

New Beginnings

A few months after John turned ten years old, Ruth Grant McDaniel tried another marriage to William Wallace Hall on December 31, 1950. She became Ruth Grant McDaniel Hall. They were married in Donaldsonville, Georgia.

One child resulted from the marriage of Wallace and Ruth Hall—a beautiful little girl named after her mother. Lucinda Ruth Hall was born on August 1, 1952. Lucinda is now a Clark.

This marriage did not last long as Wallace Hall was an alcoholic and extremely physically and verbally abusive to Ruth. Johnny recalls it as being a "hell of a mess."

During this time, Wallace had a trucking business. He had large trucks which he hauled scrap iron, watermelons, and peaches from one location to another.

As a small-framed twelve-year-old child, Little Johnny tried hard to help his step-dad, but that didn't work out very well. Nothing made a difference. Wallace Hall continued to drink more, hit more, and curse more.

Ruth divorced Wallace and took care of the children by herself for several years to come. Iris was fifteen by then and was a big help to Momma Ruth.

CHAPTER 10

Grandma & Grandpa McDaniel:
Visits to the Real Frontier

Ruth continued working and raising her four children: Iris, John, Wayne, and Lucinda. She and the children were in church every Sunday. They attended Marvin Chapel Freewill Baptist Church which was located in Marianna.

Even with John Jr. out of the picture, she still took the children every so often to Grandma and Grandpa McDaniel's.

Momma Ruth would take the children up there on a Friday and come back and get them on Sunday. Grandma and Granddaddy McDaniel never did own an automobile that they used to drive. "Uncle Jack McDaniel, who was their youngest boy, bought them a '36 Ford Sedan. They put it in the barn, and I don't think it ever came out of the barn. Granddaddy had horses and he farmed with horses, not mules."

It was a fun time; the children would stay a week at the time. They had electricity but no running water.

Johnny fondly remembers those times, "Granddaddy McDaniel had a gasoline pump that would pump water out in the shed. It had a water tower. He would sit out there with it until it would overflow over the top. The water ran down toward the back porch. There were three washtubs there for washing clothes first…then the children. Grandma had an old pot out back that she used to make lye soap with red devil lye and lard. She built a fire underneath and poked it with a stick. The stick was pure white on the end from being in the lye.

"The McDaniel's had an outhouse…. The old saying about the corncobs and the Sears and Roebuck Catalog was true out there. Granddaddy McDaniel did carpenter work and farming. He had two horses, Sally and Sara. The horses were used to plow and do his crops.

"They were also broke to pull the wagon. On Sundays when visiting the grandparents, you either went to the Baptist Church or the Methodist Church. It didn't matter which one you went to. They had alternating services. If there wasn't enough water to submerse you in, they would just sprinkle you.

"Grandma and Granddaddy would sit up front on the seat of the wagon, and all children would sit in the back. Sometimes, there would be an old, straight chair in the back for the little ones to sit." Johnny's momma and both sets of grandparents took the children to church and sat with them. They were not sent to church. "This was something the family did together. They were taught to pray, to be respectful, and to be thankful for the blessings from God."

Little Johnny loved to catch a wagon going by and jump in the back. It didn't matter if they were white, red, black, or yellow people; when they came by Granddaddy's house with an old mule pulling a wagon, Johnny would run out there and jump in the back. Nobody ever minded. He would ride it up the hill to Mr. and Mrs. Rogers's place and then walk back down. There were never any traffic jams out there at the farm.

Once when Little Johnny was visiting the McDaniel grandparents for a week, his daddy was home for a visit. It had been many years since Johnny had seen his daddy.

John Jr. caught Johnny jumping in the back of strangers' wagons and told him not to do that again. He did it again anyway and got caught. John Jr. beat the living daylights out of Little Johnny. It put a bad taste in his mouth for wanting to jump on a wagon and ride.

Granddaddy McDaniel kept his horses in a pen that had a corncrib and a walk-way. He could open a door and feed the crushed corn to the horses without getting in there with them.

"As you first went in the crib, on the right was where he stacked the corn. He had a certain way he stacked it. The butt of the corn was up next to the wall; the shuck part was out toward the center. The corn sheller was over to the side. You would pull the shucks off and put it down in the sheller and turn the wheel. A bucket caught the corn. You took the bucket and fed all the horses at one time."

Granddaddy always plowed really early in the morning. Little Johnny loved to go with him. He had a sled that he hooked to the horses. He put the plow on the sled and pulled it down to the field. He would hook the horse to the plow and start the field. This is where Johnny learned plowing to a shuck.

"You took a pole about twelve to fifteen feet tall. You would stick it in the ground with the shuck on the bottom. On the other end of the field, you had another one. Each time you reached the other end, you would move the shuck over. You would always be plowing to the shuck. Granddaddy McDaniel had the straightest rows you ever saw using this method."

One day, Johnny told his granddaddy he was big enough to plow by himself. So he threw the rope around Johnny's neck.

Johnny said, "Get up horse," and that horse started pulling and went wherever he wanted to go. Those were the crookedest rows anyone ever saw.

Granddaddy snatched that rope from Johnny and said, "Boy, you get old enough to plow, you can come out here, but you ain't messin with it no more."

That wound-up Johnny's plowing; he didn't get to do any plowing in the '40s.

Granddaddy McDaniel had a piece of property that was 120 acres. It had a sink hole. Because of lime rock formation, he had about eight to ten acres that fell in, creating a big hole. Johnny, his siblings, and his cousins would go and play in that sinkhole all the time.

"On Saturdays, if you were going to get a haircut, you went up to Bascom. They had a little barber shop up there. You would stand around outside next to the faded red, white, and blue spiraling barber pole sign until it was your turn. They would put a board in the seat so you could sit down in the chair. The razor was always dull and would pull and snatch your hair. If you pulled away, the barber would say, 'Boy be still. It ain't hurtin you.' Granddaddy paid fifty cents for our haircuts."

Men folk would stand around out front, chewing tobacco, spitting, and carrying on. The young'uns would run around and play. There used to be an old sawdust pile across from the sawmill. Granddaddy McDaniel would let Johnny go over there and play. They would get an old piece of tin, bend the front, and get on it like a bob sled, riding it down the sawdust pile. Half the time it would be wet and nasty. Momma Ruth would tear Johnny's tail up for playing in that sawdust pile.

Granddaddy and Grandma McDaniel had a fireplace which had a hearth. The young'uns would sit around it at night. Granddaddy would listen to the radio for about an hour. He had an old wire running out the window and up a tree outside. That was his antennae. He would listen to the news and then turn it off.

On Saturday night, he would listen to the Grand Ole Opry up to a certain time and then turn it off. Johnny reflects on those times, "Like I said, we didn't have indoor plumbing. We had slop jars. Lord have mercy, I remember those stinking things. You would have one under your bed, and if you had to go to the bathroom, that was what you used. Then in the morning, you went out there and emptied that slop jar. If you had to do number two, you went to the outdoor privy and went to the bathroom.

"I remember shelling, shucking, and stacking corn for my Granddaddy McDaniel. He also had a pecan orchard. We would take a fishing pole, and we would climb up those trees and whip those pecans so they would fall on the ground. Then we would get down there and pick them up in a five-gallon bucket or a cotton basket. Granddaddy would sell the pecans to make his annual payment on the farm every year.

Grandma McDaniel was a very strict woman and a very good cook. Granddaddy would kill his own hogs, and we had smokehouses there. Grandma McDaniel sewed and made mine and a lot of others' clothes. She made quilts and doilies too."

CHAPTER 11
The Value of a Hard Day's Work

Dallas Malloy had a farm behind the old store where Johnny and his family lived. Mr. Malloy had peanuts, flowers, and irrigation systems. Mr. Roberts was the straw boss man. He would pay his workers a total of three dollars a day as a laborer. A day entailed from six in the morning to six in the evening. Johnny went there and they gave him a job because they knew his momma needed the help. They expected a man's day of labor out of an almost thirteen-year-old boy.

He had to work behind a potato digger that dug up gladiola bulbs and spit them back out. The rows had stakes in them of different colors. He had a five-gallon bucket to put the bulbs in but had to keep them within those stakes because they were divided according to color. The first few days out there, he couldn't keep up with that potato digger. There was a young black boy a little bit older than Johnny that knew what to do. He would catch his row and then come help Johnny catch his row up. He kept them from running his butt off and firing him. Johnny really needed the fifteen dollars a week.

Johnny worked hard and was able to stay at Malloy's Gladiola Farm. Not only did he dig potatoes, but he hoed peanuts. Now that was a disaster. Mr. Roberts threatened his butt one day with a hoe handle. He didn't hit him with it, but Johnny got the message. Johnny was cutting the peanuts up along with the weeds. Later on, he learned how to use a pitch fork. They would turn them upside down and go over and pick them up with the fork and put them on stack poles.

Johnny remembered those long days. "Water jugs were made available to keep you hydrated. There was plenty of black boys and white boys and everybody else;

none of them knew any difference....They were all boys working for a living. It was never anything to do with race. At the end of the row, in the bushes down there, would be an old jug. It would be an old one-gallon Clorox jug that had been washed out and filled with water. It had a croaker sack tied around it with bailing wire. Everybody drank out of the same jug. You went down there and got you a drink of water at the end of the row.

"After the hoeing was completed, you had to move the irrigation system. That piece of irrigation system was about twelve or fourteen feet long. It was all light aluminum, but you would pick it up and move it, pick it up and move it, all day long."

Big old frogs would get in there where they pumped the water from the river. They would have to clean it out. When it came time to cut flowers, they had to have a long, single-bladed knife. Johnny used a yellow handled, Queen steel knife about seven inches long. He would slide down on one side and cut to his left and then slide down the other side and cut to his right, making a "v" at the bottom. He would get as much stalk as he could because he had to cut and put them in his arms, carry them until the end of the row, and put them in a bucket of water. Then they would take the buckets to the shed, laying them out by color. The women would come along and cut them off and grade them by length.

Next, they shucked the bulb. A gladiola bulb reproduces itself with a bulb. The old bulb dies, and the new bulb comes on—old ones in one tub and the new in another.

It was repetitive work every day. The hours were long and the days were hot, but Johnny learned the value of working for a dollar.

CHAPTER 12

Ground Shaking:
July 22, 1952

On July 22, 1952, a United States Air Force Boeing47-B Stratojet from McCoy AFB in Florida exploded in mid-air over Marianna, Florida. USAF was conducting a high-speed, low-level training mission.

There were two civilian fatalities:
Rufus Williams
Peggy Williams

As well as the USAF Crew:
Maj. Frederick "Fred" E. Ewing, 31 years old of Parker, Indiana (AC)
Capt. Oscar W. Yon, 28 years old of Eckley, W. Virginia (Co-Pilot)
Capt. James H. Foreman, 29 years old of Birmingham, Alabama (Pilot)
Capt. Richard E. Francis, 28 years old of Clay City, Indiana (Observer)

On the morning of July 22, 1952, Johnny got dressed and walked to work just as the sun was coming up. Typical workdays started early due to temperatures reaching 100 degrees by noon in July. Johnny and the other workers were out under the old oak trees, shucking bulbs, when they heard a large vibrating noise. Johnny felt the ground shake under his feet. Somebody said look up.

Johnny looked up to see a huge ball of fire plummeting from the sky. "An airplane had exploded over Marianna and was falling. You could see smoke and debris falling everywhere. The grown folks wanted to go and see what it was all about. All the youngsters were staring up into the sky, open mouthed. They wanted to go too but were told to keep their butts there and shuck bulbs."

The adults went up town and discovered a big four-engine plane had exploded over Marianna and killed two of Jermaine Stewart's children. The children, Rufus and Peggy Williams, were engulfed in fuel and flames when the B-47B crashed near the intersection of 4th Street and 6th Avenue. Despite all efforts of hospital staff, they were unable to be saved.

The B-47B took off from MacDill Air Force Base in Tampa, Florida. The bomber headed north over the Gulf of Mexico at a high rate of speed and was flying at an altitude of 7,500 feet when it suddenly exploded over Marianna. The plane's four turbojet engines broke away as the wings separated from the main fuselage. More than 10,000 gallons of fuel caught fire as the burning wreckage fell to earth.

U.S. military personnel arrived and sealed off the neighborhood. Body parts from the plane's crew, pieces of wreckage, and other burning debris were found as far south as the old Marianna High School building on Daniels Street, while the main fuselage crashed into the area. Pieces of wreckage were never found, and one of the conventional bombs from the plane plunged so deep into the ground that it was never found. It remains buried somewhere under northern Marianna to this day.

The Williams family was well liked and respected in the community, and the loss of the children touched everyone. Johnny learned at not quite twelve years old how quickly a beloved family member could be taken away. He also learned enough working on that farm to know he didn't want to farm for a living. He wanted to find something else to do.

CHAPTER 13

Fox Hunts and
Granddaddy Grant, the Medicine Man

Momma Ruth did not own a car. Johnny's uncle, Don Grant, went into the air force. When he came home, he had a '30s model car. "When Uncle Don went overseas again, Granddaddy Grant took that old car. A fellow named Charlie Stewart took axes and a hatchet and cut the top off of it. They turned the car into a pick up. Granddaddy Grant liked to fox hunt, so he made us a pick-up to haul the dogs."

Near the first part of November every year, a group of men—Robert Alan Willis, Sheriff Gause, Mr. Martin, the Dunnaways, and J. W. Grant—would meet up and go to the wooded areas around Dellwood, Greenwood, and Peacock Bridge. The men let the dogs out and waited, watched, and listened as their hounds searched for the scent of a fox, and then the chase was on.

Johnny's granddaddy liked wolver hounds while Mr. Barkley liked redbones. Little Johnny was the dog boy and sat by the fire, waiting to tend to the dogs when they returned. He was a little boy and found it hard to be quiet. The men were frequently telling him to "hush." The dogs' barking would get distant and then circle back around closer. The men would argue with each other saying, "Listen at that dog run. That's my dog, Ruth!" Another one would say, "No, that's my dog, Rock. Your dog is out there chasing rabbits."

Granddaddy Grant had an old one-gallon coffee can that he gave to Johnny to get some water out of the creek. He put some coffee in the can and put it on the fire. He would sit it off the fire for a bit to let the grounds settle before pouring it into a cup. Everybody swore that Jim Grant could drink the hottest coffee of anyone around…that he could spit it on a hog's back and make it squeal.

Every once in a while, some women folk would come, and they would cook fish and fry hushpuppies and French fries.

One time they cooked up a batch of onions. Little Johnny loved them and ate a bunch of them. Those fried onions made him sick. He threw up all on the floorboard of Mr. Barkley's '49 Ford Mercury. He had to sit in the back seat. Then they whipped his butt and made him get a bucket and clean it all out.

Little Johnny was Granddaddy's boy and whatever he wanted done, Johnny did it, no questions asked. Granddaddy made a septic with drain fields out of a huge culvert and made a lid to go over it. The oak tree roots would get in the drain and stop it up. They had to take the old truck and pull the lid back because it was too heavy to move by hand.

Johnny's job was to take a five-gallon bucket, dip it out, and dump it in Dallas Malloy's field. It was about thirty feet behind the store. Johnny carried the bucket toward the field, and it sloshed out, getting the contents of the homemade septic tank all over his shoes and clothes. He told his granddaddy that the mess was getting all over him. He said, "Hell boy, don't worry about it. It will wash off."

Being the active little young'un that Johnny was, he didn't like going to the bathroom. He didn't have time for that, so he would get constipated. Well, he ended up with hemorrhoids. They were external, and he was fussing with Granddaddy, telling him he couldn't work for him because they hurt.

"Hell, he didn't want to hear any of that, so he said, 'Come here boy. I'll fix ya up.'"

Granddaddy took a pint jar and put some liquid in it and a long piece of copper tubing. Little Johnny watched as his granddaddy took some gauze out of an aspirin bottle and put it on the end of the tube, attaching it with some rubber bands. He gave it to Johnny and told him to go in the bathroom and rub them hemorrhoids really good with that stuff.

Johnny did as he was told. After he got through sloshing that stuff on the hemorrhoids, they started to burn. This is how Johnny remembers it. "Son, I could clear forty acres for him in a heartbeat. He liked to have burnt me up. The liquid was turpentine. We got rid of the hemorrhoids. They were afraid to come out and show themselves again.

"If you got hurt and was bleeding, Granddaddy Grant would take a spider web to put on it to stop the bleeding. For a wasp bite, he would chew a little tobacco and put it on the bite."

Little Johnny and Jimmy Grant used to fight the yellow jackets that dug holes in the ground.

The boys would take old fishing poles with a rag on the end. They dipped the rag in kerosene, set it on fire, stuck it in the ground, and burned the yellow jackets up. Some got past the fire and stung them all over.

Jimmy Grant and Little Johnny kept fighting the yellow jackets. One of them got up Johnny's britches and was popping him all the way up to his privates. Jimmy Grant swore Johnny ran twenty miles an hour, pulling his britches off to get those yellow jackets before they could sting him anymore.

Johnny's friends, Carl Hubbard Lee and Junior Lee, lived near Stephens's old store, just down the road from Johnny's house. They had bicycles, and the boys would ride to the railroad tracks and ride down the tracks to the spring to go swimming. If the train was coming, they just pedaled faster.

The stream was small, not even creek sized. Johnny, Carl, and Junior would swim in it even in the cold of winter, getting their clothes all wet. When Momma Ruth found out, she tore his tail up, and so did Jimmy's momma.

When Johnny worked at Malloy's Glad Farm, making fifteen dollars a week, he would go to the store on Saturday and buy himself a store-bought shirt. This was a real treat for Johnny. He had always worn square shirts as a young'un. Momma Ruth and his Grandma made his shirts out of feed sacks so they were square, with no shape to them.

Most of what Johnny had was hand-me-downs. He had to put toilet tissue in the end of his shoes because they were too big. Granddaddy would wire the soles on with bailing wire.

CHAPTER 14
Marianna High School Years

Johnny got through seventh grade at Magnolia and talked his momma into letting him go to Marianna High School by riding a bus. His sister was already attending the school and talked about how good it was there. Momma Ruth gave in and let him go. All his friends played football, so he was excited when Coach Emmitt Stringer said, "Johnny, come on and join the team."

Johnny showed up to practice in his converse tennis shoes. Coach Stringer gave them all their gear and told them to put it on. Johnny was so excited, he suited up as quickly as he could and laughingly recalled, "The only problem was I had put the knee pads onto the back of my knees....They showed me how to put the uniform on and how to wear the pads. Practice entailed running around, wallowing in the dirt.

"The coach said for us to line up and get in a three-point stance. I looked around and saw how everybody was putting one hand down and sticking their butt up in the air, so I dropped on one hand and stuck my butt high in the air."

Coach Stringer came over and popped him on the butt and said, "Boy, get that butt out of the air. Get down in a three-point stance. Get low; get low." This embarrassed Little Johnny in front of everybody, and they all laughed.

But Johnny was determined and learned quickly. He got to where when he hit someone, it was like knocking the bark off a pine tree. He did pretty well in football. The team was known as the Bullpups. He could have played with the Bullpups another year, but all of his buddies had gone up to "B" team. He decided to move up with them. That was in the ninth grade.

In the tenth grade, they were the dummies for the big boys playing varsity ball. The varsity would run over them, stomp on them, knock them down, and beat the living hell out of them—just to show them they could because they were bigger.

About the end of tenth grade, Little Johnny had put on some weight and size. He turned that ballgame around. They didn't jump on, stomp, or kick Johnny Mac anymore. When they hit him, it was like running straight into a brick wall. He had worked in the fields and gained weight and strength.

CHAPTER 15

Working Hard, Playing Football, Squealing Tires, and
Picture Shows

Johnny's daddy did come back into his life. The first time he saw him was about 1954-1955 when he showed up at Marianna High School. In the late 1940s, several years after John Jr. had left his family, he had an accident which caused irreparable damage to his left hand. His left hand was amputated at the wrist when Johnny saw him again.

Johnny continued going to school in Marianna and was having a hard time getting back home after ball practice. He tried to get through in time for his momma to pick him up. Momma Ruth wasn't too fond of him playing football anyway, so he often told her to go on home and he would just catch a ride home after practice. A boy named Charles Crutchfield and a few others let Johnny catch a ride home.

Johnny got the chance to get a job at Hightower's Drug Store. They had an opening for a delivery boy to deliver medicine and put up stock. He got a total of seventeen dollars a week. His job consisted of scrubbing slats which were behind the soda fountain, scrubbing the floors, and oiling down the wood floors on the weekends. Johnny handled the sweeping and delivered medicine on his bicycle.

Later when he got his driver's license, he delivered in a standard six-cylinder 1946 Ford Club Coupe. One time Mr. Hightower called Johnny over to him. He said, "Johnny Boy, come here." Johnny was scared of him, but he was a wonderful old man—him *and* Mrs. Diddle.

He said, "I got a call that somebody was out there running around squalling the tires on a car like our delivery car. It wasn't you, was it?"

Johnny hung his head. "No sir. No sir." But it was Johnny. He was trying to make those old tires squall on the pavement.

He washed cars for them, later chauffeuring Mr. and Mrs. Hightower over to Defuniak Springs, Florida, which is about sixty miles west of Marianna. He also learned how to do sodas, malts, milkshakes, and banana splits. Johnny would go to their house, and Mrs. Hightower's maid would make lunch. She did the cooking and made really good chicken salad and ham salad. Hightower's Drug Store had a lunch bar at the soda fountain, and people from all over town came in to eat. Mrs. Maynor from Citizen's Bank would call, and Johnny would deliver lunch to them. Johnny recalled, "Back in those days, you just walked in the back of the bank, walked up the hallway, and gave the meals to them. There were no locks or anything."

Johnny told Mr. Maynor, "Somebody is gonna come in here and rob this place one of these days." He said, "Ain't nobody gonna bother this little bank."

It wasn't but a year or two later that somebody did just that. They went in the back door, robbed the bank, stole Bower Sandusky's car, and left. The case was never solved.

Back then, there were two theaters in Marianna—the Ritz Theater and the Gem Theater. Johnny would go to the Ritz Theater because he had friends working there. He would help clean up and get free tickets for movies. Movies were fifty cents. He liked watching the cowboy movies at the picture show. His friends, Donald Williams and Gerry Baggett, worked at the Ritz.

They always went in the lower section. Upstairs was the black section, and the other side was a special section. Often, the boys from Dozier Boys School—back then it was Florida Industrial School—would get to go to the show. The staff would bring them up on buses on Friday and Saturday. Popcorn was fifteen cents, admission was fifty cents, and a Coca-Cola was a nickel.

Just down the hill, below the Ritz Theater, was Otto's Diner. They had the best hamburgers in the world and the best iced-tea. The boys used to all fight to get in there at lunch when they were all in school together.

Johnny recalled, "Every once in a while, I helped Donald or Robert—whoever was working at the theater. They were projectionists and changed out the marquees. They just threw them away. Can you imagine what they would be worth today?...The one's that said Roy Rogers, Gene Autry, *Gone With the Wind*, Jimmy Dean, and all of those. They are all gone now. A fellow named Bill Brannon owned both of them."

Johnny would watch both movies at the Ritz Theater and then run across and see the last of them on the other one and then hitchhike home. His momma used to raise hell with him about this. But he never bothered anybody. He just walked out to the road and put his thumb up. Somebody would come by and think, "There's that ole crazy ass, Johnny Mac." They would pick him up and carry him home.

After he went to work at Hightower's Drug store, he turned sixteen and got his driver's license. He got a chance to buy his first car from a fellow named Julian Carter. He was married to Johnny's step-sister, Doris Carter.

Julian had a '36 Ford Club Coupe that had a six cylinder. It was painted blue and white with house paint. Johnny bought it for fifty dollars. It made it from Julian's house to Johnny's house. It was disassembled to move it to Johnny's house and was never put back together.

"Next thing I bought was a '36 Chevrolet Club Coupe. It had a little business seat right behind the driver seat and a passenger seat that would fold down. It was a six cylinder. I named it Ole Ironsides. It was disassembled later when it quit, and I never could get it back together either."

Johnny continued going to Marianna High school and played football through the 12th grade. He was a good football player and one of only five team members who made all conference his senior year. Johnny prided himself in being a guard and tackle for his coach, Harry Howell, who was probably the best coach ever in the state of Florida.

Right across the street from the school was a place called Les and Dorothy's. An egg salad sandwich, Coca-Cola, and chips cost a quarter. Mr. Les had been a boxer—a prize fighter. He always worked with the boys and put on classes teaching cut away techniques. Johnny did one once and cracked his tailbone. He could barely move for several months. He healed and was all right by the next football season.

Momma Ruth continued working hard and raising her children alone until she met a very nice man by the name of Russell Owens.

On December 12, 1957, Ruth married Lawrence Russell Owens. They were married at Marvin Chapel Freewill Baptist Church down in the Magnolia Community of Jackson County, Florida.

During this time, Russell had three children of his own and Ruth had four. Russell soon became known as Papa to all the children.

Russell's son, Lawrence Edward Owens, born October 4, 1937, was three years John's senior. Lawrence was off in the military. He would die years later as a result of cancer on December 26, 1993.

Russell had one daughter, Doris Owens—now Carpenter—born March 5, 1940, and another child by the name of Dorothy Helen Owens, born March 16, 1943. She went by Helen. Ruth and Russell joined two families together and tried to make a good life.

In May of 1958, five months after Ruth and Russell married, Johnny Mac graduated from High School.

CHAPTER 16
Military:
June 1958

In June of 1958, Johnny and Donald Williams decided they were going to join the Navy. They seemed the most glamorous military group to them. The young men were told if they joined together as a team, they would be stationed together. They were best friends, so they wanted to stick together.

They were sent to the Navy Recruiting Station in Montgomery, Alabama. Johnny wanted to be a machinist. Donald was overweight. He weighed over 250 pounds at that time and was flat footed. They accepted Johnny and sent Donald home.

So, there he was, alone. They sent Johnny to San Diego, California. He rode a train from Montgomery to California and got to see the world. He had never seen anything like that before. He went there to attend boot camp at the training center. The training center is the Recruit Training Command. There the recruit underwent his transition from civilian to military life; learned the history, tradition customs and regulations of his chosen service; and receive instruction in naval skills and subjects which would be basic information throughout his period of naval service. Johnny became Chief Petty Officer because he had been in the National Guard since age fifteen. The Guard had put him out when they found out his true age.

Johnny got in the Navy and his first duty station was Centerville. He thought it was in Northern California, got lost, and didn't know where he was. Shore patrol came by and found out where he was supposed to be and gave him enough money to buy meals and purchase a bus ticket. The bus stopped five miles from where the base was located.

In high school, Johnny had been dating Carolyn Venia Carr. She was Henry and Dixie Carr's daughter. After graduation, he went into the Navy and wouldn't see her again until his first leave in the fall of 1958. Well, Johnny came home on leave, and he and Carolyn went over to Donalsonville, Georgia, and got a quickie marriage, and then he went back to his base in California.

Johnny would soon discover that he was color blind, and his duties would be limited. After eight months, Johnny and another boy were cutting up and Johnny fell off a cement embankment. They gave him a discharge and sent him home.

Johnny managed to get to Mississippi and hitch-hiked all the way back to Marianna. He messed around at his mom's for a while until he could find a job.

Shortly after Johnny got out of the service, honorably discharged, he and Carolyn Venia Carr would divorce. It lasted as long as he stayed in the Navy. It was something that shouldn't have happened, but they both wanted to get married and they both regretted it later. She went on with her life, and Johnny went on with his life. Their divorce was final in November of 1960.

CHAPTER 17
Career in Dry Cleaning

After returning to Marianna, Florida, from serving in the military, John P. McDaniel III searched for a job in an economically troubled Jackson County. The Air Force had decided to close Graham Air Base in late 1960, despite the efforts of the influential Congressman "Bob" Sikes. The community lost not only a combined civilian and military payroll of $6 million but also several hundred families who added significantly to the social life of the surrounding cities and communities.

Johnny got a job at Nifty Cleaners. It was owned by Fred G. Wiley at that time. Mr. Wiley had a job open as a route man. Johnny would pick up laundry and return it to the store. Johnny ran everywhere, picking up on all aspects of the dry-cleaning business quickly. Mr. Wiley trained him to do everything, so within a year, Johnny was his manager.

Johnny said, "Mr. Wiley was tickled to death with this turn of events. He would sit over at Henry's Sweet Shop and not do a damn thing while I did everything.

"The cleaners had an old water tubed boiler and the alkali would get so bad from the city water if you didn't put the proper treatment in it, it would rupture the tubes. We had to call Bob "Boiler" Bill out of Jacksonville, Florida, to come and repair the boilers."

Those boilers leaked water down in the firebox. Crates of empty Coke bottles people had returned to get their nickels back had gotten placed near them on the floor. Johnny recalled, "Fred got mad one morning when he tripped over one of those bottles and drug them out in the middle of the floor and started kicking them everywhere. He had Coca-Cola bottles bouncing off the walls. Most of the people that were pressing clothes were black and sang while they worked. But, buddy, you talk about it getting quiet; it got quiet when Mr. Wiley threw his fit. You could have heard a pin drop."

Mr. Wiley made his way out there to the old boiler and called for Johnny. They messed around with it until they finally got it going. A little while later, Mr. Wiley left. He wouldn't stay anywhere long. Boiler Bill was called again.

When Fred Wiley left, those black people would start singing gospel songs like "Swing Low Sweet Chariot," "Amazing Grace," and those old hymns. They were always so quiet except singing gospel music. Johnny said, "They sounded so good. I loved hearing them sing."

Mr. Fred Wiley didn't pay Johnny very much. A fellow named Dorcey Goode was the owner of Southern Laundry and Cleaners, a big-time operation. He talked Johnny into coming over and working for him. Around this time, everyone referred to Johnny as Johnny Mac.

Mr. Dorcey thought Johnny Mac was going to steal Mr. Wiley's business, but Johnny wouldn't do that to Mr. Fred. He ran the plant for Mr. Goode, worked on the equipment, and kept it all running.

In 1961, that's how Johnny Mac met a man by the name of Jay Y. Folsom. The presses had a counter balance on the back of them. When you pulled the head down and locked that head, those counter locks would lock over. They were made out of cast iron. Once in a while, they would hit, and it would break them beyond repair. They would have to be replaced.

Johnny recalled, "Those steam irons would burn you all the time…constant damn problem."

Mr. Goode told Johnny to take the counter balances over to Jay Y. Folsom and to tell him to get on them really quick—that he had to have them right back. Being a young'un of twenty-one years old, Johnny didn't know any different, so he went to Mr. Folsom's.

He said, "What can I do for you, boy?"

Johnny said, "I work for Mr. Dorcey Goode, and I've got these counter balances here. They've got to be welded. They broke. He said to tell you to get right on them. He has to have them."

Well, Jay Y. ran Johnny Mac out of that shop with those damn things. He said, "You tell Dorcey Goode to bring me a damn check."

Johnny was scared to tell Mr. Dorcey that, but he did. He went back and told Mr. Goode what Jay Y. said.

Then Mrs. Elizabeth Goode got on the phone to Mr. Jay Y., and he told her to send him the money they owed. He didn't ease off a bit. They got Jay Y. his money and then sent Johnny to Mr. Doyle Green to do the welding on the machine pieces.

About a year later, Mr. Fred Wiley got a chance to buy a little laundry from Mrs. Williams over in Tallahassee on Persian Street. It wasn't anything but a small laundry. He approached Johnny and wanted them to go into business together. He was going to guarantee Johnny so much money a week if he went to Tallahassee and ran the laundry.

CHAPTER 18
Love of His Life

Johnny and some of his friends started going to a place called the Green Lantern. They would dance to the jukebox. He, Hamburger, Phillip, and a bunch of boys would go there to hang out with a bunch of girls they knew from high school. There wasn't any drinking, except maybe a Coca-Cola. They would put a quarter in the jukebox for seven songs and dance the whole time.

Johnny and Phyllis Scott got to enjoying each other's company and dancing every weekend. She graduated high school and went on to Tallahassee to Lively Vocational School to become a beautician.

By then, Johnny had saved up enough to afford a car. He was working at Nifty Cleaners. Phyllis liked his '56 Star Chief Catalina. Johnny let her drive it back and forth to beautician school.

There is never an exact time and place for true love. It happens accidentally with the beating of single hearts. And so, it happed that Johnny Mac met the love of his life, the woman that would be the mother of his children....Johnny decided he was going to get married.

The Alford Methodist Church was the setting for the special wedding ceremony of Miss Lois Phyllis Scott to Mr. John Perry McDaniel III on July 28, 1961.

Johnny's parents, Mr. and Mrs. Russell Owens and Mr. J. P. McDaniel Jr. watched as their 21-year-old son, Johnny, stood nervously in a dark suit and tie with a pale carnation in his lapel...awaiting his bride's entrance. Phyllis was given away by her father, Mr. William Leslie Scott, as her mom, Myrtle Blanch Davis Scott, wiped tears of pride and joy from her eyes. The petite figure graced the church aisle in a white sheath dress with long, pointed sleeves tapered at the wrists. Her small, nervous fingers gripped a white Bible topped with an orchid and streamers of white satin ribbons.

Mr. W. L. Scott relinquished his nineteen-year-old daughter's hand at the front of the sanctuary amidst floor vase arrangements of white gladioli and gold branched candelabras supporting burning white candles.

The double ring ceremony was performed by Rev. L. Milton Cutchen, who was the pastor of Grace Methodist Church in 1961.

John's heart stopped briefly as he lifted the short veil to reveal the glowing porcelain face of his wife just seconds before the union was sealed with a kiss. The couple made their home at 1421 Fairway Drive in Tallahassee, Florida, where Johnny went into business for himself.

John and Phyllis opened up the little laundry that Fred Williams had purchased. Johnny started with a Willys Jeepster, driving out to contact customers. Mrs. Williams had sold them that thing and provided them with a list of people to see. They quickly realized they couldn't make a living on laundry alone. They ended up having to contract out the dry cleaning.

The old equipment kept tearing up and breaking down. It was such a mess that it ate up all the profits.

Fred Williams finally came over to Tallahassee and said, "We're out of business. I ain't putting no more money in this place. You just gonna have to get out and find you a job."

Phyllis and John were living in a one-bedroom apartment on the golf course. John was now unemployed, no money, no nothing, except a beautiful new bride. Mr. Fred just said, "I'm shutting it down."

John's sister, Iris, lived in McClenny, Florida. She asked them to come there and she would see if she could help them find jobs in Jacksonville.

John was too proud; he didn't want to go back to Marianna. They moved and John walked the streets of Jacksonville for about three months trying to find a job. Finally, a friend of his, Lloyd Johnson, offered to help him out. Lloyd was working with Interstate Life Insurance Company on Riverside Avenue. He worked as a debit route salesman. Lloyd said he had an opening if John wanted it.

John went to Interstate Life Insurance Company and was hired by Lloyd's brother, Lavon. Lavon was an outstanding insurance man. He taught John how to sell. John had to get a license, so he studied hard and passed the test to become a licensed insurance agent. He received his own debit, which was a route book with directions.

The company then transferred John. He and Phyllis came back home to Marianna. John lived in Marianna and worked all the way over to Bonifay (two counties east of Marianna). He had his own route, but the route was so big it ate up everything he made.

The Marianna, Jackson County, Florida, area was seeing more growth in the early 1960s when J. C. Rainey built Carol Plaza on the west end of Marianna. The Piggly Wiggly store was first housed there but later relocated to the adjacent Lafayette Plaza. The Sunland Training Center opened on the site of the old TB Sanitarium near Greenwood in 1961. The growth in the area did little to help John in the insurance business as the McDaniel's struggled to make a living.

Phyllis, bless her heart, was a trooper. She worked as a beautician—cutting hair, curling hair, and doing shampoos to bring in extra money. She worked for Inez Beauty Shop in Marianna. Maddie Hall and Mrs. Simms took the struggling, newly-married young couple under their wings and tried to help them make a living. They survived off of Phyllis's tips their first year of marriage.

CHAPTER 19

Finance Career Begins As 1962 Ends:
Relocations for Family

As the year of 1962 was coming to a close, the country was seeing a series of diverse events. The United States and Great Britain were performing nuclear tests at the Nevada Test Site; President Kennedy addressed the nation in a televised speech, announcing the presence of offensive missile sites in Cuba; in one of her last public appearances, the memorable birthday song by Marilyn Monroe was sung on May 19th of 1962 at a birthday celebration for U.S. President John F. Kennedy; Mariner 2 made the first United States fly-by of another planet (Venus); the Beatles released their first song; the Beach Boys introduced a new "Surfin'" musical style; USSR performed nuclear tests at Novaya Zemlya USSR; President Kennedy banned all goods to Cuba (except food and drugs); and the US and Cuba reached an accord—Cuba started returning US prisoners from the Bay of Pigs invasion.

Even with all the changes in politics, music, science, and culture the world was seeing, John P. McDaniel III still couldn't make a go of the laundry business in the capital city of Florida, and he couldn't make a go of the insurance business either in the panhandle area.

Then, Hulan Lamar had a job opening for a collector for Union Finance Company. It was a collector and assistant loan officer, neither of which John had prior experience. He went to Union Finance, and Mr. Lamar hired him the 12th day of December, 1962.

Hulan Lamar trained Johnny in collections from calling the customer to visiting their residence in attempts to collect debts. Johnny received six cents per mile reimbursement. "This was what they called chasing bad credits and slow pays. Sometimes you would chase those slow pays; they might owe thirty dollars, and you would get five or seven dollars."

In Marianna, Florida, the following year, Union Finance Company sold out to Seaboard Finance and then to Avco Finance Company later. Johnny had worked his way up to assistant manager for Hulan at Union Finance. The second year he was there, he was sent to fill in for a manager that was on leave.

They paid him $200.00 a month when he worked at two offices in Panama City and when he moved to Pensacola as assistant manager. Johnny continued working hard until he managed to work up to six hundred dollars a month.

The office in Ft. Walton Beach came open. Mr. Kendricks was the district supervisor, and he hired Johnny. He was the manager of Avco Finance in Ft. Walton Beach on 8 Perry Blvd. for about a year and a half before they built a new office due to location. Johnny said, "There was a strip joint called Kitty Cat Corner across the street from the old location. The new office was on Avon Park. I worked in Ft. Walton for two years, 1963-1965."

During those two years, Phyllis and Johnny had two children. The apple of his eye, a blond-haired, blue-eyed little angel named Machelle was born on May 2, 1963. And the apple didn't fall far from the tree….John's mini-me, John P. McDaniel IV, was born on October 14, 1965.

One month before Machelle was born, John returned home due to the loss of his grandmother, Lessie W. McDaniel, on April 24, 1963. Lessie was born on June 22, 1887, and was 75 years old at the time of her death. A small service was held as John Jr. mourned the loss of his mother and John III said his final goodbyes to his grandmother. Graveside services followed at Bascom Methodist Church Cemetery in Bascom, Florida.

John and his good friend Ray Mixon would often go over to Foley, Alabama, on Saturdays. Ray's daddy had a place they could hunt and shoot doves. On the day Little John was born, Johnny was in Foley shooting doves. He arrived at the rental home in Ft. Walton to the phone ringing off the hook. It was Johnny Mac's momma. "You better get your tail to the house. Phyllis is having that boy."

Johnny jumped in the car and hauled ass to Marianna. When he got to Marianna, Phyllis had already had their son....She was mad as hell at John P. McDaniel III.

At that point, the McDaniel's had a boy and a girl, so they went back to Ft. Walton Beach, Florida. Johnny bought a house on a GI Bill. The house payments were $113.00 a month in 1965.

They were making a living. Avco Finance had an opening in Pensacola. They were firing the manager and wanted Johnny to take that office. It was a much bigger office with a large salary increase. Johnny took the job, and the company paid his moving expenses.

They left Ft. Walton Beach and moved over to Pensacola. The new office was downtown on Intendencia Street in the heart of the city. The books for Avco Finance in Pensacola were out of balance by twenty to thirty thousand dollars, and they had been unable to locate the error. Johnny stayed up until midnight every night for weeks, reconstructing every day's work back to where it was in balance. He finally found it. "They thought I was a hero at that point," he recalled.

The house in Pensacola had a huge pine right in front. Being near the coast, Johnny knew it had to come down. He paid to have the tree cut down but couldn't afford the stump removal as that was extra. The children watched the week-long project of their dad. He chopped some, sawed some, sang some, drilled some, sang some more, and did a whole lot of burning to get that old stump out of the ground.

Johnny took a short leave on August 16, 1968, to return home due to the death of his grandfather and namesake, John Perry McDaniel Sr.; J.P. was born on September 1, 1884, and was 83 years old at the time of his death. John Jr. returned from Pennsylvania for his father's funeral. Family and friends attended the service at Bascom Methodist Church with burial following at Bascom Methodist Cemetery.

While living in Pensacola, during his time away from work, John loved to ride the dirt roads. Once when his daughter was about five years old, they were driving down a desolate stretch of dirt road with Machelle begging to drive. Johnny stood his little girl in his lap and let her help with the steering. She felt like big stuff peering over the steering wheel as they eased down the road flipping dust up behind them.

Johnny used to sing to his children. Their favorite was "Little Brown Jug." Little did the children know at that time that the song was about liquor.

Johnny was back at work less than a year when his mother Ruth's father passed away. Johnny took a short leave to attend the funeral of his grandfather James W. (J. W.) Grant on April 20, 1969. J.W. was born on February 23, 1884, and was 85 years old at the time of his death. This hit Johnny really hard as he was very close to his grandfather. A beautiful service was held at Marvin Chapel Freewill Baptist Church in Marianna with graveside services following at the Church Cemetery.

Due to Johnny's success, Avco decided to send him to Gainesville, Florida. They were going to pay him even more money to go there. Phyllis wasn't happy, but they decided to move the family from Pensacola to Gainesville. Johnny was promoted to a regional supervisor. He wasn't afraid of hard work and always looked for ways to get ahead.

On Main Street, right across from the Gainesville office was a place called McDaniel Furniture Store. The owners were of no relation to Johnny, but he always remembered the store. John had that office for a year before the other Avco Finance Office downtown got into bad trouble, so he left the one on Main Street and went to the troubled location to attempt repairs.

Shortly after the family's move to Gainesville, Phyllis lost her father, William Leslie Scott, on February 16, 1972. He was eighty years old.

In a year's time, Johnny had the Gainesville office straightened out. Avco then called and needed him back in Pensacola. The location over there had blown up. It took a lot of talking for Johnny to convince Phyllis to move the family again. The only reason she agreed was that it would put them back closer to their hometown of Marianna, so they went back to Pensacola.

Johnny bought a house at Eleven W. Intendencia Street off of South Street. This would be home for a year. Things were going well. On May 2, the family celebrated Machelle's ninth birthday with a trip to the beach in Pensacola. The finance company built a new office on N. Palofox. Johnny always had a love for music and would come home late from work and lie in the floor listening to music over an old earphone headset so as not to wake the children. Machelle would sneak out of bed and lie on the floor next to her daddy listening to old Engelbert Humperdinck pieces.

The dust had no sooner settled at the new office building in Pensacola before the Finance company sent Johnny to West Palm Beach to run a big office down there which was deplorable. During that period of time, Phyllis was very unhappy. Johnny didn't blame her; he had moved her around relentlessly, working eleven branches in ten years.

After eleven years of marriage, they were just about to the point of getting a divorce. John P. McDaniel III was worried about success. He wasn't worried about what his ambition and desire to succeed was doing to his wife and children.

Avco Finance promised they would make Johnny an assistant district supervisor. They dangled that carrot in front of Johnny until he finally talked Phyllis into another move. She never agreed to it, but she went anyway in July of 1972.

The family lived in Lantana, and Johnny worked in West Palm Beach. Lantana encompassed an area of approximately three square miles in Palm Beach County and still retained the charm of its origins as an old Florida fishing village. Despite the city's charm, things got even worse with Johnny and Phyllis. She was giving up on him and their marriage. Johnny really tried to spend more time with the family. Every Saturday and Sunday he would take the children to the beach. They loved playing in the water and fondly laughing at their dad in his dark dress socks and "Jesus Sandals," building sand castles on the beach.

On Wednesday, October 4, 1972, ten days before Little John's seventh birthday, Phyllis received a call. All of a sudden, her mother, Mrs. Myrtle, who still worked at Sunland in Marianna had died. Lightning had struck the electrical service going into the house and set the house on fire and burned Mrs. Myrtle to death in the house.

Johnny put a shattered Phyllis on an airplane and sent her home to Marianna. Johnny had the children, Machelle and Little John, until he could get them to their mother. He couldn't afford plane tickets for all of them. Johnny found someone to run the office in West Palm and drove home to Marianna with the kids.

He tried to be there for Phyllis. The service for the 68-year-old Mrs. Myrtle Blanch Davis Scott was beautiful with family members and friends arriving to show their respect. On Monday, October 9, Johnny spent his thirty-second birthday trying to persuade his wife to not give up on their marriage. It took Johnny several days after the service to even attempt to talk Phyllis into returning to West Palm Beach.

After much talking, Johnny convinced her to go back with him. On Saturday, October 14, 1972, they celebrated Little John's seventh birthday in West Palm.

CHAPTER 20
Beginning of Life-Changing Career

The McDaniel family wasn't back in West Palm but a couple of months after Phyllis lost her mom. One evening when Johnny came in late from work, Phyllis just said, "Johnny, I'm going back to Marianna. If you can't go back to Marianna, we will just have to get a divorce. I can't keep this pace, living down here like this and being away from my family. I've already lost my daddy and my momma this year...."

Well, about that time, a friend and local business man in Marianna, George Darrell "G.D." Yon Jr., called John. Ronnie Craven had gotten elected as sheriff in Marianna. Craven had defeated the incumbent sheriff, Barkley Gause, and would assume duties in January of 1973. They wanted to know if John could do budgets, run ledgers, and handle the financial aspect of a sheriff's office. Johnny informed them that he could do that. He had been doing that for the past ten plus years, dealing with $100 dollars to $5,000,000 dollar financial offices. Mr. Yon asked if Johnny would come up to Marianna and speak with Craven about being his administrative assistant. Johnny told Yon he didn't know....He needed time to think about it. Johnny knew it would be a huge cut in pay, but it might be the only way to save his marriage.

Johnny thought about it and prayed about it. Within a week, the family drove all night one night to come up to Marianna. He met with Jackson County Sheriff Ronnie Craven. They talked, and he agreed to hire Johnny.

At the end of December, 1972, Johnny left Avco Financial in West Palm Beach and moved his family back to Marianna to begin work at the Jackson County Sheriff's Department.

January 1973
Jackson County Sheriff's Department
Ronnie Craven – Sheriff
Benjamin Lavaughn (B. L.) Parmer – Chief Deputy
John P. McDaniel III – Administrative Assistant

Johnny's salary in January of 1973 was $525.00 a month. He was making $700.00 a month with Avco Financial, but he took the cut in pay to move home and try to save his marriage. He had completed ten years with Avco Finance Services. They gave John mustering out pay—a prorated pension pay out.

He had enough to make a small down-payment on a house in Dogwood Heights, a small, quiet subdivision just north of Marianna. He bought it from Kelso Gillenworth, who was editor of the local paper. Living next door to them was Sid and Judy Riley who owned a local bed and breakfast. Across from John was Roy and Margaret (Libby) Hutto. Roy served in the Marines and then became a Florida state trooper where he would serve for 25 years before retiring in 1989. It was a wonderful, safe family community to raise their children.

This decision in December of 1972 started John's law enforcement career and changed his life. John, Phyllis, Machelle, and Little John tried to start a different life.

John took Phyllis and the kids to Chipola River, Blue Springs, and Compass Lake. The whole family loved all types of water activity. Once a friend with a boat met them at Compass Lake; Little John was about eight years old and recalled his mom and dad skiing on the lake with just one ski. The two pulled off at the dock, circled the lake, and his mom would come gliding in and walk ashore with not a hair out of place.

But no matter how hard John tried, moving back never mended the feelings between him and Phyllis.

Unfortunately, things kept getting worse and worse. John had already turned Phyllis sour on him and his lifestyle. Too little, too late. He knew it was his fault.

CHAPTER 21
The Craven Administration

The Craven administration started out with Lavaughn Parmer as chief deputy and Frank Bylsma and Sonny Dean as investigators. As the administrative assistant, John was tasked with learning the budget process, paying the bills, and preparing a budget for the upcoming year.

Mrs. Harris and Abbie Jean Burdeshaw worked for the Jackson County Board of County Commissioners. Between those two ladies, they helped John learn how to prepare a budget, submit a budget, and know a little something about finances in law enforcement. They had taken over Mr. Gause's budget, which was $212,000 dollars to operate for a year. That included the jail, patrol, civil process, court system—everything. The budget was a nightmare.

The old jail was a horrific mess—built in 1947 from a plan that Mr. High, the Architect, had gotten from the 1920's. It was outdated and antiquated the day Craven took office. They had to operate with it and do the best they could.

The old jail housed 12-21 inmates with exception of women. They didn't have the facilities to house females. If a female prisoner got sentenced to jail time, the sheriff would beg the judge to let her out. The departmental budget didn't allow the money to hire a female correction officer (matron). They would hire a female to cook for the inmates, and she would also serve as the matron. Mildred Christmas served as the first cook/matron under the Craven administration. She was cantankerous as could be but could cook anything, but if she got mad at you, dogs couldn't eat the meal.

However, she could be a sweetheart and helped staff make it through those times. She got there at four in the morning, cooking biscuits and bacon, and then everybody in the courthouse starting coming for breakfast. They had to stop that because the department couldn't afford to feed the whole courthouse every morning. The department bought Ronnie a new car. The first one was a Buick. Sheriff Gause had bought a Chrysler 300 when he was in office, and it was issued to Chief Deputy Parmer.

The rest of the department drove whatever: 1969 Chevrolet, couple of old dodges, and old highway patrol cars. They did the best they could with their assets. Inmates that knew anything about mechanics helped keep the departmental vehicles running. Occasionally, the Department of Corrections would help and let them use their mechanics. They didn't have to pay an electric bill except at the jail. The sheriff's department and offices were housed in the county courthouse. They had to pay the telephone bill, but electricity in the courthouse was paid by the Board of County Commissioners.

In 1973, Ronnie Craven's salary as sheriff was $24,000 a year. Lavaughn Parmer's salary was about $600 a month. He had left the Department of Corrections after twenty-plus years to come there and work as chief deputy. John had spent ten years in the financial business and came home for $525 a month. Frank Bylsma and Sonny Dean both made $500 a month as investigators.

Chief Parmer was basically in charge of everything except the administration. John hired two ladies, Glenda Parmer and Linda Hatcher. They helped with bookkeeping, civil processes, warrants division, evidence, and more. That was their job, and they both were fantastic. They would even act as matrons if a female prisoner had to be transported. At night, the department would have to hire someone. Usually that was State Trooper Marvin Wagner's wife, Nancy.

Years before John came to work at the sheriff's office, down below the old jail on the east side was an elderly black woman. She did moonshine by the shot. Every six months, they would put her in jail for selling moonshine whisky. She would be the cook for six months. She would get out and they would catch her again. She always stayed at her house, so they didn't have to hire a matron. She acted as the cook, the matron, or whatever was needed.

During first appearance under the Craven administration, they would walk the inmates up the hill from the old jail up to the courthouse. Sometimes if there were eight to ten inmates, they used a long log chain and chained them all together.

Don Grant, John's uncle, was in charge of the jail. He would handcuff all those inmates to the chain. If one ran, they would all have to run. Mr. Grant would walk inmates up to the courthouse and put them in the holding cells to wait their turn in court.

The warrant division was a nightmare. They had warrants which had never been served and warrants that had been served but were still showing active in the file.

According to John, "Those were quite different times. If you arrested a person twice for the same charge, they didn't rush out and get a lawyer and sue you for false arrest before you could resolve the issue and release the person."

There were a lot of issues facing the new administration which would require time and hard work to resolve and clean up over the years to come.

The sheriff's office didn't work much traffic. They were usually the first responder to accidents and just stood by until the trooper arrived on scene.

Typical deputy duties at that time included working burglaries, thefts, family disturbances, and loose livestock. All deputies had their turn at being a wrangler.

They had their turn chasing cows to get them off the road. There was a stock law in place, but it was rarely observed or enforced.

The first year of the Craven administration, John recalled Chief Lavaughn Parmer as not being afraid of the devil and one of the bravest men he ever knew. Parmer would work 24 hours a day. He didn't care what it was because he loved it so much. Basically, if it hadn't have been for Parmer, his knowledge, and the hours he gave to the department, they would not have succeeded in turning the office around.

Sheriff Craven was the smartest man John ever knew in his life. Ronnie was a very, very intelligent man but had a hard time coming to work during the day. He liked to ride around at night and listen to what was going on and be a part of the night life of law enforcement. He didn't care anything about the courthouse or being there in the day. That created some problems with the judge and other issues as well.

They managed to work through the problems. In 1973, Article 5 mandated the placement of a bailiff in the courtroom and the appointment of an attorney for everyone charged. As part of the legal process, first an information document had to be filed. Florida Attorney General Robert L. Shevin (1971-1979) and the State Attorney's Office got together and tried to work out a uniform complaint system. A complaint would be filed against an individual for the sheriff's office to file an information document with the clerk's office. The clerk's office sent this to the state attorney. The state attorney reviewed to determine if they would prosecute the case. If they elected to prosecute, they would send the file back to the clerk's office with an information file, and then the warrant would come back to the sheriff's office. The sheriff's office would log it in and assign it to an officer to locate the person and put them in jail.

At that time, there were no standardized complaint forms. Everything was on canary yellow pads or even worse, scrap pieces of paper or napkins. The former chief deputy, John J. "J.J." McCrary, carried a canary yellow pad and pen with him everywhere he went. Everything was done by hand.

John P. McDaniel III had the opportunity to work with the State Attorney's Office to develop a uniform complaint form system. He studied the Florida statutes just as hard as he could and was successful in the development of a standardized form still utilized today.

If there was a shooting, for example, the new form would have a list of who the victim was, who the witnesses were, age, and all other necessary information. They developed a form cross referencing statutes to decide about burglaries, bad checks, etc. The new form took the guesswork out of it for the law enforcement officer, and it insured that no information or details would be omitted.

In 1973-74, Jackson County had more bad checks than anywhere in the whole state of Florida, it seemed. Local businesses would call and notify the sheriff's office they had fifteen or more bad checks and they were bringing them up to fill out the proper complaints.

John studied the whole "bad check" process. It was very time-consuming to create the information complaint with the store name, address, date, time, name, and narrative information. For instance the information in the complaint might be "John Doe came in to said store to purchase household groceries and products that cost 'X' dollars and tendered check in 'X' number of dollars which later was returned from the bank marked insufficient funds (or closed account or no account)." When this process was complete, John would send it to the clerk's office, and the clerk's office would make it an official document and send it to the State Attorney's

75

Office. The SA would review it and decide if they would or would not issue a warrant for worthless checks. Well, there was too many of them, and politically, you couldn't put everybody in jail. John, as administrative assistant, was told by Sheriff Craven to get on the phone and call the writers of bad checks, as he didn't want to put them in jail.

John did as the sheriff advised and called offenders to work something out. John would call and say, "John or Jane Doe, you got a bad check down here at the IGA. You got one day to bring me the money. If you don't, I'm going to get a warrant for you and put you in jail."

That went on and on and on. John became a collection agency for the sheriff's office for bad checks. John recalled, "It became a nightmare because, again, they didn't want to put offenders in jail. Most of the people with bad checks and so forth were hard-working people; they had to work for a living. If you put them in jail, they couldn't post bond. If they couldn't post bond, they would lose their jobs. Then their wives and children wouldn't have groceries, electricity, etc....

"Back then, on Friday nights, there was a fella named Jimbo. He worked like a dog all week long, but come Friday night, he would give his wife money to buy groceries and pay bills for the week. Jimbo took what was left, shoved it in his pocket, and headed to the pool hall. He would drink and drink and drink until he got drunk. Early morning hours, when Jimbo finally rambled home, his wife would start fussing and cussing at him. She would follow him from room to room just cussing and hollering until he beat the pure tar out of her. She would call the sheriff's office. 'Jimbo is down here beating the hell out of me. You better get somebody down here, or I'm gonna kill him.'

"The Sheriff's Office would send a deputy out there and find that Jimbo had indeed beat the hell out of his wife. They would arrest him and put him in jail. Jimbo's wife would nurse her bruises, and by Sunday, she would be at the jail saying one of two things. 'Sheriff, we got to get him out of jail so he can go to work in the morning' or 'let him out at five o'clock in the morning.' This was weekend after weekend. Same scenario, over and over."

A lot of that behavior passed on over the years from generation to generation and became a process known as learned behavior. During John's tenure in law enforcement, he would eventually work two or three generations, starting out with the daddy and then next to the son and grandson—case after case of domestic violence.

"A lot of the people arrested and placed in jail in the '70s and early '80s were very talented at a specific trade. Some of the best pulpwooders, equipment operators, contractors, licensed carpenters, and welders ended up in jail. They were good at their trade. They just had to blow off steam on the weekends and they would just beat the hell out of whatever or whomever got in their way. This happened over and over and over."

Back then, the janitor at the courthouse had a son that was bad to get drunk and stay drunk. Well, he committed a crime. Chief Parmer was actually the one that went to arrest him. He pulled a knife on Parmer and said, "I'll cut your throat if you come after me." Parmer just eased closer and closer as he kept him talking. Finally, as quick as lightning strikes, Parmer hit him upside the head and knocked him out, took the knife away from him, and put him in jail.

When it came to armed robberies, they all worked together. John was on the administrative end but had gotten to the point where he enjoyed law enforcement. He talked Sheriff Craven into sending him to the law enforcement school at night, on his own time, in Chipley. The sheriff agreed to pay for the school. In April of 1973,

77

John began attending Washington-Holmes Adult Vocational Training Center to become a certified law enforcement officer. He drove back and forth; the course was 280 hours at that time. Later, the State of Florida came up with a law that said that any law enforcement officer had to be paid $600.00 a month. That helped John as he went from $500.00 a month to $600.00 a month in salary.

During those months, Johnny Mac had come to love law enforcement. He found something he enjoyed and wanted to learn more and more about it.

With that being said, Johnny branched out and did a little work here and there in all areas of law enforcement under the supervision of Sheriff Craven.

In August of 1973, Lavaughn Parmer decided he wanted to go back to the Florida Department of Corrections. He gave them until October before he vacated the chief deputy position with the sheriff's department and went back to corrections to finish out his state retirement. Needless to say, it was a huge loss to the sheriff's department. Parmer knew everybody, was everywhere, and did everything; he was a great man.

Johnny Mac claimed they *did* butt heads from time to time, but they did it as gentlemen. "Parmer would be mad as hell at you one minute and then walk up and say, 'What the hell's wrong with you. What's wrong?'

"I'd say, 'Parmer, me and you just got through having bad words.'

"Parmer would just shake his head. 'Awe, don't worry about that. Nothing to it. Don't worry about it.'"

CHAPTER 22

Chief Deputy at the Wild West of Jackson County (Billie Clubs, Drunks, Shoot-Outs, and Roadblocks):
October 1973

In October of 1973, Sheriff Ronnie Craven made a decision that would change Johnny Mac's life once again. "Johnny, I'll pay you $1,000.00 a month if you will be chief deputy and administrative assistant and take on the job of captain."

Well, that was right down Johnny's alley. He didn't really know enough about law enforcement. He wasn't a seasoned law enforcement officer, but with his eagerness and desire to learn, he was just tickled to death with the opportunity.

Johnny Mac took the job of being chief deputy/captain in charge of patrol and administrative services. They hired Lil Hollis away from the school board. She came in and took over most of the administrative services. John still did the budgets, grants, and so forth. He spent most of his time looking after finances, followed closely by supervision of patrol and the jail. He continued to go to law enforcement schools, whether it be drug enforcement, customs, or whatever was offered. He would take advantage of the opportunity to learn as much as he could.

One of the first things he did when he took office as chief deputy was to order uniforms. At that time, he purchased gray pants with white shirts. He always thought that looked like marine patrol uniforms. He loved them, thinking those were the prettiest uniforms they ever had. He got a gun belt and his own weapon, a Smith and Wesson .357 model 19 revolver with adjustable sites and a four inch barrel.

He donned his uniform and went on the road. He had to prove himself as chief deputy to all the staff, to

79

Ronnie, and the public. He also had to prove himself to himself. There were times he was scared as hell. But he never asked anyone to do anything he wouldn't do himself. It meant in the event of a hostage situation, he was going to be the lead man. He would help with cases without interfering, however. He was a working chief deputy/captain who made mistakes like everyone else.

John learned quickly he could get a lot more by asking cooperation from people—inmates, prisoners, violators of the law—by dealing with them and bargaining with them rather than trying to run over them and bark orders. He managed to put it together without too much use of force. From 1973 through 1977, John continued to learn and grow in his law enforcement career.

John recalled one particular fellow up in Greenwood in the north end of the county. The fellow was racing up and down the roads, showing his butt big time. Officers responded to the citizens' complaints, went out there, and got him stopped. They got him out of his car, and he proceeded to fight the officers.

After much tussling, they got him in the back of the old '69 Chevy patrol car. Once the deputy arrived at the jail, he called dispatch. "You better get me some help out here; he's trying to kick the cage out."

Johnny Mac was at the jail. He walked up to the patrol car and told them to roll the back window down. He leaned over to the open window. "Okay, now I got everybody out of the way but me. I'm gonna open this door and you're gonna come out of there and act like a man, or I'm gonna beat the living hell out of you."

The fellow cursed Johnny a bit but finally he respected him enough to get out and go inside the jail.

***

Another time, an inmate was on work release and had gotten drunk. Johnny Mac went to get him, and he got combative. John forcibly man-handled him, picked him up, threw him in the back of the patrol car, and carried him to the sheriff's office.

John got him out of the car and started up the steps with him when the prisoner turned around and charged Johnny like a bull. John had not handcuffed him. Johnny Mac always had pretty good strength, and this guy was going to put him to the test. When the prisoner came back on John, he grabbed the boy and bear hugged him as tight as he could. John almost squeezed the life out of the boy as he carried him up to the catwalk area and threw him down. John told the deputy to lock his ass up and that he would see the prisoner when he got ready to see him. John got the prisoner's attention as well as other officers by showing them he would go the extra mile and do what he had to do in order to get the job done.

***

Bill Reddoch was a local farmer and successful businessman. He was instrumental in the growth of Jackson County. Bill would occasionally sponsor cookouts for law enforcement personnel. John was at one of those cookouts once when he received a call from the Sneads Police Department. A fellow named Danny was in his yard, drunk on the north end of Sneads, and he was shooting high-powered rifles at anything that moved. The officers were pinned down behind an ambulance. John rushed over to Sneads and used his car to get up close enough to help the officers and to get closer to where Danny was perched. John kept trying to talk to him, but Danny kept cussing and shooting everywhere.

John hid his gun in the pit of his back, stepped out with his hands up, and said, "I want to come up there and talk to you."

Danny let out a string of explicit words you could hear a county away before replying. "All right, you come on, but don't none of the rest of you SOBs come up here."

Johnny drew in a deep breath and turned to look at the officers before taking steps toward Danny. "Boys, if he kills me, I want y'all to make damn shore you kill him now."

Johnny went toward Danny, hands held up and his .357 in the small of his back, praying that he could get to it quickly if he had to. Danny was drinking beside an old station wagon he owned. The tailgate was down, and every now and then, he would ease over and sit on the tailgate. He had a rifle in one hand and a bottle of Lord Calvert in the other. He would grab that bottle, take a drink, fire off a few rounds, and cuss everybody. Johnny realized this situation was getting worse and tried to keep talking to him in order to divert his attention away from the others. The ambulance he was firing toward had oxygen tanks aboard. Danny would listen to John, but he kept cussing and drinking.

Finally, not sure it was a good thing, Danny warmed up to Johnny just a little bit and shoved the Calvert bottle toward Johnny Mac. "Have a drink with me."

Johnny shook his head back and forth. "I don't believe I want to have a drink right now."

Danny swung the liquor bottle in the air a little closer to Johnny. "You're gonna take a drink with me."

"No, I'm not gonna take a drink right now."

"Well, damn you! I'll drink it my damn self." Danny took him a big swallow as he placed his rifle on the tailgate next to his pistol.

About that time, John heard a rustling noise at his feet, and it was Deputy Duane Davis crawling up to help subdue Danny. As Duane got there, Danny had his bottle up in his right hand. Johnny reached and grabbed him under his armpit and over his left shoulder, pulling him down so he couldn't do anything.

He couldn't get to his rifle or pistol, so Johnny and Duane wrestled him down and brought him in without any further incident. They managed to come up with a successful end to that one. Johnny said, "If Danny had shot the ambulance the officers were using as cover and hit an oxygen bottle, it would have killed the hell out of a bunch of them."

They didn't have sense enough to think about things like that back then, often rushing head first into situations. When adrenalin kicked in, they were incapable of comprehending the extent of the danger.

***

Another case early on in Johnny Mac's career when he was a chief deputy was the case of Willie Tom. Jackson County Sheriff's Office received a call from Bay County that a man by the name of Willie Tom had shot at his neighbors, pulled a knife on them, and threatened to kill them. Bay County, being immediately south of Jackson, meant they didn't have much time to assist their neighboring agency. Willie Tom had left the scene at a high rate of speed headed toward Jackson County with a Bay County Sheriff's Deputy in pursuit and needing back up.

Johnny Mac had his wife, Phyllis, and two children in the car with him when this started. He stopped at the closest safe place he could find, Investigator Frank Bylsma's house, and left them there. The high speed chase was coming north from Bay County onto Hwy 167. Frank lived on that road, so the whole road by his house was blocked off.

Investigator Frank Bylsma had a new Pontiac the department had just bought him, Deputy Buck Edwards had a marked car, and Johnny Mac was in his new 1974 department car.

Frank was first in line, then Buck Edwards. Johnny radioed them to leave just enough room between them so if they couldn't stop Willie Tom, at least he'd have to whirl in and out between them. Johnny would stay in the back and catch him if he got past the road block. Sure enough, he got past them and came right past Johnny. It really pissed Johnny off, so he flipped his car around and caught Willie Tom. They didn't know it was called a pit maneuver back then, but Johnny hit his left rear quarter panel, spinning him out to the right side and Johnny spun to his left, crossways to the road where he was at.

Johnny forgot to take his seatbelt lose and was caught up, trying to get out of his car. Willie Tom started shooting with a .22 pistol. He shot the whole damn windshield out trying to shoot Johnny. It didn't penetrate the windshield, just spread glass everywhere. Johnny managed to get out of his car, get on the ground, and come across the hood with his gun cocked up. Frank Bylsma had already fired one time, shooting through Johnny's car.

Johnny hollered, "Woe, ya'll don't shoot me."

Deputy Buck Edwards was jumping up and down, waving his radio mic like he was doing calisthenics, yelling. "He's gonna kill you. He's gonna kill you."

After Willie Tom had fired all of his shots, Johnny could hear him firing on a dry cylinder. So he started to approach him. The minute Johnny got to him, Willie Tom pulled out a large Barlow-looking knife. Johnny had a 36" Billie club and came across the hood of his car striking Willie Tom with that club knocking the living hell out of him.

Willie Tom started at Johnny again. When he came at him the second time, Johnny cracked down on him.

Then Mr. Davis, a deputy from Bay County arrived and got in between them. Now this man had tried to shoot Johnny, cut him, and everything else, so Johnny fully intended to put him down.

Deputy Davis got in between them right when Johnny was coming down full force on Willie Tom. The downward force broke the deputy's arm. Davis never let Johnny forget that he broke his arm when he was trying to help him.

Johnny was just trying to subdue the man without killing him. They got him, but it wiped Johnny's car out. The new 1974 Pontiac had the whole front end torn off. A wrecker came to pull Johnny's car and went by Bylsma's house on the way out. Johnny's wife and daughter were standing on the front porch and saw the wreckage being towed. The women in Johnny's life went to pieces.

By the end of 1977, Ronnie Craven ran for sheriff again with Charles Applewhite running against him. Charles's daddy, Robert Applewhite, was a very popular man and a very good, well-respected man in the county. Charles had gained a wonderful reputation as a law enforcement officer.

So Charles, being a civil process deputy, politicked and campaigned everyday against current Sheriff Craven. Johnny tried to tell Ronnie that he was doing it, but Ronnie didn't believe him. Craven said Charles wouldn't do that.

When election time came closer at hand, Ronnie hadn't stayed in the office like he was supposed to and hadn't done some of the things he was supposed to do....He just had some problems. Johnny knew Ronnie Craven was fixing to get his butt beat, or he thought he was, because some of the people that had helped elect Ronnie had come to Johnny and asked him to run for sheriff. Johnny told them no, he would not run against

Ronnie. Not only was Ronnie Craven his sheriff, he was his friend.

CHAPTER 23
Civic Involvement /
Mason and Shriners

J ohnny became a master Mason in 1975. Masonry is the oldest and largest fraternity in the world. No other organization has a man walk into a room full of strangers, anywhere on earth, and immediately receive welcome and honor as a friend and brother. Many Masons are well-known throughout history: Benjamin Franklin, John Hancock, Paul Revere, Winston Churchill, Douglas McArthur, General Winfield Scott, Davy Crockett, Wolfgang Amadeus Mozart, John Wayne, Roy Rogers, Henry Ford, Arnold Palmer, Edwin E. "Buzz" Aldrin Jr., Oscar Wilde, and many, many more.

Freemasonry does not recognize differences in race, color, creed, or station, and its history dates back from antiquity. Masonry has two purposes: 1) inspire members to live by the tenets of brotherly love, relief, and truth, and 2) endeavor to build a world where justice, equality, and compassion shine for all humankind. Even though Masonry's founding philosophy is based upon religious principles, they do not serve as a religion nor as a substitute for one, but they do believe in God.

Sometimes people confuse Masonry with a religion because they call some Masonic buildings "temples." But they use the word in the same sense that Justice Oliver Wendell Holmes called the Supreme Court a "Temple of Justice." Neither Masonry nor the Supreme Court is a religion just because its members meet in a "temple."

Johnny worked his way through the chairs—different positions within the Masons. Members have to be elected to each position and be a part in different activities.

In 1978, Johnny was elected Master, which is like the president of a club. This was Harmony Lodge #3, which is the Masonic Lodge in Marianna. It is the second oldest lodge in the state of Florida.

Johnny also went through Chapter Counsel and Commandery. This takes you into the Shrinedom. He went through the Scottish Rite, 32 degrees. Then he went to Aja Temple. When he left Aja Temple, they decided to start their own temple in Panama City, Florida. With that being said, they have a temple in Panama City named Shaddi Shrine Temple. Johnny is also a charter member of that group.

A lot has been said about Masons, the secrecy, and all of those things. The one thing Johnny knows about Masons and is close to his heart is "You can't be a Mason unless you believe in God. The only secrecy to it is the catechisms. There is no secret group to do anything. All they do is take a young man and make a better man out of him. Their mission in life is to make better people in life out of young men."

The Shriners Hospitals for Children, specializing in burn injuries, have been leaders in burn care, research, and education since opening in the mid-1960s. Thanks to the cutting-edge medical care provided at these hospitals, every year thousands of children have a greater chance of surviving from all types of burn injuries. With the help of Shrine Temple, hospitals all over provide services to children, and it doesn't cost the family anything. Johnny used to serve on the Burn Children Committee in Marianna. It was his job in Marianna—if they had a burn victim to make arrangements through the Shrine Temple in Panama City or Pensacola—to get the child to a burn institute or hospital.

Once they had a small, black female child up near Bascom that fell into an open fire and was burned very badly. Johnny got in touch with Harold Foran of Chipola Aviation. He took his leer jet and they loaded the injured child up and got her quickly to Cincinnati, Ohio, for the best burn treatment possible.

Historically, as far back as King Solomon's Temple in Biblical times and the things that went along with building the temple, different people went into different apprentices, fellow crafts, and masonry. The only basis of "secrecy" is how they received their wages for what they had done.

Johnny took a lot of pride in being a Master Mason, a York Rite, a Scottish Rite, and a Shrine. Each organization has one ultimate goal—to reinforce the United States of America, the Constitution of America, and God almighty.

CHAPTER 24
Elections Lost /
Endings and New Beginnings

Charles Applewhite *did* run against Ronnie Craven in the sheriff's election, and John McDaniel ran for tax collector in 1976.

September of 1976 was the first-time John Perry McDaniel III ran for a political office. He ran against Foster L. Jennings for the office of tax collector. John was still trying to save his marriage and didn't want to be in the middle of the turmoil about to occur at the sheriff's office, so he elected to run for tax collector, but Jennings won the race. It was close with Jennings receiving 5525 votes to McDaniel's 4824.

On September 7, 1976, when the polls closed for the first primary election, six candidates for the office of sheriff were narrowed down to two opponents. Applewhite received 2410 votes to Craven's 4174. The votes cast for Brock, Everett, Glass, and Goodson would be divided between Applewhite and Craven on the second primary on September 28, 1976.

During one of those first years working at the sheriff's office, John recalled living in Indian Springs; he had bought some toys for the young'uns and one or two things had to be put together. He was sitting in the floor, assembling toys, when he got a call that there had been a shooting in the house behind him. A woman had shot her husband with a shotgun and killed him. They responded on the basis of the initial report that it was self-defense. When John arrived on scene, he quickly realized it wasn't true. The female had mental problems and had shot the man in the back and killed him.

John stood there looking at him and noticed that he had a bulge in his shirt. He was lying face down, so John reached down and lifted his shirt. She had blown his lungs completely out of his body.

He and other officers worked that case right up until ten o'clock Christmas morning. He finally got to go and have Christmas with his children.

As chief deputy, Johnny regularly stayed out all night, but they weren't working all the time. A lot of time they were playing, doing things they didn't have any business doing but nothing against the law. They would spend hours just riding up and down the dirt roads, having a drink, and doing target practice down at Iron Bridge.

They were spending time with one another at the sheriff's office but not with their families. It cost Ronnie Craven the election and was costing John his marriage.

During Charles Applewhite's four-year term as sheriff, Johnny went to work for Peacock Motor Company. Mrs. Irma Stone gave him a job. Johnny helped her with the showroom and learned how to run the office and sell cars.

Well, Johnny Mac got to missing law enforcement. He had found something in the job that filled a void in his life. Sneads Police Department, just east of Marianna but still in Jackson County, needed someone to run the radio. Johnny was willing to do anything to get back to that career.

A few months into 1977 found John's marriage deteriorated beyond repair. Phyllis and John divorced on May 17, 1977. John moved to a little, old house out in the country that belonged to his momma. His children wanted to come and live with him. In the beginning, his daughter Machelle was adamant she was living with Daddy. His son, Little John, moved in with his dad and Machelle soon followed.

John was working at Peacock Motor Company in the daytime and Sneads Police Department at night. They had an officer working at Sneads PD that decided he didn't want to be a patrolman anymore. The chief at Sneads asked John to get a uniform and be a patrolman for him.

Well, that was right down John's alley. He got to be a patrolman. Every minute away from Peacock Motor Company, he was at Sneads Police Department.

By early 1978, John was able to do better for his children and bought another house in the Dogwood Heights subdivision, just a block or so from their original family home. The children got to pick out their colors for paint, and they had a good time fixing the house up. Both Machelle, fourteen years old, and Little John, eleven years old, had their own rooms.

Deputy John Dennis came to help Johnny Mac one time. Dennis worked for Sheriff Applewhite. Johnny Mac had a problem with a trucker one night. The trucker refused to get out of the truck. Johnny Mac talked him out and had turned his back on him. Dennis was there to back him up. The trucker tried to hit Johnny Mac, and when he did, Dennis creamed him, put him in the dirt, and handcuffed him. If it hadn't have been for Deputy Dennis, Johnny Mac could have gotten hurt that night.

Johnny Mac met John Dennis for the first time that night, and they became good friends. Johnny Mac said that Dennis "saved my bacon." John said there were many more times that John Dennis had his back. Johnny Mac continued working both jobs and living down in that little house until he ran for office in the next sheriff election.

On May 3, 1978, Jackson County citizens and local law enforcement were shocked and sickened by the discovery of two bodies. The soil down a deserted country road just outside the town of Cottondale was covered in blood, following the brutal double murder of Bonnie Myrle Ward and her twelve-year-old daughter, Donna Lynn Strickland.

On May 1, 1978, two days prior to the discovery of the bodies, Jimmy Lee Smith had aroused the suspicions of a bank teller when he attempted to cash a check drawn on another bank. Although law enforcement officers responded promptly and chased the vehicle Smith was driving, he evaded capture.

The next day, May 2, law enforcement officers found the vehicle abandoned. The vehicle belonged to Bonnie Ward. The same day on which law enforcement officers found the abandoned vehicle, they arrested Smith and charged him with forgery. Pursuant to a search incident to Smith's arrest, law enforcement officers seized a pocket knife and a ladies' watch. The watch would later be identified at trial as that of Bonnie Ward.

Upon arrival at the jail, Smith requested to speak to a lawyer. An assistant public defender, Herman D. Laramore, was at the jail and conferred with Smith. At the conclusion of their conversation, Laramore advised Smith that he should make no statements to law enforcement officers.

On May 3, when Smith appeared for his first appearance hearing on the forgery charges, the court appointed the public defender's office to represent him. Later that day, Deputy Ron Steverson of the Jackson County Sheriff's Department telephoned Laramore and advised him that the bodies of Ward and Strickland had been found and that Smith was a prime suspect in those murders.

That same day, Steverson questioned Smith about the homicides. Steverson advised Laramore that he had interrogated Smith.

The next day, May 4, law enforcement officials arrested Smith for the Ward and Strickland murders.

Deputy Steverson again interrogated Smith. This time Smith confessed to both homicides. Deputy Steverson notified Laramore.

On May 5, Deputy Steverson filed complaints against Smith for the murders of the two victims. At his first appearance on the murder charges, Smith signed an acknowledgement of rights form and requested the appointment of counsel.

This is an excerpt from the findings of fact made by the trial judge:

In the case of Bonnie Myrle Ward, the evidence shows that prior to her killing, she cried and begged the defendant to please leave her alone; that thereafter, he coolly and deliberately strangled her while he looked directly into her eyes; that he noted her kicking and gasping for air; that he noted while strangling her that her tongue bulged and protruded from her mouth; and that, while pitilessly strangling his helpless victim, he exhorted her to "Die, bitch."

Upon twelve-year-old Donna Lynn Strickland coming to her mother's aid and seeing the defendant's vicious attack upon her mother, the evidence shows that the defendant then calmly and deliberately strangled the said Donna Lynn Strickland, and upon experiencing difficulty in choking her unconscious with his hands, held her by the throat with one hand while he wrapped an antennae cord about her throat with the other hand so as to more easily complete his wicked and vile purpose.

The court further finds that after choking both victims to the ground, the defendant removed all the clothing from each of the totally helpless females so that both were completely nude and then proceeded to utilize a large stockmen's type pocket knife to brutally stab and hack at each of his still-living victims until they were dead.

Bonnie Myrle Ward was stabbed six times in and around her left breast, after which her throat was cut. Donna Lynn Strickland was stabbed ten times in and around the left breast, and her chest was then slit open by the defendant so that he could look at and touch this poor child's heart. These were slayings committed without any pity or pang of conscience, requiring cold, brutal, and heartless calculation so as to inflict a high degree of pain and suffering. The defendant's actions clearly reflect his total and utter indifference to and enjoyment of the suffering of his victims.

Jimmy Lee Smith had been a guest in Ward's Cottondale area home the night before the murder and Smith had accompanied Ward, her daughter Donna, and two of Ward's younger children on some errands the next day. The trip became ugly when Jimmy Lee became agitated about comments made about his girlfriend. Somewhere along the way home, Smith convinced Ward to drive down an abandoned country road and made her get out in a remote field where he performed his vile acts.

After he killed Bonnie and her daughter Donna, he drove the two younger children home, fed them, and put them to bed. In the days following the double murder, he threatened to finish off the rest of the family.

Over the next several days, Smith made five additional statements—both an oral and a written confession on May 5, a videotaped confession on May 6, a written confession on May 9, and a written confession on May 16.

On June 6, 1978, a grand jury indicted Smith for the murders of Ward and Strickland. After pleading not guilty to each count, Smith was tried before a jury and convicted of both murders.

The brutality of these murders hit home for John. He had small children at home and it terrified him to think someone could harm one of them. He took additional

96

measures in coaching the children regarding strangers. He also taught his children how to shoot and respect guns at an early age.

This case was so horrific that all law enforcement officers throughout the county were impacted. By the traumatizing images—whether they were on scene first-hand or exchanging information as part of the investigative process—it had an impact. Unlike the general public, officers are often called to disturbing crime scenes where they see numerous traumatizing images. Whether officers deal with a suicide, murder, assault, or even a rape, law enforcement officers see far more disturbing images than the average citizen. Officers are often the first people to arrive on scene, and those who are at the scene look to the officers for stability and leadership in the midst of chaos. Officers must learn to control their emotions in order to efficiently carry out their duties. Unfortunately, the repressing of emotions can lead to the future growth of disorders correlated with stress. The repressing of emotions doesn't just end at work; it can eventually impact the home.

From atypical work shifts and high-risk situations to the effects of post-traumatic stress disorder, law enforcement takes a toll on both law enforcement officers and their marriages.

The stress incorporated in law enforcement work often does not just stay at work. Eventually, the marriages of law enforcement officers suffer.

John continued to be deeply disturbed by the senseless violence and total disregard for human life surrounding the Jimmy Lee Smith case. He continued working in law enforcement and raising his children, giving them an extra hug when he could.

His ex-wife, Phyllis, moved from the area, and John returned with the children to a family home in Dogwood Heights. Momma Ruth told him about a pretty young lady that worked with her that was recently divorced. She just wouldn't let it go. "Johnny, why don't you ask her out? You don't need to be single and all alone."

Well, one day when Johnny Mac was visiting his mom, she gave him a small piece of paper with a phone number and the name, Linda Stevens.

A week or so later, Johnny called Linda and asked if she would like to go out on a date. She did. They had many more dates over the next year, and John fell head over heels in love.

He asked Linda to marry him. Momma Ruth was just as excited as Johnny. John P. McDaniel III and Linda Pagenkoph Stevens married on February 28, 1979. Judge Robert L. McCrary Jr. performed the simple ceremony. John's two children, Machelle, fifteen years old, and Little John, twelve years old, were living with him, and Linda had two children—

Terry, ten years old, and Dana, five years old. When he and Linda married, John bought them a home on the corner of Greenwood Hwy and Odom Drive. They attended Eastside Baptist Church and tried to blend into a happy, healthy family.

Just three months after their marriage, John, Linda, Little John, Terry, and Dana all celebrated a big family event on May 2, 1979. It was Machelle McDaniel's sixteenth birthday. Johnny Mac had found a convertible mustang which he purchased and restored for his little girl.

Johnny Mac was a very happy young man with his new bride and children. He and his father were forming a good bond and making up for lost time. Johnny Mac's son, Little John, was very close to his grandfather, John Jr.

On April 6, 1980, the front sideline page of the local newspaper, the Sunday *Floridan* read, "FDLE Investigates Sheriff's Department." Apparently, two tape recordings made by former Jackson County sheriff's deputies during their own investigations of Sheriff Charles Applewhite led to a full-scale investigation of the sheriff's department by the Florida Department of Law Enforcement.

The tapes, made by former deputies Ron Steverson and Devan Land, allegedly contained recordings of Applewhite making sexual advances to a job applicant and mismanagement of property under the control of the sheriff's office. Sheriff Applewhite went to the Governor's office asking that Steverson and Land be investigated for possible violations of Florida Statue 934—the state law governing the procedures for recording conversations without the knowledge of everyone involved. State Attorney Leo Jones added that the "overall situation in the [sheriff's] office is under investigation. The recordings were from August of 1979."

The moral at the sheriff's department in 1980 was at an all-time low in light of the approaching election.

John P. McDaniel knew what he had to do. He was going to be the next sheriff in Jackson County, and he would make a difference.

CHAPTER 25
Working toward a Dream

Once John's daddy rejoined their lives when John was in high school, he had returned each year on his vacation until he began to have some health problems. John McDaniel Jr. was a male nurse working in New Jersey. John Jr. had studied and became a physical therapist. He soon began to have blood flow problems in his legs and had to wear circulation stockings. Due to health reasons, he had to retire, so John Jr. moved back home to Marianna to be close to his family.

John Jr. really and truly wanted to come back and make amends for the times Iris, John, and Wayne didn't have a daddy. In the late 1970s, John Jr. rented a trailer in Eastgate Trailer Park near where the Hopkins dealership is on Hwy 90, on the east side of Marianna. He had re-married a very nice woman named Helen. John Jr. and Helen would live in the rental while their home was being built in Malone, across from the ballfield.

John Jr. tried to be a part of Johnny Mac's life and became actively involved with the sheriff's department and became Mayor of a little town called Malone, just north of Marianna in Jackson County.

John Jr. started a program called meals on wheels. The senior citizen center would prepare meals for seniors that were shut in and couldn't get out, and they would deliver the meals. When his grandchildren visited their grandparents, Granddaddy Mac would make sure they chipped in and helped with the meals on wheels program.

John Jr. also started his own Christmas program. They collected money from different places and purchased gifts, getting the welfare department to provide names of needy families that were eligible.

They managed to collect enough money to make sure those children had Christmas. It made everybody in the county proud.

John Jr. quickly fell in love with his new daughter-in-law, Linda. He thought she was perfect for Johnny. John Jr. spent time taking Little John hunting and fishing when not working or involved in non-profit fund-raising events. When the men went on hunting and fishing trips, Machelle would stay with Helen. She and Helen would go out to dinner in Dothan and catch a movie.

On Tuesday, July 1, 1980, John III lost his grandmother, Laura Belle Davis Grant. John's mother, Ruth, was devastated by the loss of her mom. Both of her parents were gone. She was saddened that her mother wouldn't be able to witness the results of the sheriff's race in which her grandson, Johnny, was working fervently to win. Laura Belle was born on September 18, 1889, and was ninety years old when she died. Family and friends attended her service at Marvin Chapel Freewill Baptist Church in Marianna. Laura Belle was laid to rest next to her husband, J. W., who left her to be with the Lord eleven years earlier.

John Jr. continued helping with his son's political campaign for sheriff by actively putting up "Vote for Johnny McDaniel" signs all over the county. John's main campaign promise was to be a working sheriff for the people, and he pledged fairness to all county citizens.

On September 7, 1980, the Jackson County *Floridan* ran an ad in the local newspaper next to an article regarding the campaigning drawing to a close. The following is a handwritten letter from Johnny's wife Linda:

Dear Jackson County,
In a few days, you will be going to the polls to elect the man you would like to be your next

sheriff. Before that time, I would like to tell you about my husband, Johnny McDaniel.

Johnny wants to be your next sheriff. Why sheriff? Because he worked as chief deputy and administrator for the sheriff's department here in Jackson County, and he loves law enforcement. Those of you that knew him as chief deputy know that he was there whenever he was needed.

Johnny knows what the job as sheriff means. He knows the pleasures of the job and the problems involved in that job. Johnny has solutions for many of these problems. Solutions that will work!

Johnny will be a sheriff Jackson County can be proud of. He is a man of integrity, fairness, and honesty. He will be a sheriff for all the people of Jackson County.

I say this not because I'm his wife but because no one knows him better than I. No one will work harder for the people of Jackson County.

Please vote for my husband, Johnny McDaniel, on September 9th.

Linda McDaniel

Two days after the ad ran, the voter turnout on September 9, 1980, was great for the first primary election in Jackson County. Candidates for sheriff included Charles H. Applewhite (incumbent sheriff), Ernest T. Brock, Sonny Dean, Paul Dudley, W. A. (Billy) Dykes, Cairl Goodson, and Johnny McDaniel. Charles Applewhite received 2883 votes, Billy Dykes received 2938, and Johnny McDaniel got 3764. There would be a run-off in October.

It was the largest voter turnout in Jackson County history with 12,520 people voting in the sheriff's race.

Johnny had to face Billy Dykes, and it still appeared the runoff election would be close.

John's wife Linda responded with another handwritten letter which was published in the local paper.

Thank you Jackson County,

Before last Tuesday's election, I wrote a letter to you, asking for your vote and support for my husband, Johnny McDaniel, candidate for sheriff.

Boy! Did you come through for us! And now I want to tell each and every one of you thank you. It's taken a lot of hard work on our part, but no amount of work could make victory possible without you. Johnny and I will never forget our many, many friends.

Again, thank you, and we look forward to seeing you at the polls again on October 7th.

Gratefully,
Linda McDaniel

The McDaniels continued to campaign over the following weeks. Momma Ruth prepared pounds and pounds of cheese grits and hushpuppies for the fish fry fund raising events.

Johnny Mac's daddy was a big help. Once daddy, always daddy to his children, but John Jr. still felt like he had something to prove.

John Jr. had a very limited income, so he took a clerk job at night at Sheffield Oil Company north of Campbellton. Johnny Mac's son, Little John, had come to idolize his granddaddy. All the things that John Jr. missed out on doing with Johnny, he tried to make up for with Little John.

October seventh arrived with 32 precincts reporting for the second primary and special election. Johnny McDaniel had defeated Billy Dykes for the office of sheriff. McDaniel led the polls with a total of 7779 votes to Dykes's 4338. Johnny carried all of the county's 32 precincts and 66% of the vote.

All of Johnny's family and friends celebrated this huge victory. Johnny had the world by the tail, and his dreams were becoming reality. The family celebrated Little John's fifteenth birthday just five days after the election.

Johnny began riding with deputies at night to get a feel for what was going on in the county. Training began for John by the first of November. There was little doubt that Johnny McDaniel still wanted very badly to be Jackson County's next sheriff and that he would spend long hours preparing for his January 6, 1981, takeover of that office. Sheriff Applewhite very graciously offered Johnny the opportunity to work with him and observe the department in action.

Johnny came to work in November of 1980 for $800.00 a month until he assumed the duties of sheriff on January sixth. Johnny had begun preparing for this honor on the day after the polls closed. He had already developed an organizational chart, revised the budget, and prepared a standardized pay scale. Additionally, he had met with a large number of local law enforcement officials in an effort to establish a network of cooperative investigative alignment. Sheriff Applewhite gave Johnny a walkie-talkie radio to keep with him, and Johnny had his badge and gun. If anything bad happened, department personnel were instructed to call Johnny Mac.

On November 13-15, 1980, John attended a "new sheriff seminar" sponsored by the Florida Sheriffs Association in Tallahassee. This put Johnny McDaniel one step closer to becoming the county's chief law enforcement officer. The first thing Johnny Mac may have done on January 6, 1981, at 12:01 a.m. may have been to pin on the five-pointed gold star...but the rest of the things he had to accomplish to assume office were much more technical. He would be commissioning deputies, implementing operational staff, conducting inventory of departmental assets, and assuming custody of prisoners in the jail.

Johnny gained a wealth of information from the seminar. In addition to the technical and professional services provided by the Florida Sheriffs Association, Johnny learned that the Association also provided legal services. As a sheriff, he could call with questions and get legal opinions from staff attorneys with specialized knowledge of law enforcement agencies.

Everything was falling into place.

CHAPTER 26
Hands of Death

December of 1980 found Johnny working hard to learn the duties he would assume as sheriff.

Johnny helped his dad with the Christmas Program. John Jr. had already collected quite a bit of money and had received the list of needy families for the county. He was intent on making sure that every family on the list received Christmas. Johnny was doing his Christmas shopping for Linda and the children. Life was good, and the spirit of Christmas filled his heart.

On a cold Monday night on December 15, Johnny received a call in the middle of the night from the sheriff's office. There had been a robbery and shooting at Sheffield Oil Company just north of Campbellton, Florida—up near the Florida/Alabama State Line. Johnny asked for a status of the situation.

Dispatch advised they had one down and may have the bad guys pinned down. Johnny said he would be 10-8 (in service) and be to them shortly.

***

At approximately 1:59 a.m., Graceville police officer, Patrolman Charles J. Shumaker, was dispatched to the Sheffield Oil Company. There was an armed robbery in progress. Upon arrival, Shumaker was advised that there was a black male subject inside the station and also a white male. The white male was lying on the floor with an apparent head injury. Graceville Police Chief Robert Whitehurst arrived on scene with Patrolman Shumaker. They were the first officers to arrive. They were quickly joined by an Alabama highway patrolman, five units from the Houston County Alabama Sheriff's

Department, and three Jackson County Sheriff's Office deputies. Jackson County Sheriff's Department Chief Deputy David Turnage arrived shortly and took over the lead in the investigation. The suspects were gone from the area. The initial report that suspects were pinned down was inaccurate, the only person inside was the wounded store attendant. The truck driver who called dispatch was still at the scene.

***

Johnny Mac snatched some clothes on and headed out the door toward the scene in Campbellton. All he had was the handheld radio, so he lost communication not too far from his house. When Johnny arrived, he didn't know what was going on.

He pulled up and one of the deputies, Donnie Branch, walked toward him. Donnie was a young man that had worked under the Craven administration.

Johnny asked. "What's the situation, Donnie?"

"We got one down," Donnie said softly.

Johnny looked puzzled, thinking Donnie was acting a little strange. "What's going on?"

Donnie just looked at John, his face a total question mark. Johnny could tell Donnie didn't know what to say or how to say anything, but he didn't know why.

Johnny kept approaching the store. He was looking in the door and saw some shoes on feet at the door and a male lying in front of the service counter just inside the station.

Several officers had gathered around. Johnny looked at the man on the floor in a pool of blood and said, "It looks like those same old-type shoes my daddy wore."

Johnny looked again and saw gray pants and his daddy's old goatee. "DAMN; DAMN. That's my daddy!"

Donnie hung his head and said, "Yes, sir. We've got rescue coming already."

"God, almighty, he's been shot. Let's go to Dothan with him."

They said, "No, you can't go to Dothan with him. That's across the state line, and he needs immediate medical transport."

"The hell, you say!" Johnny knelt down, talking to his unresponsive daddy. "Daddy, I'm gonna get you some help. You're gonna be okay."

They said again, "No, you can't move him. Rescue said we could further injure him."

Johnny demanded, "Get the doctor on the phone and tell them what the situation is…that he's been shot in the head, above the right ear. And tell them I'm wanting to go to Dothan with him now."

Donnie called, and the doctors in Marianna were kind enough to agree to let them go on to Dothan with him.

Johnny escorted the Jackson County Fire and Rescue unit to the Southeast Alabama Medical Center in Dothan, Alabama.

Johnny got there and went in the emergency room. The doctor came in and was examining Johnny's daddy. He said contact needed to be made with some of the family members and to get them up there because he was bleeding internally and filling up inside. They would have to relieve the pressure immediately.

Johnny said. "Go ahead and do it. I'm his son."

The doctor looked at him and said, "What the hell are you doing in here?"

"I'm also the sheriff-elect of Jackson County."

The doctor shook his head. "All right, God almighty. Let's get busy."

Johnny made contact with his brother and sister and advised them what was going on. They came right away. Iris was living in Macclenny, Florida, which was about three hours east of Marianna, and William was living in Tallahassee.

They went ahead and did a cut down and tried to relieve the pressure because he was bleeding internally. It was just terrible. He was in surgery for a little over two hours, but doctors were only able to relieve the pressure and the bullet remained lodged in his brain.

Both of Johnny's siblings headed immediately to him, and by noon that next day, they were all together. They sat quietly waiting and praying.

John's older sister was a registered nurse and had taught nursing. She was about to take over as hospital administrator in Daytona Beach. Iris looked over at John and squeezed his hand. "He won't ever make it, Johnny. The doctor told me if he lives, he'll be a vegetable. He's on the ventilator now."

John, Iris, and Wayne talked it over and after much discussion and a flood of tears, they came to a decision. They tried to get with the doctor to tell him to just unplug their daddy. They all knew John Jr. would never want to be kept alive by machines.

The doctor didn't want the children to feel like they had killed their father by removing the plug to the ventilator. He said, "I tell you what we'll do. Let's just leave him on the ventilator until seven o'clock. If he doesn't get any better by seven o'clock, we will unplug him."

Johnny and his siblings continued to pray for a miracle. Well, at about five minutes before seven in the evening, John Jr. passed away. All of his children were with him. The doctor saved them from having to make the decision to remove life support. That was a very kind thing he did for the family, and they were grateful for his consideration.

The Jackson County Sheriff's Office was having a hard time doing anything with the murder case because there were no witnesses...nothing. A couple of truck drivers had seen some people, but it was all really sketchy. The driver who initially discovered the robbery and notified dispatch provided a description of a couple he saw leaving the area.

John and his family made the arrangements for the burial of their father. John Perry McDaniel Jr. was buried in the family cemetery at Bascom Methodist Church. John Jr. was born on June 8, 1916, and died on December 15, 1980, at the age of 64. He left behind a loving wife, Helen D. McDaniel; an adoring daughter, Iris Iden; two loving sons, John Perry and William Wayne; and seven grandchildren that idolized him.

On Thursday, January 1, fifteen days after Malone Mayor J. P. McDaniel was brutally beaten and shot in the head with a .25 caliber pistol, the Jackson County Sheriff's Department released a composite of the killer. The composite of the suspect was developed from a description by an unidentified truck driver who came into the station about the time the attempted robbery and murder had taken place. He observed a black male behind the counter and just assumed he was the station attendant. When he went in the station to pay for his gas, he found the station attendant wounded and lying on the floor.

Agencies in Florida, Alabama, and Georgia worked virtually around the clock in an effort to apprehend the murderer. Captain David Turnage, chief deputy at Jackson County Sheriff's Department, released the composite of the man believed to have murdered the popular Malone mayor. Turnage said law enforcement officials were looking for a black male, possibly from the area, who was between five feet, eight inches to five feet, eleven inches tall. He was described as having brown eyes with a black "longish" type afro haircut.

Turnage said the truck driver worked with a law enforcement artist to come up with a composite. Turnage reported that the gunman was unable to open the cash register but did take an undetermined amount of cash from McDaniel's wallet.

Sheffield Oil put up a $1,000.00 reward leading to the arrest and capture of the person(s) who killed McDaniel. In addition, the local Panhandle Citizens Band Radio Club established a J. P. McDaniel Fund at Citizens State Bank. McDaniel was a member of the club and was known by the CB handle "Happy Pappy."

By Sunday, January 4, 1981, two suspects had been charged in the murder of the former mayor. A black male and female were held in the Jackson County Jail without bond. Jessie L. Wilson, 21, and Mattie Catherine Russ, 26, of Campbellton were formally charged in the McDaniel murder on Friday, January 2, at 6:15 p.m. after the two were arrested in Campbellton on Thursday.

The search for the two began after Trooper Randall Jones of the Florida Highway Patrol received a tip from an informant sometime Wednesday night. Law enforcement officers spent New Year's Day looking for a 1974 Mercury station wagon believed to have been occupied by the couple.

Trooper Jones and Deputy Dale McSwain were riding in the Campbellton area along with Trooper E. E. Finch and a friend, Cliff Whitfield.

Whitfield spotted the station wagon belonging to Ms. Russ as it turned off of Hwy 231 onto Hwy 2. The troopers followed the vehicle onto a dirt road before affecting the stop as Wilson was reported as being armed and dangerous.

Ms. Russ was driving at the time of the stop. Trooper Finch ordered all occupants out of the vehicle. Several officers arrived at the scene, including Sheriff-Elect John P. McDaniel. Trooper Finch brought the suspect to the jail in Jackson County.

Wilson was charged at that time with uttering a forged instrument and worthless checks and was held for Houston County, Alabama, and Washington County in Florida. Ms. Russ was charged with grand theft. Officers and investigators worked with evidence through the night and the next day until the formal murder charge could be made.

Sheriff Charles Applewhite's crew arrested the couple as they felt they were prime suspects in the case. A press conference was held on Friday night with Doug Sullivan, manager of Sheffield Oil Company, Firemen Paul Ladecour, Lt. Jimmy Smith, and Investigator John Dennis listening as Captain Turnage, Sheriff Applewhite, and Trooper Jones provided the details of the December 15 shooting. Sheriff-Elect McDaniel sat in the back of the room during the press conference. He only watched and quietly listened.

CHAPTER 27
Sheriff of Jackson County:
January 1981

At midnight on Monday night, 12:01 a.m. to be exact, John McDaniel and his administrative assistant, Jim Williams, held their first meeting with their 28- member staff—the exact moment the McDaniel administration officially took over the responsibility for the office.

On Tuesday, January 6, 1981, John P. McDaniel III was officially sworn in as the new sheriff.

Jackson County would see a few new faces in the political arena. The courthouse had an overflowing crowd of family, friends, and well-wishers to watch Judge Robert L. McCrary Jr. administer the oath of office to three recently-elected public officials—John P. McDaniel III as sheriff, Daun Crews as clerk of the court, and Jim Appleman as state attorney.

McDaniel kept many of the department officials the same. He announced his list of officials after he was sworn into office. Jim Williams, a former lieutenant with the Marianna Police Department was head of the new sheriff's administrative team. He was assisted by Zolinda Russ, who already handled the warrant division; Frances Malloy, who worked in the tax collector's office for about fifteen years; and Sheila Vickery, who resigned her position as city clerk in Alford to take the position at the sheriff's department.

J. J. McCrary, who worked for former Sheriff Roy Robinson and was an investigator and administrative assistant to former Sheriff Barkley Gause and was an investigator with the state attorney's office for eight years, was the head of McDaniel's investigative division.

David Turnage, who was chief deputy for the past four years, continued to work in the investigative division along with Harold Glisson, who had twelve years' experience.

Fran Nunnally continued as the secretary in the investigative division.

Lowell Spooner, who had twenty years' experience, continued to be the department's chief dispatcher.

Sgt. Dale McSwain, who had eight years' experience with the S.O. and several with the P.D., would be over one shift with CPL John Mader, Lou Roberts, Dale Jones, and Donnie Branch assisting.

Sgt. Duane Davis was in charge of another shift with Sgt. Henry Keith, James Bevis, Leonard Norsworthy, and CPL Claude Widner assisting.

Don Grant was the criminal intake officer for the department. Jailers were Rusty Booth and S. J. Peacock.

By Friday, January 9, 1981, Sheriff McDaniel had settled smoothly into his new position. He did much preparation for assuming office prior to being sworn in as sheriff. A lot of his hard work made the transition seem like a piece of cake.

Things John P. McDaniel III implemented during his first three days included:

- Arrangements made to repair blown engines in five of fifteen vehicles
- Uniform pay scales established
- New tires for some of the department vehicles
- Development of a personnel manual
- Revision of a communications manual
- Preliminary work done on establishment of property control records

- Issuance of uniforms and equipment
- Series of meetings with staff and other law enforcement agencies

John was extremely pleased with his new department and the cooperation he was receiving from other agencies and the people in the community. Still, something was deeply haunting the sheriff, and he just couldn't back away from it. He kept going back to the promises he made while campaigning "to be a working sheriff for the people [who] pledged fairness to all county citizens."

He missed his father greatly and was still having difficulty dealing with his murder. But something about the case just didn't sit right. John had reviewed the entire investigation over and over. He had pledged fairness to all county citizens. There was not enough evidence to have charged Jessie Wilson and Mattie Russ with the murder of his father. He knew it. As much as he wanted justice for his father, it had to be just that—justice.

The more he looked at the facts, the less it seemed to fit. The arrest had been made days before he took office as sheriff. He had some friends come to him and say, "Johnny, you won't ever win that case, and you're wrong to keep pressure on those people."

This had nothing to do with race; it was two black people in the community that were in trouble. A lot of the community thought it was them that robbed the store, but that wasn't the case.

After a lot of investigating, praying, and soul searching, Johnny made a decision. It upset his sister and his brother, but in his heart, he felt it was what needed to be done...drop the charges. They really and truly did not have a case. If it went to court, they would not win.

On Friday, January 23, Sheriff McDaniel dropped the murder charges against the couple accused of killing his father. He said there was insufficient evidence to hold Wilson and Russ. The subjects were still tried on other charges of grand theft and issuing worthless checks. Johnny Mac was handling the case as a sheriff and not as "the son."

CHAPTER 28
Jackson County:
A Sheriff's Department in Crisis

In February of 1981, it was discovered that Former Jackson County Sheriff Charles Applewhite apparently left office in January owing about $50,000 in unpaid bills. This was according to Deputy Court Clerk Larry Spivey who served as Applewhite's fiscal officer until November of 1980. Spivey estimated that only about $10,000 was still available in the Applewhite budget to retire the debts. Back on March 10, 1961, an attorney general's opinion ruled that such debts are the responsibility of the former sheriff unless the county commission approves a budget supplement.

Sheriff McDaniel assumed office with major bills still outstanding in excess of $55,000. These included bills for Department of Corrections meals, fuel purchases, medical treatment for prisoners, external housing of female prisoners, and fleet and utility expenses.

On Tuesday night, March 10, 1981, the Jackson County Commission held its regular meeting. The top item on the agenda was the ex-sheriff's bills. Ex-Sheriff Applewhite and current Sheriff McDaniel were present along with the County Commission board members. Chairman Teamon E. Durden, Commissioners Durelle Johnson, Alva Mercer, Ernie Padgett, and Frank Bylsma were present. By unanimous vote, the commission passed a motion made by Commissioner Bylsma which essentially told more than 75 creditors that the county would not be responsible for bills left unpaid because of over-expenditures in the sheriff's department. Applewhite appeared before the commission to explain that inflation, particularly in the areas of fuel and medical cost, had been responsible for increased costs within his department. The one-term sheriff said he had tried to curtail expenses but had been unable to keep up with the rising prices.

John McDaniel was concerned about the effect of the commission's decision on his new administration. He pointed out that five oil companies had already stopped departmental use of gas credit cards, and he felt certain more would follow. Sheriff McDaniel advised the commission that if he experienced financial problems, he would not hesitate to ask the commission for a budget supplement.

Jail problems still plagued the new sheriff. Responding to a state mandate, Sheriff McDaniel searched out and met with architects in the area. On Tuesday, February 24, 1981, the new sheriff and architect Paul Donofro presented the commission with preliminary drawings outlining three possible approaches to the jail problem with costs ranging between $200,000 and $417,000 dollars. Both McDaniel and Donofro urged commissioners to select one and proceed immediately. McDaniel felt that if action was not taken immediately, the county ran the risk of falling under a federal court order that would require them to build an all-new facility at a cost of millions of dollars. The commission agreed to review the plans and to render a decision at a later unspecified date.

By March 24, 1981, the Jackson County Jail was still receiving negative inspection reports and threats of impending closure. Sheriff McDaniel met with commissioners again. This time, the county commission committed itself to begin work in January of 1982 on a jail remodeling project that would cost upwards of $417,000. Voting went back and forth with several commissioners voting against the expenditure.

Sheriff McDaniel refused to give up and urged the commission to provide him with a letter of intent, stating the letter should be enough to keep the present facility from being closed. In the end, the commission committed to the remodel project with a start date of January 1982.

Before the end of the March 24, 1981, meeting, Mr. Phil Shuford and Mr. Gordon Revell from Florida Department of Corrections appeared before the board, requesting both assurance that what happened with the prior sheriff would not happen again and requesting the past bill be paid. The board could not give that kind of assurance, nor did they agree to pay the prior bill.

After the staff from Department of Corrections (D.O.C.) left the meeting, Sheriff McDaniel advised the board that he felt D.O.C. intended to terminate their contract to provide meals for jail prisoners, following the refusal to guarantee payment. Commissioner Bylsma advised that it would cost approximately $30,000 more in operating expenses per year if D.O.C. terminated their contract.

In April of 1981, Sheriff McDaniel requested assistance, stating legislators, juvenile authorities, and the State Attorney's Office were not the only ones concerned with the recent escapees from Dozier, the juvenile justice facility in the county. They had a tremendous impact on the sheriff's department as well.

The Florida School for Boys, also known as the Arthur G. Dozier School for Boys, was a reform school operated by the state of Florida in the panhandle town of Marianna from January 1, 1900, to June 30, 2011. For a time, it was the largest juvenile reform institution in the United States.

As a result of changes in the law, the majority of the 125 juveniles who had escaped from Dozier in previous years ended up in the county jail. During the month of April 1981, nineteen Dozier escapees spent time at the county jail, awaiting disposition of cases. They averaged staying thirty days at a cost of $10 per day. This equated to local taxpayers paying $5,700 to house Dozier

121

juveniles. McDaniel's already strapped budget could not handle the additional strain. The sheriff also was concerned for the welfare of the citizens of Jackson County due to the high escape rates. His department expended all available manpower to initiate the search and apprehension every time a juvenile escaped, but he still worried that an escapee would harm a member of Jackson County.

Sheriff McDaniel gained a short-lived extension from D.O.C. regarding the preparation of meals for the jail. The Commission tabled the decision until the following month, and D.O.C. terminated the contract. The jail kitchen was renovated, and Jackson County Jail resumed the preparation of their own meals on May 1, 1981. Sheriff McDaniel hired Mildred Christmas as the jail cook with dual duties of matron/correctional officer.

In light of these events, Sheriff McDaniel would be forced to ask the county commission for a supplement of $60,000 to his $461,000 budget. The jail kitchen renovation, cost of meals, and additional staff to prepare meals, as well as the increased cost of utilities and fuel were attributing factors. The Commission would only approve half of the request with a supplement of $30,000.

May 1 of 1981 would see success as Sheriff McDaniel had made several large drug arrests and cleared out the evidence room of illegal drugs at the sheriff's office. McDaniel observed the large burning pile of marijuana and other drugs confiscated by his department and Marianna Police Department. The cleaning house resulted in the destruction of more than $70,000 in illegal drugs, some dating back as far as 1977.

John's daughter, Machelle, celebrated her eighteenth birthday on May 2, 1981. Shortly afterward, the family celebrated Machelle's high school graduation.

During the latter part of May in 1981, John McDaniel would participate in an officer memorial ceremony for two fallen Jackson County deputies. With just five months under his belt as sheriff of Jackson County, John P. McDaniel felt it was important to recognize those who had given the ultimate sacrifice. Sheriff McDaniel, along with Judge Robert L. McCrary, former Sheriff Barkley Gause, and Marianna Mayor J. D. Swearingen presented plaques to Mrs. Alan Finch and Mrs. Aaron Creel.

On July 4, 1961, Deputy Sheriff Allen Finch and Deputy Sheriff Aaron Creel were shot and killed by a prisoner in Jackson County Hospital. The suspect, under a life sentence for robbing a service station in Marianna, set fire to a mattress in his cell. He and three other prisoners were taken to the hospital for minor burns. Deputy Finch escorted the suspect to the rest room where he gained control of Deputy Finch's weapon and shot and killed him. He then walked to a nearby room and shot Deputy Creel twice in the head as he was guarding the prisoners. He then shot and killed an innocent bystander.

Sheriff McDaniel spoke from scripture. "Blessed are the peacemakers, for they shall be called the children of God." Matthew 5:9

***

In June of 1981, John's daughter, Machelle, married and moved to Tallahassee to start a new life. John would later sell the home on Odom Drive after completion of the new family home in Indian Springs.

Johnny built his wife a house—not just any house, but her dream home in Indian Springs. Linda worked for Harold Huff, who was one of the co-owners of the Indian Springs Subdivision. Johnny purchased a small lot at a reduced price and built their house. She and Johnny designed it. Basically, it was her house.

By the end of June, Sheriff McDaniel requested a 1981-82 budget of $892,000— an increase of $224,000.

123

The major deficit-causing factors in the original budget were attributed to the jail, termination of a federal program which funded officers, meal preparation in house for jail inmates, vehicles, equipment, radios, salary for 35 staff (compared to 28 in prior administration), and inflation. The original budget did not take into account the more than $50,000 overspent by the Applewhite administration.

CHAPTER 29
Dozier Escapee Brutalizes
Local Family

Sheriff McDaniel had expressed prior concerns about the high escapee rate at Dozier School. His worst fear manifested itself on Monday, June 22, 1981, when tragedy struck in Jackson County. Three members of a Jackson County family were hospitalized in critical condition, after being severely beaten by a fifteen-year old Dozier School escapee. Curtis E. Jackson, 64, his wife Jewel, 56, and their son, Richard, 18, were transferred to Tallahassee Memorial Regional Medical Center where they would undergo treatment and lengthy surgeries for massive head injuries.

An extensive manhunt for the juvenile, John Jay Bruschayt of Deland, would culminate a few hours later when the 1977 Chrysler Cordova stolen from the Jackson residence would crash 140 miles north of Marianna. Law enforcement officials in Homerville, Georgia, just north of Valdosta, notified local authorities that the juvenile apparently fell asleep at the wheel and ran into a road grader, overturning four times before coming to a stop. Bruschayt only received minor injuries and would later be transported to Bay County Jail for security reasons.

At the time of Bruschayt's hearing, he was housed at the Dozier facility lock-up. Due to the lack of security at the facility and the high number of escapes in prior months, Sheriff McDaniel placed armed deputies on site during the entire time the youth was at Dozier.

McDaniel would continue to work with State Attorney Appleman and demand fencing be erected at the Dozier Campus. Dozier Superintendent Lenox Williams advised that bids were being taken on a $495,000 project which would include a twelve-foot perimeter fence around the compound along with electronic monitoring capability within a fifty-foot area of the fence. Superintendent Williams also advised they were in the process of obtaining funds for additional staffing at the Dozier Facility.

Bay County Sheriff Lavelle Pitts contacted Sheriff McDaniel early on Monday morning, July 6. John Bruschayt, the fifteen-year-old boy charged with the near-fatal beatings, was found dead in his Panama City jail cell. He apparently hung himself with pieces of a bed sheet. The Bay County jailer discovered the boy hanging in the juvenile wing of the jail at approximately 5 a.m. Bruschayt was the sole occupant of his cell.

Sheriff McDaniel advised the suicide occurred just a few hours prior to a 9 a.m. hearing which would have been held at the Jackson County Courthouse where Circuit Judge Robert McCrary would have decided whether or not to waive the youth to adult court for trial on charges of attempted murder in the first degree, armed robbery, and burglary.

John continued to urge the commission to re-consider regarding its budget decision. He needed the total amount requested ($896,000) to protect the citizens of Jackson County adequately, run the sheriff's office, and run the jail. Sheriff McDaniel was ready to appeal the county commission's decision to award him $734,000 for the next years' operation. He would have the paperwork ready to go to Tallahassee before August 25th for the Department of Administration to review. The Cabinet and Governor would make the binding decision.

On the eve of August 25th, a compromise was reached, and the Commission awarded McDaniel $775,000 for his departmental budget. He began immediately reaching out to area legislators for any relief possible regarding the operation of the jail. The expenses for the jail alone would eat up close to $300,000 of his yearly budget.

McDaniel next started his war on drugs. The end of August, 1981, yielded the confiscation of 1,073 marijuana plants with a street value of $321,000 and five additional arrests in unrelated drug operations which yielded the confiscation of a tractor-trailer and two personal vehicles. Four more drug arrests were made the first week in September with additional vehicle seizures.

CHAPTER 30

"Angel Flying Too Close to the Ground"

John was so proud of his older sister, Iris. She worked hard and advanced up to hospital administrator in Macclenny, Baker County, Florida. She had so much love to give. Iris and her husband adopted two children—a son and a daughter. They became her whole world. She was always there for her little brother, Johnny, and her own family as well as meeting the needs and demands of a large hospital.

Nine months after John's father was murdered, he was awakened by the ringing of the phone late Friday night on September 18, 1981. Late night calls still sent his heart racing since he received the call of the robbery when his father was murdered.

His older sister was returning home from work at the hospital, exiting the Interstate off-ramp toward her home. Bright lights were headed directly toward Iris. A drunk driver was coming up the off ramp at a high rate of speed. The head-on collision killed Iris. Iris Iden McDaniel Parish was born June 3, 1937, and was laid to rest at age 44 in the family cemetery at Marvin Chapel Freewill Baptist Church in Marianna. No truer words were ever written than those inscribed on her headstone: "An inspiration to all who knew her."

John had buried his father the prior December and his sister nine months later, but that was just the beginning of the pain and heartbreak he would endure.

Iris was a good Christian woman. John reflected on his big sister's life and honestly felt Iris was "an angel flying too close to the ground" and was called home to live with God…too soon for her loved ones left behind.

129

John continued to develop ideas and implement changes to make Jackson County a safer place to live. The month following Iris's death, Johnny Mac requested a change in the curfew ordinance. The current ordinance left him with hands tied as it allowed him to only enforce the midnight curfew on licensed establishments selling alcoholic beverages. This did not take into account the private clubs, such as bottle clubs.

CHAPTER 31
Impersonating the Sheriff

In October of 1981, John had the opportunity to attend a two-week FBI training seminar at the FBI Academy in Quantico, Virginia. He was married to Linda and they had been unable to spend much time together due to the demands of the job, but Johnny decided to go as the training would be immensely beneficial.

Johnny enrolled in the class as a sheriff and would be up there for two weeks, with the weekends free.

Linda went to visit her family in Elgin, Illinois, and was headed back to Marianna when Johnny Mac came up with a plan. It was four months before their three-year wedding anniversary, so they decided to meet in Asheville, North Carolina, at the foot of the Smokey Mountains.

They got an exclusive room at the Biltmore. The Inn on Biltmore Estate is housed on 8,000 acres adjacent to Biltmore House, George Vanderbilt's 19th-century chateau. It had the finest amenities and was an oasis of service, style, and charm. A stay overnight on the estate meant experiencing the same gracious hospitality enjoyed years earlier by George and Edith Vanderbilt's guests.

Once John and Linda confirmed their plans and made their reservations for the weekend, John had one thing left unfinished. He had to keep the sheriff's office notified of all the things he did and where he was in case there was a major problem requiring him to leave and go home.

John and Linda enjoyed elegant dining, specializing in regional cuisine. Specials included estate-raised beef and lamb and fresh-picked ingredients from the Biltmore kitchen gardens. They ate in a setting of white tablecloths, beautiful views, and gracious service.

After dinner, John and Linda walked hand in hand, admiring the beautiful gardens and mountain views. From the wicker porch rockers outside their suite, the couple sipped wine and watched the sun slide down behind the Blue Ridge Mountains. Upon returning inside their suite, they enjoyed the luxurious bathing accommodations and had just gotten in bed when there was a knock at the door.

Linda looked at John and he looked at her, both wondering who in the hell it could be.

"Yeah, who is it?" John asked.

"Sheriff McDaniel?"

At this, John became concerned. There must be something wrong. He ran and opened the door, forgetting to even put his pants on.

On the other side of the door stood two huge officers.

"Good evening, sir. We're officers with the sheriff's office up here," the larger of the two said.

"Give me a minute and let me put my pants on. Is something wrong?"

"We just need to talk to you."

John yanked his pants on and invited them in the room, thinking something bad had happened back in Marianna.

"Are you Sheriff McDaniel?"

"I am Sheriff McDaniel, and that is my wife right over there." John pointed at Linda sitting in the chair.

"How you doing, ma'am?" they both said nicely as they touched the tips of their hats.

They turned back to John and asked if he had any identification or credentials verifying him to be Sheriff McDaniel.

"Why, hell yes I do." John was becoming aggravated by their challenging tones.

"We need to see your credentials."

"Shit. I left my credentials in the car. Let me go down and get them."

When he returned, the officers looked down at the credentials and then at each other.

"Officers, one of you needs to tell me what the hell is going on here because something is up!"

The one officer straightened, standing all of 6'4" with a massive gorilla frame and said. "Well sir, I'm going to tell you. We got a call from Florida that somebody had stolen the sheriff's car and the sheriff's credentials and they were impersonating the sheriff here in Asheville, North Carolina."

"That's bullshit!" Johnny Mac was irate.

"It's for real. We're going to have to carry you downtown to the police station," one of officers said in a stern voice.

"No, hell, you ain't gonna carry me nowhere." John looked at the two guys. Those officers were gorillas; they were *big* boys.

Johnny said. "Hold on, hold on….We are not going to do that."

People on the outside of the hotel began to notice what was going on. The deputy sheriffs were up there talking to Johnny, and it was taking quite some time. People were getting concerned and anxious. Local law enforcement never came to the Biltmore. They never had a reason to.

"I tell you what we're gonna do. We're gonna call the sheriff's office in Marianna, Florida…"

Before Johnny Mac could finish what he was saying, the officers said, "No, no…you can't call the sheriff's office in Marianna."

"Well, by God, we're going to call the circuit judge down there, Judge McCrary. Robert L. McCrary. You ever heard of him?" John was beyond pissed at that point.

The one officer looked over at the other and then back to John. "No sir, no sir. We don't know who Robert L. McCrary is....Never heard of him."

Johnny Mac looked over to see Linda with a very anxious expression on her face. He said, "You officers look up Judge McCrary's number and get him on the phone. Let me talk to him, and you can listen to the conversation..." Both officers started laughing—deep, belly laughs.

"What's so damn funny to you guys?" John demanded.

They said, "Do you know a fellow by the name of Cowboy Morris?"

Johnny Mac shook his head. "I'm gonna kill him. I'm gonna kill him...just as sure as I get home."

The officers went to laughing again. "Cowboy, one of your officers back in Jackson County, and a few others were the masterminds of the impersonating an officer scenario."

Johnny Mac thought to himself..."I need to kill Cowboy, just as soon as I see him. I'll just take his head off."

Well, the big gorilla officers left and went about their business. John and Linda got up the next morning and were looking forward to spending another night in the luxurious hotel. But when they went to the office to extend their stay, the office staff refused to let them check back in.

They said, "Sir, we don't know what's going on, but we can't have ya'll staying here with the deputies coming up here. This hotel prides itself on being prestige..."

"For God's Sake..." John just shook his head and walked out of the lobby. They had to find another hotel to stay in because of the crap his deputies pulled. John didn't know who all was part of it, but that whole bunch had it coming when he returned home.

Needless to say, that practical joke didn't make any points with Linda. She had never been exposed to anything like a bunch of deputy sheriffs and their pranks.

John swore he was gonna kill Cowboy when he got back to Jackson County. But it was all done in good clean fun. Everybody that worked for Johnny Mac was his friend but also part of his family. They could pull jokes on each other, and it was taken in the light it was done in—good clean fun.

John had learned that the jokes and pranks were a way for the deputies to release the tension and stress of their daily jobs. "The horrific things they saw and dealt with on a daily basis would drive you crazy if you didn't find a means of release."

CHAPTER 32

Sheriff Returns to Problems in Jackson County:
November-December 1981

Johnny returned from his FBI training seminar and the Biltmore Hotel fiasco to find a bad situation at the department. He didn't kill "Cowboy" Morris as he had to contend with other issues.

On Tuesday, October 27, while he was attending the seminar, two prisoners escaped from the county jail. Steven Kenny and Michael Shockley were reported missing when jail officials discovered their cell empty at approximately 6 a.m. Their escape route reportedly was through an air conditioning duct from which a window air conditioner had been removed. The two were able to avoid apprehension for 24 hours before being captured in Marianna by the Marianna Police Department and returned to the county jail.

Due to the escape, the board of county commissioners decided to use $23,995.86 in grant money for building funds instead of for department vehicles.

Sheriff McDaniel had taken many measures to prevent an escape. Prior to leaving for the training seminar, he had put bars around windows at the jail. Upon his return and learning of the escapes, he had a wire cage installed around the air conditioner.

Johnny Mac's biggest need at his department was automobiles. John would have to try to find another solution for the problem. The legislative grant money for law enforcement was clearly earmarked for equipment and not for use in the jail. Sheriff McDaniel was not consulted regarding the appropriation of the funds changing while he was out of town.

It was not an uncommon site to travel the roads in Jackson County and see two patrol cars hooked up with jumper cables or have a wrecker pass, towing a patrol car in for repairs.

John received news that his alcoholic beverage ordinance request was being tabled. He had wanted the ordinance to allow him to go into private clubs without a search warrant to make sure there was no selling of or consuming of alcoholic beverages after midnight Monday through Saturday and all day on Sunday. The ordinance prepared by County Attorney J. Paul Griffith would not allow these actions by law enforcement personnel.

This denial was extremely upsetting to Sheriff McDaniel in light of the most recent local night spot slaying which occurred just one week earlier. Edward Eugene Crutchfield was fatally shot in the face with a small caliber pistol in the parking lot of Club 77, located between Chipley and Graceville. The shooting occurred shortly before 2 a.m. John felt this could have been prevented with the proper monitoring of private clubs as related to the alcoholic beverage ordinance he requested.

In light of the problems John returned home to find, he remained focused on the positive while trying to implement sustainable changes for the good of the county.

The official J. P. McDaniel Christmas Fund was established on November 24, 1981. A county wide program to provide Christmas gifts for the needy kicked off with joint sponsorship from the Dept. of the Jackson County Sheriff's Department. The program was named the J. P. McDaniel Christmas Fund in honor of John's father.

Sheriff McDaniel was proud such a great cause was named after his late father. Regardless of the losses he had suffered, Christmas was a special time for John.

On December 9, 1981, the local newspaper, *The Monitor*, shared John III's thoughts on what Christmas is:

"Christmas is a time to celebrate the greatest gift of all times, our Savior. A time to do as God did and show our love through giving. A time to share our love and joy with others.

"Christmas is a time to enjoy being with our loved ones and sharing the sweet memories of the ones who have gone on before us.

"A time to stop and look around us and see all the beautiful things that we really have to be thankful for— our loved ones, our health, life, and happiness.

"A time to be thankful for our freedom, our country, and this great nation.

"A time to thank God for Jesus who gave his life that our sins might be forgiven."

***

While the J. P. McDaniel Christmas Fund marked high donations and pledges, the murder of its namesake remained at a stalemate. December 15, 1981, marked the one year anniversary of John Jr's murder. The case was still being worked, but due to the lack of key evidence and the gun used to commit the crime, an arrest could not be made.

***

On Monday, December 21, 1981, at approximately 6 p.m., Sheriff McDaniel and Graceville Police Chief Robert Whitehurst learned of a plot to steal drugs from the small hospital located in Graceville, Florida— Campbellton-Graceville Hospital. Preparations began immediately in anticipation of the robbery which was to take place during the early morning hours between 1 a.m. and 2 a.m. on Tuesday.

A dozen officers from the two agencies were staked out in and around the hospital. Jackson County Sheriff's Department officers involved in the investigation and stake-out were Sheriff McDaniel, Chief Investigator J. J.

McCrary, Investigators Devon Land, Harold Glisson, and John Dennis. Graceville Police Department officers in the case were Chief Robert Whitehurst, Danny Pitts, Charles Shumaker, Aubrey Martin, Bruce Ward, and Jeff Skinner. At 1:30 a.m., the robbers were spotted in a pickup truck belonging to one of the suspects near the hospital. At 2 a.m., the three robbers, wearing ski masks, climbed over a fence near the rear of the hospital facility. One suspect, Russell E. Kirkland, was carrying a 30-30 rifle. Investigator Dennis was positioned in the shadows on the ground next to a building and saw Kirkland coming straight at him. Reaching for his gun, he yelled a halt command, followed by "sheriff's department." As he did, Kirkland turned on him, aiming his gun. Dennis immediately fired his weapon, striking Kirkland in the chest.

When shots were fired by Dennis, suspect Ronny Grissett turned, aiming his sawed-off shotgun. Investigator Glisson ordered the suspect to halt, and when he did not, Glisson fired a shotgun, striking Grissett in the shoulder, hand, and foot. The third suspect, Larry Hendrix, immediately fell to the ground, surrendering and relinquishing his possession a .22 caliber pistol.

Russell Kirkland died at the scene as a result of his injuries. Ronny Grissett was treated at the hospital for non-life-threatening wounds, and Larry Hendrix was taken to Graceville Police Department and then to Jackson County Jail. Johnny Mac praised the officers for a job well done. The shootings were turned over to the state attorney's office for investigation as a matter of procedure.

***

With his first year as sheriff coming to a close, Johnny Mac finally received praise from the Florida Department of Corrections for the many improvements made in the Jackson County jail since it was inspected in January. Even though the jail inspection report was better than it had ever been, there was still improvement necessary. There were six areas of focus: 1) classification of prisoners 2) facilities for prisoner exercise and programs 3) additional supervision of food preparation and delivery to inmates 4) additional personnel to provide constant supervision on both floors of the jail at all times 5) need for constant supervision of juveniles in custody and 6) female officer on duty at all times.

The report also addressed inadequate lighting and ventilation in the structure which was built in 1947 and renovated earlier in 1981. Plumbing fixtures were listed as not being clean and not in good repair.

McDaniel felt his staff did an excellent overall job in operating the jail facility.

***

By the close of 1981, the J. P. McDaniel Christmas Fund was deemed a "huge success" by all participants and volunteers and all associated with the charity. The inaugural year netted the fund approximately $4,000 in cash, which was utilized to purchase groceries, clothing, and toys along with special needs such as utility bills for senior citizens. Over 300 families and 800 individuals benefited from the 1981 charity.

CHAPTER 33
"Linda on My Mind"

Johnny was sheriff only one year and three months when everything unraveled at home. He loved Linda with all his heart, but things didn't work out. The demands of the job had him away from home too much, and when he was physically home, he was still at the department mentally.

John's son and Linda's son couldn't get along; it was a mess. Little John would move around a bit with his mom, Phyllis. He went to Arizona and came back to live with his daddy. He went to Panama City and came back again. Everything Linda tried to implement by way of a loving, structured home life seemed to be undermined. Little John had a hard time adjusting to not having both his parents at the same time, and he missed his Grandfather McDaniel.

They tried everything to make it work, and it just could not be fixed. On April 12, 1982, after three years and two months of marriage, John and Linda McDaniel divorced.

John continued being the best sheriff he could be for the people of Jackson County. He continued to love and worship God, never losing his faith. He did however, for a long period of time, break down somewhat anytime the country song, "Lying Here with Linda On My Mind," was played on the radio. His moments of sadness and grief were personal and not shared with anyone.

Little John stayed with his daddy in Indian Springs for a little over a year.

Johnny threw all of his energy and attention into the job of sheriff and tried to get Linda off his mind. The first few years at the sheriff's office, he tried to be everything to everybody, and that belief would continue his entire administration. "Honestly, that is what the job of sheriff is all about, being everything to everybody. *And*, if you do that, you will not have a personal life or a private life at all. You will go 24 hours a day, 365 days a year, just as hard as you can go."

CHAPTER 34
POW, POW, POW
More and More Gunfire in
Jackson County

Mid-morning one day, Deputy Ray Allen called for assistance regarding a boy named Ronnie Wilson. Ronnie lived down off Mill Springs Baptist Church Road in rural Jackson County.

Ronnie was quite a character. He had been in Vietnam and liked that way of doing things. Ronnie could train a dog to go and get him a pack of cigarettes, a beer, or whatever. Ronnie had a grandson that he taught to shoot a BB gun when he was so little he couldn't even hold it up to his shoulder. The little boy would have to choke it down real close to shoot the gun.

Ronnie had gone off with another old boy, Greg Cook, and they got to drinking and cutting up, carrying on with one another when according to Greg, Ronnie pulled a gun out and fired it around. Greg took the gun away from Ronnie and shot him. Ronnie fell off out of the car. Greg stopped the vehicle, got out, and went around to where Ronnie lay bleeding on the ground. Greg straddled him and began to beat him.

By then, the nearby neighbors who had heard the gunfire and commotion called the sheriff's office. The first officer to arrive was Deputy Allen. Allen tried hard to calm things down. Greg Cook had shot Ronnie a couple of times and was down over him beating him. As soon as the deputy got there, Greg was hollering at Ronnie and cussing at the deputy.

The deputy was unable to calm him down and de-escalate the situation. Johnny Mac was sitting at the sheriff's office, talking to a psychiatrist from Florida State Hospital who was inquiring about the things they did in law enforcement and how they handled things in a crisis situation when the call came in from Deputy Allen. "Get me some help down here now."

The psychiatrist said, "This is exactly what I'm talking about. This is the thing that I want to see and know about."

Johnny Mac reluctantly agreed. "All right, you can ride with me, but you have to do exactly what I tell you to do."

They got in the car and hit interstate 10 and headed east over to the Grand Ridge exit on the east side of the county. At that time, Johnny smoked.

The psychiatrist made the comment, "I never seen anybody drive 120 miles an hour, take a cigarette out, and light it while flying down the road."

As they got off the exit and went down toward the old Ocheesee Pond Landing and headed toward Mill Spring Community, Johnny Mac radioed dispatch to get deputies Glisson and Dennis headed to back him up. Those were the two best shots in the county. As Johnny turned the last curve before the church, running his lights and siren, he was met by a bunch of people standing in the middle of the road waving Johnny frantically toward the fight.

They motioned him around. Johnny whipped around the crowd, and the fight was right in front of him. Johnny jumped out and was basically in the fight. He told Greg Cook to stay down. Cook was straddling Ronnie, his pistol in Ronnie's mouth, telling him, "I'm gonna shoot you. I'm gonna pull this trigger."

"Listen here, you're not going to shoot anybody. Get up and give me that gun. Now let me have it," Johnny commanded.

The fellow didn't say anything.

"All right, get up and let me have it. Give me that gun. Don't hurt that man no more." Johnny was trying his best to de-escalate the situation until Dennis and Glisson

146

got there. If they had to shoot him, those were the two that could do it successfully with no one else injured.

Greg Cook looked all wild eyed. "Get your ass out of here, or I'm gonna shoot you next."

Well, about that time, *click*, he pulled the trigger. It snapped. When it snapped, Johnny rushed him. Johnny got Cook off Ronnie and tackled him to the ground, taking the gun away from him. He held Cook to the ground until help arrived from some of the deputies.

When Glisson and Dennis got there, Johnny turned the fellow over to them and went to Ronnie who was making a gurgling sound, lying there on his back choking on his own blood. Johnny rolled him over on his left side, reached in his mouth with his finger, and cleared his passageway by getting all the blood and mucus out of him so he could breathe. The paramedics, fire, and rescue arrived and took Ronnie to the hospital in Tallahassee.

Johnny had forgotten about the psychiatrist he left huddled in the patrol car. That gentleman didn't ask again to see first-hand how crisis situations were handled.

Johnny didn't think that Ronnie Wilson would live through the night because he had been shot two or three times, but he did.

The hospital called Johnny a few days later and said Ronnie was awake and wanted to talk to him. Johnny headed to the hospital with camera in hand to take pictures of the shots and wounds. When he arrived, he told Ronnie that he had to take some pictures for the court records. Ronnie agreed but asked Johnny to give him a minute. Ronnie fixed himself up and said, "Okay, do I look pitiful enough now?"

Johnny said, "Yeah, you look pitiful."

They sent the man to prison for shooting Ronnie, who never really recovered from his injuries.

***

Later problems would arise in a small community called Sinai. A fellow down there by the name of Joseph had a lot of mental problems. He was supposed to be on medication and had gotten to the point where he refused to take the medicine. His mother couldn't get him to take it. She even tried putting the meds in his food, but he wouldn't eat. Officers went down there on an ex-parte' to get him and bring him in. He snatched lose from the deputy and climbed a ladder into the attic closing the hatch behind him.

Every time they started to go to the car, he would shoot at them. Joseph had an arsenal of guns and ammo in the attic. They managed to call out for help, stating they were pinned down in the house. Johnny went down in an old car that belonged to Sneads Police Department. He intended to get up to the house using that car as a shield and help get those officers out.

When Johnny drove toward the house, Joseph shot the windshield out of the car. Johnny started backing out as fast as he could. He forgot he had left the driver's door open and tore the door off the car as he backed. Johnny said, "Gosh dog, it was a mess."

They managed to get some more help to divert Joseph's attention. Johnny had to get those two officers out of the house and get them to safety.

By then, a dear friend of Johnny's named Roy Hutto arrived. Roy was a sergeant with the Florida State Troopers. Sgt. Hutto heard the radio traffic and came down to help out with the situation. There was an old unused road bed—a pig trail—that led down beside the house. Every time they tried to walk down it, Joseph would fire off at them...*POW, POW, POW.*

Roy was ahead of Johnny, and Joseph kept firing over their heads until he clipped a limb. The limb came down on Roy's bald head.

Johnny laughed at Roy. "I don't believe he likes highway patrolmen."

Roy said, "You just shut up."

Roy was a typical former U.S. Marine. He looked and acted the part. Johnny looked up to Sgt. Hutto. "Son, he was a man and not afraid of anything."

Johnny and Roy got off the main part of the trail, just in the edge of the wood line, and continued to ease toward the house, but Joseph kept shooting at them.

"Roy, you got that python, and you're a damn good shot. Put a couple of rounds up there in the end of the house where he's at and see if you can scare him and make him come down." Johnny pointed to the south end of the house.

Roy took good aim and *POW, POW*.

Well, they didn't hear anything. They waited and waited and still didn't hear anything.

"Roy, you reckon you killed him?" Johnny asked.

"Dang, Johnny Mac, don't you even start that now. I don't want to listen to that....I won't ever get through with the paperwork. Don't go there...." Roy shook his head as they continued to listen.

It wasn't but just a little bit and State Attorney Jim Appleman called. He wanted to get involved and use negotiation skills to bring the situation to an end. Johnny told him to bring it on.

Within minutes, Appleman arrived and wanted to talk to Joseph and see if he could talk him into coming out. Johnny motioned down the trail toward the house and said, "Have at it."

Jim went down that same road that Johnny Mac and Roy had gone down earlier.

Jim hollered, "Joseph... Joseph...I'm a lawyer."

Man, Joseph let loose with a barrage of bullets...*POW, POW, POW, BOOM, BOOM, BOOM, BOOM.*

Johnny smiled at Jim, "I don't think he likes state attorneys either."

Steven Anderson came with Jim. He also worked for Jim at the State Attorney's Office. Johnny Mac and Steve and a few others used an ambulance as a shield to back in to the house to try and get Joseph out.

They tear-gassed the house in an effort to get him out of there. Well, Johnny had gotten overcome by carbon monoxide and tear gas. He was down on all fours and couldn't breathe.

Steven Anderson said, "Are you all right?"

"No, I can't breathe."

Johnny requested Deputy Ingram to get up to the attic trap door opening, climb up the steps, and grab Joseph's legs out from under him when he went by. They had to put an end to the mess before someone was killed.

Somehow, Eddie got up there and got that trap door open while everybody else kept Joseph distracted. Eddie grabbed Joseph and threw him down the trap door where he landed on the floor with a thud on his head. They resolved that incident without having to kill or shoot anyone and no one getting seriously injured.

***

Tuesday night, September 14, 1982, in the regular session of the Jackson County Board of Commissioners, progress was on the horizon. A motion was made by Commissioner Bylsma, was seconded by Commissioner McDaniel (no relation), and was carried unanimously to approve the sheriff contacting the Department of Corrections and advising of the board's intent to begin the preliminary work on phase II and construction of up to $120,000 on the jail project after January 2, 1983. John had worked very hard for the jail renovation.

Sheriff McDaniel also presented the board with an ordinance for their review on morality. Motions were made, seconded, and carried unanimously to advertise the intent to adopt an ordinance on morality.

**

By January 7, 1983, the wheels of progress regarding the jail project were still moving slowly. Sheriff McDaniel present the board with a check for $415.50 for the contraband fund, and also reported on the current jail inspection. The sheriff commented on the property behind the jail owned by Mrs. Nunnery. He informed the board that the property could be purchased for $10,000 for the forty by ninety foot lot. A motion was made by Commissioner Mercer, seconded by Commissioner John Padgett, and carried unanimously to grant the request for $2,000.00 to be used as a binder to pay Mrs. Nunnery for the property. A contract would be prepared with the balance paid when available.

**

Twelve-year-old Holly Celeste Kolmetz drowned on March 26, 1983. The tragic event occurred during a severe storm. Sheriff McDaniel was there and stayed through the torrential down-pouring rain, waiting until the moment search parties could go out and find Holly. Johnny Mac's call to duty did not end there. The child and her family were from Washington County, Florida, one county west from Jackson. Holly's father was in the Jackson County Hospital. Sheriff McDaniel went to the hospital and spoke with Holly's parents. He then gave up his home for the Kolmetz family to reside during Mr. Kolmetz's stay in the hospital. Johnny's heart, drive, intelligence, and determination would advance Jackson County more than any leader had in the past. Seeing a need in the community, he would make sure his department could fill those needs going forward. His next venture in the near future would be a dive and recovery team for the sheriff's department.

***

May 14-21, 1983, found Sheriff McDaniel demonstrating the proper fingerprinting techniques. The Jackson County Sheriff's Department in conjunction with the Pilot Club of Marianna and McDonalds held a voluntary fingerprinting program as an aid to missing children searches. All children who participated received free helium balloons and French fries, compliments of McDonalds. Johnny Mac felt the program would relieve a lot of parents' minds knowing that they had actual fingerprints of their child or children.

***

A county commission board meeting on June 14, 1983, would still find John McDaniel thinking outside of the box for ways financially affordable to protect the citizens of Jackson County. He presented the board with the Lake Seminole Project.

The proposal broke out at $15.00 per man hour as follows:

- $4.00/hour paid to sheriff department for expenses, gas, oil, etc.
- $3.00/hour for administrative costs incurred by the board of commissioners, check writing, etc.
- $8.00/hour paid to off duty deputies to patrol Lake Seminole

Motions were made, seconded, and carried unanimous approval to accept the proposal on the Lake Seminole Project.

***

On Tuesday, June 28, 1983, Sheriff McDaniel addressed the Marianna Lions Club, of which he was a member. Johnny Mac provided a slide slow with information on drug abuse—locally and nationally. He showed different types of drugs, explaining the effects of each.

Locally, he defined marijuana as being the biggest problem—along with alcohol. In 1980-81, Florida was the drug capitol of the world. Due to the organization of the Drug Task Force and its effect on the state, Florida no longer held that horrible record.

Johnny Mac concluded as guest speaker for the Lions Club by saying, "I hate drugs. Over ninety percent of those in jail are there because of drugs. If I don't do anything else as your sheriff, I'm going to give the dopers hell."

CHAPTER 35

Jackson County Sheriff and Deputies
Subject to Wrongful Death Suit:
July, 11, 1983

A little over a year had passed since John's divorce from Linda. Little John still lived with him in Indian Springs in Linda's dream home.

John was still battling problems with the jail. The Department of Corrections had implemented new guidelines regarding sight and sound in relation to monitoring prisoners. This was a somewhat impossible task, considering the structure of the late 1940s built jail. The jail renovation project was moving at a snail's pace.

Two and a half years as sheriff of Jackson County had brought many changes to the sheriff's department. Jail conditions were improved, department vehicles were a fraction better, contracts providing assistance with patrol had been implemented, a few new pieces of equipment had been purchased, and John met each problem hard, fast, and head on.

He loved his job as sheriff and had decided he would run for the office again in 1984 at the end of his first four-year term. Jackson County had seen an increase in burglaries over the past year. John restructured his deputy's hours and divided the county into zones with a specific deputy designated to work a particular zone. When staff permitted, the patrol lieutenant would remain center or "float" as needed. His idea was to provide more protection during the windows of time which rendered citizens more vulnerable.

Sunday night, July 10, found Jackson County deputies reporting for the second shift as usual. Lt. Deputy Duane Davis provided his crew with the usual updates prior to beginning their shift.

Something had occurred late Sunday evening that the sheriff's department nor the deputies had been made aware of—a front window of the Marianna Video Store was broken. Owner Richard Lundgren (a Jackson County auxiliary deputy) cleared the broken glass and replaced it with a sheet of plywood. That night, Richard and his wife, Margaret, slept in the store behind the desk.

The usual building checks were performed with nothing amiss until 2:00 a.m. on Monday morning when Deputy Davis and Ricky Cloud arrived at the property of the Marianna Video Store on Hwy 90. Deputy Sheriff Davis noticed the broken window in the storefront and suspected that a burglary was in progress. Deputy Cloud was nearby and immediately responded as a backup unit.

Due to the increase in burglaries the county had been experiencing, the deputies entered the store without announcing themselves. The store was only faintly illuminated by a small television.

What happened next would be sharply disputed by the parties. Deputy Davis testified at trial that he saw a large shadow or silhouette rise up from behind a desk, saw a flash of light from a gun, and felt a blast of hot air on his forehead.

After being shot at, Davis testified, he fired three times in return. When the shooting stopped, Davis went around the desk, shining his flashlight. Davis saw Richard Lundgren lying on the floor with blood trickling from his head and saw a gun on the floor. Davis testified that Margaret Lundgren then reached for this gun and that he told her not to touch it.

Deputy Ricky Cloud stated at trial that he saw a man stand up from behind the desk with a pistol in both hands. Fearing that he would be shot, Cloud turned his head and wheeled backward. As Cloud was wheeling backward, he heard the first shot. The shot sounded to Cloud like it came from behind the desk. According to Cloud, he then fired repeatedly in return.

On direct examination at trial, Margaret Lundgren testified that she woke up her husband when she heard someone walking on the broken glass outside the store. Margaret testified that her husband Richard "was raising up when someone started shooting and that Richard never made it all the way above the desk before he was shot."

She testified that Richard never fired a shot and that she never fired a shot. Margaret denied having later reached for a gun. In a prior deposition, Margaret had stated, "I recall him reaching for his gun." She later retracted, stating she did not know whether Richard reached for a gun and that Richard could have fired a shot.

Forensic examinations revealed that Richard Lundgren had been struck by one bullet in the right temple and that this bullet had first passed through the desk. Investigators found no physical evidence suggesting that Richard or Margaret had fired a shot. The pistol found in the store had lint in the barrel. No ejected shell casings were found. No gunshot residues were found on Richard's hands.

John McDaniel would arrive at the scene and immediately notify the State Attorney's Office to assist with the investigation as well as notifying Florida Department of Law Enforcement. His heart went out to his deputies and the Lundgren family. Richard Lundgren had served as an auxiliary deputy with the Jackson County Sheriff's Department. Sheriff McDaniel would find himself in court trials and appeals for years to come regarding this unfortunate turn of events.

The Grand Jury convened and cleared both Davis and Cloud. However, the decedent's wife, Margaret Lundgren, would sue on behalf of herself and the decedent's children. A civil lawsuit was brought against

157

the two deputies, Davis and Cloud, as well as Sheriff McDaniel.

After a jury trial, the district court entered judgment in favor of the plaintiff. The court held Deputies Davis and Cloud liable for $16,565.13 under 42 U.S.C. 1983, and Sheriff McDaniel liable for $198,750.00 under the pendent state law claim for wrongful death. In addition, the court awarded attorney's fees in the amount of $34,606.50 against defendants, allocating 8% of these against the two deputies, and 92% of these against the sheriff.

Plaintiff's would appeal on several grounds: violation of fourth amendment issues, qualified immunity, and eleventh amendment issues.

With regards to the violation of fourth amendment, on appeal, appellants argued that the officers' conduct in returning fire was justified and violated no constitutional right. According to appellants, the officers had probable cause to believe that the decedent or plaintiff posed a threat of serious physical harm to themselves or others. Appellants contended that it was uncontroverted that either the decedent or plaintiff rose up from behind the desk with a pistol with apparent intent on using it on the deputies.

If the facts were as appellants claimed, then the deputies' conduct would violate no constitutional rights. The Supreme Court has indicated that "if the suspect threatens the officer with a weapon…deadly force may be used." Tennessee v. Garner, 4714 U.S. 1,11, 105 S. Ct. 1694, 1701, 85 L. Ed. 2d 1 (1985).

But the factual disputes in the case—whether the plaintiff or the decedent had stood up behind the desk and had threatened the officers with a weapon or fired a shot—were sharply contested by the parties.

The jury could have reasonably believed that the officers were neither threatened by a weapon nor appeared to be threatened by a weapon nor were fired upon but rather that the officers without provocation shot at a non-dangerous suspect. It is probable that this is what the jury did conclude since it answered "yes" to special interrogatory questions regarding whether the deputies violated one or more of plaintiff's or decedent's constitution rights. Under the version of facts apparently believed by the jury, defendants violated the fourth amendment right to be free from unreasonable seizure when they fired at Richard Lundgren.

The Florida Constitution indicates that a sheriff is a county officer.

This judgment was affirmed in district court. Funds were paid from the state treasury rather than from county funds.

U.S. Court of Appeals for the Eleventh Circuit—814 F.2nd 600 (11th Cir. 1987) April 13, 1987.

CHAPTER 36
Serving the County
With Limited Resources

A little more than two weeks had passed since the tragic shooting of the Marianna shop owner by Jackson County deputies when Sheriff McDaniel had to attend a special meeting of the Board of County Commissioners. The approved budget of $900,000.00 needed to be increased to $921,000.00 if the sheriff's department was to continue working efficiently.

Jim Williams, the sheriff's administrative assistant, took a few minutes to again present their position on the budget. A motion was made by Commissioner McDaniel (no relation) to fund the $921,000, but the motion was withdrawn for lack of second. The board agreed to remain at $900,000.00

Sheriff McDaniel presented the board a check for the contraband account in the amount of $85,000.00 and additionally requested $2,500.00 to pay an informant. The monies to pay an informant passed with unanimous approval.

Over the next few months, John would continue to come up with ideas to resolve the funding issues surrounding the department and jail.

Departmental vehicles were still breaking down beyond repair. Rebuilt engines could not withstand the vigorous assault of running 24 hours a day, seven days a week. The department was working with old Highway Patrol cars which resulted in high maintenance costs to the county. With no increase in the budget, Johnny would have to continue rebuilding the older cars.

CHAPTER 37
Back in Time...

A two-day event was held on September 24-25, 1983, commemorating the Battle of Marianna which occurred on September 27, 1864. On Saturday, September 24, Marianna history was changed as Confederate troops and local militiamen put some would-be Union looters on the run during a skirmish before approximately 500 spectators. On a sunny warm afternoon, spectators watched as the skirmish broke out near the bottom of the hill.

Back in 1864, the battle actually was a raid on the relatively unprotected town by Union troops—many of them freed slaves from the federal Naval base in Pensacola.

The approximately 500 Union soldiers, led by General Alexander Asboth, were on a looting mission— raiding towns and taking metals, food, and anything else of value.

Attempting to defend Marianna was a force of about 180 gunmen composed of a few local militiamen, farmers, businessmen, store owners, and others.

Because he was wounded during the battle, Asboth ordered that all of the buildings in the town be burned. That order was partially carried out, with St. Luke's Church and two other buildings being razed.

The battle's toll included nine Confederate soldiers and fifteen Union soldiers killed and sixteen Confederates and forty Union soldiers wounded.

The federal troops captured 54 prisoners during the battle. The troops held the city only overnight, fleeing in the predawn hours as Confederate soldiers moved into the area. However, during the short time they stayed, the Union troops looted the town so badly that it literally took years for local residents to recover.

While the rebels won the Saturday re-enactment, they lost during the Sunday re-enactment, just as they did during the Civil War.

The sheriff for the town during the re-enactment was none other than Sheriff John P. McDaniel. Jackson County Sheriff McDaniel was observed telling a group of boys where to flee when Union troops started attacking. Johnny Mac was among fifty people involved in the battle re-enactment in which the Confederate forces successfully defended Marianna.

***

On Thursday night, October 14, 1983, father and son celebrated Little John's eighteenth birthday in style—a fire in the backyard, a huge barbeque, and plenty of good ole country music.

By Halloween, Little John and a bunch of boys moved in together at a little house in Cypress on the east end of Jackson County. Little John would work at several jobs over the next few years, driving a truck and later running a dry-cleaning business.

John felt truly alone at home. He found himself working even more hours than before. By the first of December, 1983, Johnny Mac was full force participating in the J. P. McDaniel Christmas Fund Project for the under-privileged children. The mere effort made him feel closer to his daddy whose murder was still unresolved after three years.

CHAPTER 38
Last Year of First Term as Sheriff:
1984

Johnny Mac had grabbed the horns and held on tightly in January of 1981. He had a vision for the department and grabbed the bull by the horns and never let go. He was bucked off a few times but climbed right back in the saddle, fighting for a better-protected future for the citizens of Jackson County.

He had lost his father, his sister, and divorced his wife since becoming sheriff three years earlier. He never stopped praying or believing that God would provide a way.

Johnny Mac implemented the McGruff Crime Dog program in Jackson County. John dressed up as McGruff the Crime Dog and went into the schools and taught the youth to "Just Say No to Drugs."

He stepped up his "War on Drugs" by working out a deal with Harrell Foran, owner of Chipola Aviation. The department would rent the plane to fly surveillance and do spotting maneuvers in search of dope fields. Johnny Mac utilized Deputy Wayne "Cowboy" Morris as his pilot. He had hired Cowboy back in May of 1983. Prior to '83, Cowboy had given many hours to the department as an auxiliary officer. He had an eye for the terrain and could spot marijuana plants anywhere. He was an excellent pilot and donated many hours of his own time to the sheriff's department and the citizens of Jackson County.

The contracts for service Johnny had entered into with some of the smaller municipalities and the Lake Seminole Project had afforded additional deputies with a cost split, so the county didn't have to absorb the whole salary and benefits package for the officer.

The jail renovations were being implemented, keeping DOC and the feds from forcing closure of the old jail. It was still a continual bad problem. The more rules and regulations implemented by DOC pushed the old Jackson County Jail further from compliance each quarter. It was an exhausting drain on the county finances and short of building a new jail, the problems would eventually be insurmountable.

Johnny announced his candidacy for re-election for sheriff. He participated in campaigning cook outs and the distribution of campaign signs, but he did not change his day to day operations. Johnny Mac campaigned every day he was in office—meaning, he tried to be everything to everybody, every day of the year.

The first primary election for Jackson County was held on September third. The office of sheriff had four contenders: Ernest T. Brock, George Cannady, John P. McDaniel, and Steven Underwood.

Momma Ruth, Machelle, and Little John all gathered around Johnny Mac as the results began coming in from the polls. The excitement was beginning to build. John P. McDaniel took 84% of the vote in the 1984 election compared to 66% when he ran for the first time in 1980. With the polls tallied, John P. McDaniel won with 10,634 votes. Steven Underwood had 1346, George Cannady with 282 and Ernest T. Brock with 405. Johnny Mac carried every precinct by a very large margin and was excited to serve the people of Jackson County Florida for another four years.

Jim Appleman won the State Attorney's race against Ed Miller. Sam Mitchell took the State Representative race, and Dawn Crews won out against Raymond R. Bruner for the Clerk of Circuit Courts.

There was one record-setting turn of events in the election of 1984. A news reporter for WTOT-WJAQ Radio had decided to seek one of the five seats on the

Jackson County Commission. Gloria Moreland defeated Lucious "Cap" Pooser in the District 3 run-off race to become the county's first woman commissioner.

**

John continued squeezing the life out of his departmental budget in order to protect and serve the citizens of Jackson County.

With Christmas approaching, it brought about a time for fulfilling the needs of others. John dove into the J.P. McDaniel fundraising project with all his heart.

The Sneads Christmas Parade was getting ready to kick off. Johnny Mac got all suited up in his McGruff Dog outfit. Investigator John Dennis drove the patrol car in the parade so Johnny Mac could hold onto the outside mirror and walk and wave at the children. It was a pretty warm evening for the Christmas Parade. The squeals of children's laughter and a group of Christmas carolers filled the air.

Johnny Mac began to get very hot in the McGruff suit and thought to himself, "This parade sure is moving fast." He continued holding onto the mirror and walking and waving at the children. The suit's dog head was so large it made it impossible to see anything.

Faster and faster he walked, hanging onto the side mirror. Finally, Johnny Mac said, "John Dennis, why are you driving so fast?"

"Johnny Mac, I'm just keeping up with the flow of the parade," John replied with a tiny grin.

Johnny Mac kept walking faster and faster and then stopped. "Wait a damn minute, John. You're the lead car!"

John died laughing. "Just keeping you on your toes, Sheriff!"

"When I get out of this suit, I'm gonna kill you John…" John slowed down and Johnny Mac finished the parade walking at a slower pace, and he didn't kill Dennis afterward. He was used to their jokes by then. It was all done with love.

***

On Sunday, December 16, 1984, a local newspaper, the Jackson County *Floridan*, ran an article entitled: "J.P. McDaniel Made a Mark on Lives." The article detailed the personal account of Beverly B. Conrad, assistant project director for the J. P. McDaniel Christmas Fund.

Mrs. Conrad stated, "The last time I saw J. P. McDaniel was on December 13, 1980, at a Christmas party. He wore a bright red and white checkered shirt and seemed to be enjoying himself immensely; so was his lovely wife seated beside him. It's still hard to believe that just a little over 24 hours later, he would lay dying of a robber's gunshot wound to his head. Only a few days earlier, this gentle man had begged my forgiveness for not seeing me sooner upon learning of the death of my father. Never can I forget his cheerful calls on the C.B. radio as he went about town delivering meals to the sick and homebound. Very appropriately, his radio 'handle' was Happy Pappy.

"J. P. gained his greatest satisfaction in life by doing things for and helping others. J. P. didn't preach about it being more blessed to give than to receive. He lived it. He advised me to never grieve over past mistakes. He admitted making some serious ones in his younger years, and [he] had vowed to spend the rest of his life not grieving about them but making up for them. J. P. McDaniel made a mark on me, a mark that I hope time will never erase."

John P. McDaniel III definitely inherited some great qualities from John Jr.

Johnny Mac lived to help others.

CHAPTER 39
Back in the Saddle Again
1985

Johnny started the year in 1985 beginning his second term as sheriff of Jackson County. He was pleased with the accomplishments his department had made during his first term. Even though there had been much money spent renovating the old jail and attempting to bring it up to code, inspection results still fell short. Johnny Mac began reaching out to members of Tri-States' Law Enforcement Sheriffs and Chiefs in an attempt to resolve the issues and come up with a plan.

Department vehicles and radio equipment were still a source of contention. John would continue asking the commission for assistance in upgrading the department fleet and the communication system.

The year would bring much excitement for Johnny. His daughter, Machelle, was expecting his first grandchild in May. He could hardly wait. His son, Little John, would turn twenty and was making a good living driving a truck. He stopped by to see his dad almost every day. Unless he was out of town, John stopped by to see Momma Ruth every morning before going to work.

Jackson County was battling a rash of robberies and burglaries all over the county. Johnny did an analysis of the times most incidents were occurring and increased deputy presence during the most vulnerable time for citizens and businesses. By the end of February in 1985, investigative efforts had paid off and several warrants were issued for subjects on some of the burglary cases.

At approximately 7:30 p.m. on the evening of March 4, 1985, Deputy Wayne "Cowboy" Morris was traveling south on Highway 231 when he observed Thomas "Jack" Fitzgerald standing in front of the Sand Hills Tavern in the Round Lake area of Jackson County. Cowboy easily recognized Fitzgerald as one of the subjects Jackson County Sheriff's Department had a warrant on for burglary. Also, Fitzgerald had made several threats on Morris's life. The threats were due to Officer Morris finding and destroying Fitzgerald's dope fields on several occasions.

Cowboy called for a marked unit to respond as he was driving an unmarked, 1968 Chevrolet blazer, white over green, belonging to the Jackson County Sheriff's Department. Fitzgerald left the tavern driving north on Highway 231 in a blue and primer-colored 1958 pickup truck with Alabama license plates. Cowboy followed Fitzgerald up to Alford where Fitzgerald turned west on County Road 276. After approximately one mile of travel on C-276, Cowboy flashed his lights and blew his horn, trying to get Fitzgerald to stop. Fitzgerald slowed down but would not stop. At that point, Cowboy was becoming concerned that he was being set-up by Fitzgerald who was known to be armed. His most recent threats against the officer were that Fitzgerald was going to blow Cowboy's head off to stop him from disturbing his dope fields.

Cowboy followed Fitzgerald across the Washington/Jackson County line where Fitzgerald turned left onto the first unpaved road and stopped. Cowboy pulled up to the side of Fitzgerald's truck and said, "Halt, Deputy Sheriff."

Fitzgerald then pulled off. Cowboy yelled, "Stop, Deputy Sheriff." Cowboy then fired two or three warning shots, but Fitzgerald did not stop. Cowboy then fired at the left rear tire, but the subject still did not stop. Cowboy got back into his vehicle and pursued Fitzgerald again. Approximately ½ mile down, the vehicle turned left. As Fitzgerald made the left turn, Cowboy observed the driver's door open and Fitzgerald exiting the vehicle as it was still moving. Fitzgerald bailed out of the vehicle and jumped a hog wire fence. Cowboy stopped and made it to the fence, telling Fitzgerald to stop again and again identifying himself. Fitzgerald did not stop. Instead he ran east. Cowboy fired one shot toward Fitzgerald's legs and struck him on the left leg just above the ankle.

About that time, back up arrived, Deputy James Bevis. Cowboy told Fitzgerald again to halt, not knowing at the time that he had shot him. Fitzgerald hollered, "Don't shoot again, Wayne. You done broke my leg."

Cowboy responded, "Thomas, don't you move."

"Just don't shoot me again. You done shot my leg," Fitzgerald hollered.

Deputies Bevis and Morris went to Fitzgerald and handcuffed him. Bevis then began to give him first aid as he summoned an ambulance and his supervisor.

Shortly, Washington County Investigator James Gollehon arrived at the scene. An examination of Morris's weapon revealed five empty rounds and one live round. The live round and the five spent rounds were removed from the weapon and taken into evidence and retained by Investigator Gollehon. The weapon was released back to Deputy Morris.

Jackson County Fire and Rescue arrived and transported Fitzgerald to Jackson Hospital in Marianna.

The deputies immediately notified Sheriff McDaniel of what had occurred. Johnny Mac notified Florida Department of Law Enforcement that he had an incident occur involving an officer-related shooting of a fleeing felon. He advised he was allowing Washington County Sheriff's Department Chief Deputy Roger Haddix to oversee the complete investigation. FDLE was welcome to investigate the shooting themselves or accept the findings of Chief Deputy Haddix.

By 11:00 p.m., Judy E. Gilliland, who was with Fitzgerald during the incident, was also booked in the county jail on burglary charges.

Johnny Mac was still battling with the legal ramifications from the last officer-related shooting from the Lundgren case. He knew this one would probably follow suit and took measures to ensure the investigation and all evidence be handled properly with no possible hint of any improprieties.

In this case, the plaintiff, Thomas "Jack" Fitzgerald, provided notice of civil action suit to the Florida Department of Insurance and to Sheriff John P. McDaniel on November 20, 1985.

Cited below are some of the same issues used as grounds for Fitzgerald's civil suit which were identical to those used in the Lundgren case:

- *Violation of Constitutional Right to Due process – 14th Amendment*
- *Violation of 4th and 5th Amendment*
- *Assault and Battery*
- *Negligence*
- *Qualified Immunity*

Fitzgerald filed this civil action against John P. McDaniel, Sheriff of Jackson County, Florida, and Wayne T. Morris, Deputy in the United States District Court of the Northern District of Florida pursuant to 42 U.S.C. 1983 for violation of rights guaranteed by the fourth, fifth, and fourteenth amendments to the United States Constitution (Count 1). Fitzgerald's complaint also stated state law causes of action for assault and battery (Count 2) and negligence (Count 3).

At the conclusion of the evidence, the district court instructed the jury that Fitzgerald's arrest was lawful; consequently, the jury should determine "whether a lawful arrest was accomplished by using excessive force under the circumstances."

The jury returned verdicts of $1 punitive damages against Morris personally under Count 1, $120,375 *compensatory damages, $1,500 punitive damages against Morris personally under Count 11, and $28,087.50 against Sheriff McDaniel in his official capacity under Count III. Sheriff John P. McDaniel presented four issues on appeal: (1) whether Morris's conduct was reasonable (2) whether this action should have been dismissed because of Fitzgerald's failure to comply with the notice provisions of Florida Statue Sec. 768.28(6) (3)whether the district court lacked jurisdiction to hear this case because the state of Florida had not waived sovereign immunity and (4)whether the district court erred in granting a motion in limine, restricting testimony of threats Fitzgerald allegedly made against Deputy Morris.*

In looking at the issue of whether Morris's conduct was reasonable, a review of Florida statutes sec. 776.05 provided:

A law enforcement officer, or any person whom he has summoned or directed to assist him, need not retreat or desist from efforts to make a lawful arrest because of resistance or threatened resistance to the arrest. He is justified in the use of any force which he reasonably believes to be necessary to defend himself or another from bodily harm while making the arrest...

McDaniel and Morris contended that Morris's conduct was reasonable because Morris was acting under the specific authorization of section 776.05. Nelson v. Howell, 455 So.2d 608 (Fla. 2d D.C.A. 1984) was cited which concluded that if a private citizen may use deadly force in preventing a felon from escaping, then a law enforcement officer must also be permitted to use deadly force in preventing a felon from escaping.

The jury did not find Morris's use of deadly force to be reasonable under these circumstances. The jury's assessment of the reasonableness of Morris's conduct was a factual finding by which the court was bound.

173

With regards to the dismissal of the claim based on the failure to comply with the notice provisions in section 7768.28(6), the district court held that the issue of Fitzgerald's noncompliance with the statue is moot.

With regards to the sovereign immunity issue, McDaniel contended that he was sued in his official capacity as sheriff of Jackson County, Florida, and that this lawsuit was barred because the state of Florida has not waived its sovereign immunity for civil rights actions brought under 42 U.S.C. 1983. Fitzgerald contended that he sued McDaniel and Morris individually, not in their official capacities, and that whether Florida waived its eleventh amendment immunity is irrelevant. His contention was that this issue had been resolved by Lundgren v. McDaniel, 814 F.2d 600 (11th Cir. 1987).

In Lundgren, Sheriff McDaniel argued that his deputies were sued in their official capacities and that the lawsuit was barred because Florida had not waived its eleventh amendment immunity. The Lundgren court cited Kentucky v. Graham, 473 U.S. 159, 105 S. Ct. 3099, 3106 n. 14, 87 L. Ed. 2d 114 (1985) in which the Supreme Court observed that when a compliant does not clearly specify whether state officials are being sued in their individual capacities, in their official capacities, or both, often the course of the proceedings will indicate the nature of the liability sought to be imposed. The Lundgren court then concluded that because the qualified immunity defense was raised, litigated, and submitted to the jury, Lundgren's claim was tried as a claim against the deputies solely in their individual capacities. Examining the record in this case, it was concluded that because McDaniel and Morris raised, litigated, and submitted to the jury a defense premised on qualified immunity, the lawsuit was filed against them in their individual capacities. Qualified immunity is available only in an individual capacity lawsuit, not in an official *capacity. Ruling by district court was affirmed on this issue.*

With regards to the issue motion in limine (request of judge/court to allow or disallow inclusion of evidence), McDaniel and Morris contend that the district court erred in granting Fitzgerald's motion in limine, restricting testimony concerning threats Fitzgerald made to Deputy Morris. McDaniel and Morris argue that they proffered the testimony of five witnesses regarding threats, and that by restricting all references to marijuana or drugs, the district court emasculated the probative value of their testimony. McDaniel and Morris assert that the district court misapplied rule 403 of the Federal Rules of Evidence by finding that the probative value of this proffered testimony was substantially outweighed by the danger of unfair prejudice, confusion of the issues, or misleading the jury. Ruling by district court was affirmed on this issue. The district court properly restricted the testimony of the witnesses to avoid the danger of unfair prejudice. No abuse of the district court's exercise of discretion was noted.

The latter was of great detriment to Sheriff McDaniel and Deputy Morris in this case. The five witnesses who had firsthand knowledge of the threats made by Jack Fitzgerald to shoot and kill Deputy Morris were brought in and instructed by the court that their testimony could make no reference to drugs, marijuana, or illegal activity with regard to Thomas Jack Fitzgerald.

In The United States District Court Northern District of Florida, Panama City Division, Thomas "Jack" Fitzgerald, Plaintiff, v. John P. McDaniel and Wayne "Cowboy" Morris, as sheriff and deputy sheriff of Jackson County, Florida, respectively, Defendants— MCA 86-2002-RV—final jury verdicts were rendered on December 17th, 1986, as follows:

- *Federal Claims – Section 1983 – Punitive Damages awarded against the defendant, Wayne Morris in the amount of $1.00*
- *State Claim—Assault and Battery—Damages sustained by the plaintiff, Fitzgerald, were legally caused by the conduct of the defendant, Wayne Morris, in the amount of $120,375.00*
- *Punitive damages were awarded against the defendant, Wayne Morris in the amount of $1,500.00*
- *Negligence – The percentage of negligence which was a legal cause of damage to the plaintiff was calculated at 70% against the defendant, Deputy Wayne Morris, in the amount of $40,125.00*
- *State Claim of Negligence – Plaintiff Thomas "Jack Fitzgerald" awarded the recovery of $28,087.50 from the defendant John P. McDaniel, in his official capacity as Sheriff of Jackson County, Florida.*

Sheriff McDaniel was very upset. Surely the jury must have wondered why Fitzgerald would have made threats of serious bodily harm or death against a *deputy sheriff without giving any reason whatsoever for making those threats. It was a reasonable conclusion by Deputy Morris on the night of the shooting that he was being set-up by Fitzgerald for him to commit the promised act of murder.

Johnny Mac would ponder these two cases over and over again. "As an officer, you were required to make split second decisions regarding the use of force." Johnny didn't second guess his officers' decisions. He simply

176

stood behind them and made sure a thorough and impartial investigation was completed to the fullest extent. The truth was the truth. They learned from each case and moved forward.

CHAPTER 40

Force vs Deadly Force

Over the years, Johnny Mac always wanted to find an alternative to deadly force—having to shoot and kill somebody.

He had heard about bean bag guns. "You could shoot the bean bags out of a specially made gun and they would incapacitate the suspect without killing them." Johnny got with another officer, Joey Rabon, and told him to order some of them for the department.

They took some of the drug money funding (money gained through drug seizures) and bought the guns and bags. They received training until they were proficient at handling the new weapon.

Then an old boy up off Highway 2 in the north end of Jackson County got drunk and was sitting out beside a fire. He was going to kill himself, kill his daddy, and just kill everybody in the world. Johnny went there with some of his officers and the boy kept threatening to shoot everyone.

He would hold the gun in his mouth, then take a drink, then hold the gun to his head, then take another drink. His daddy came and tried to help talk him down. That was the wrong move because he was still mad with his daddy about something.

His girlfriend came and tried to talk to him, but he was mad at her too. He threatened to shoot the cops if they didn't leave.

Johnny Mac told Officer Joey Rabon to get where he could get in position to do something with him. A couple other deputies followed Joey as back-up. Darkness had already fallen upon them. The officers could see Joey as they crawled on the ground near where he was sitting by the fire.

He stood up with his whiskey bottle in one hand and a gun in the other hand. Officer Rabon shot him with that bean bag gun, and it immediately knocked him down, knocking the gun out of his hand. Johnny ran over to him, and the old boy said, "God damn, Johnny Mac! You 'bout killed me."

Johnny said, "What? Weren't you just talking about shooting yourself?"

The old boy said. "Aww, hell. I wasn't gonna kill myself."

They managed to get the old boy the help he needed without having to shoot anyone.

**

On another occasion, a young boy robbed a bank in Malone at gunpoint. The young man came from a very nice family and just went wrong. Johnny and several of his officers all set up at different locations with a plan to get the young man out of the car and utilize the bean bag gun to subdue him.

The young man flew past a trooper.

The trooper turned around on him with his lights and siren. The young man started shooting at the state trooper. The trooper returned fire hitting the boy in the back of the head and killing him.

The trooper was justified in what he did; it was just tragic that it ended in death. In that particular case with a suspect armed in a vehicle, the bean bag gun would have been ineffective.

Johnny later learned that the young man had become a heavy alcohol user. He felt the bank robbery was more alcohol than anything. Johnny had seen alcohol end up hurting a lot of young people and their families and was working hard to implement more programs in the jail to assist in beating the addiction.

CHAPTER 41
Regional Jail Concept Entertained:
March 1985

On Tuesday, March 12, 1985, Sheriff McDaniel once again pled with the Board of County Commissioners regarding another failed jail inspection report. Sheriff McDaniel came up with a way to meet the federal prison board standards without hiring the fifteen additional personnel the prison board required.

Johnny Mac sought and won approval from the board to purchase two monitoring systems, new locks, and smoke alarms for the jail. The monitors would allow the jail to operate in compliance without all five female matrons the prison board originally required. The cameras would allow the dispatcher to see and hear the female prisoners housed just a few feet away from the dispatch office. The total $3000 cost for this project would have to come from the contraband fund, since the jail maintenance fund was already over-spent by approximately $1,181.00.

Johnny Mac additionally added that five area counties, frustrated by the threat of federal lawsuits because their jails didn't meet federal prison board standards, were meeting on March 19 to discuss the possibility of a regional jail. The regional jail would house prisoners from all five counties. Sheriff McDaniel elaborated that a lot of details would need to be worked out in considering the concept. Just a few included 1) staffing and construction 2) where to locate the facility 3) transporting prisoners back and forth 4) staffing ratios 5) dollar amount for each county's contribution.

***

The Tuesday night, March 19, 1985, meeting in Chipley with area sheriffs discussing the regional jail concept went well. A committee was formed with various county commission liaisons in an effort to come up with solutions to some of the problems. Future talks were scheduled with the Department of Corrections, prison inspectors, and other agencies to identify and iron out problems.

The number one problem that needed to be addressed was that of a location for the facility. Three counties of the five were willing to participate—Jackson, Holmes, and Washington counties. It could only be built in one county, and that raised questions for the other two counties. The problem of the eroding authority of the other two sheriffs whose counties the facility was not built would have to be addressed. Calhoun and Walton County sent representatives to the meeting but declined to participate in the concept. How to fund, staff, and construct as well as the booking process would also need to be decided.

As the sheriff of Jackson County, Johnny Mac wanted to keep them from engaging in needless legal battles that would cost the taxpayers and still result in their having to build another jail.

Washington and Holmes counties were already subject to lawsuits, and Jackson was under threat of a lawsuit for violations of federal prison standards, related mainly to understaffing charges.

Johnny remained optimistic, stating, "If we continue to work together in an effort to help our citizens, we should be able to come up with some good solutions to the problems we face."

CHAPTER 42

Officer Down:
April 4, 1985

S heriff McDaniel was in Pensacola, Florida, on the fourth day of April, 1985, doing research on jail population and construction in preparation for the possibility of a new jail. As he was eating his evening meal, things were turning bad in Jackson County. Eighteen-year-old Morris Lavon Brown and nineteen-year-old Edward Lee Cotton entered the Jr. Food Store in Malone, Florida, with stockings on their faces and a .22 caliber pistol. They robbed the clerk at gunpoint, and Brown fired a shot at a customer who entered the store during the robbery. The two suspects fled the store at approximately 9:38 p.m. in Cotton's blue and white El Camino, headed toward Campbellton.

Robberies had escalated in Jackson County, so the deputies had devised a plan when the next robbery occurred. Investigator John Dennis had met with Deputy Bevis earlier in the evening at the hospital to take a statement from the victim of a domestic. A postmaster over in Cypress had shot her husband. Deputy Bevis had asked Investigator Dennis for film to take pictures of the victim. The two had gone out to the trunk of Dennis's car and gotten the film. Bevis had asked Dennis if he was upset with him as he was going through a divorce and had two small handicapped children. Dennis had told him he was one of his best friends and of course he wasn't mad at him.

The two talked briefly about their plan regarding the strategic locations they were to go to in the event of a robbery, and they both left the hospital. Deputy Bevis's location was Old U.S. Road (Hwy 167) and Hwy 162. John Dennis went toward Hwy 90 and Hwy 69 near Grand Ridge.

Later that night, Dennis heard the call on the radio: "Robbery, shots fired, suspects leaving Jr. Food Store in Malone." Dennis turned on Hwy 69 North, headed toward the area. Dispatch advised the suspects were driving a blue and white El Camino.

The almost ten-hour ordeal began at 9:38 p.m. on Thursday night, April 4, when Bevis, an eight-year veteran with the Jackson County Sheriff's Department, received a call that two black males armed with a gun had robbed the Jr. Food Store in Malone fifteen miles north of Marianna.

The 40-year-old deputy, James Bevis, met up with the suspects at the intersection of Hwy 167 and 162 in Jackson County. He advised he had them spotted and described the vehicle to the dispatcher, Hayes Baggett, as being a Blue and White El Camino and gave the tag number. At 9:49 p.m., Deputy Bevis advised he would be 10-50 (stopping the vehicle).

Investigator Dennis called Deputy Bevis on the radio and advised him, "I'm coming to you. Just hold them down."

Bevis pulled the El Camino over and asked Edward Cotton to exit the car. After obtaining Cotton's driver's license, he asked Brown to step out of the car. He found the clerk's purse and other items from the Jr. Food Store robbery. He placed both suspects with their hands on the hood of his patrol car—Cotton on the driver's side and Brown on the passenger side.

Deputy Bevis radioed, "I got them. I recovered the purse from the robbery."

Dennis responded, "Put your gun on them. I'm headed to you, turning on 162 now."

At 9:59 p.m., Dispatcher Baggett checked with Bevis after two minutes from his last transmission and received a 10-4 / 10-6 (okay but busy), advising that he was arresting the suspects. Baggett advised Bevis that he would send another officer his way.

In another two minutes, Dispatcher Baggett checked on Deputy Bevis again. "Jackson to 9; 10-4?"

There was no reply.

Dispatcher Baggett tried again. "Jackson to Jackson 9; 10-4?"

No response.

Dispatcher Baggett immediately contacted all available units to respond and continued in his attempts to reach Deputy Bevis via radio.

Investigator Dennis reported that he had Deputy Bevis's flashing blue lights in sight at 10:06 p.m., but the suspect's vehicle was nowhere in sight. Dennis went to go around Bevis's car and saw James on the other side of the road. Within the same minute, he called for an ambulance. He utilized his low band radio in the car and advised, "James is down. Put a bolo out for the El Camino."

Investigator Dennis will never forget the horror of what he found. Deputy Bevis was across the road from his car, shot three times—flat on his back with his mouth and eyes full of blood. Dennis unzipped James's shirt to check for vitals and attempt to help him. James was wearing his vest.

Sheriff McDaniel had just finished eating supper in Pensacola and had gone up to his room when he received a phone call. "Sheriff, Deputy Bevis was just murdered."

John rushed out the door in a haze, handed his room key to the front desk, and advised them he was checking out. He had a new Oldsmobile which had just been purchased from Mr. Hopkins at his dealership in Marianna. The Olds was equipped with an FHP radio.

Chill bumps still run over John today when he repeats what he said when he checked on over the radio that night. He called Florida Highway Patrol in Pensacola and told them, "This is Sheriff McDaniel from Marianna. I just had an officer killed, and I will be exceeding the speed limit from here to Marianna, Florida."

As it worked out, the FHP Dispatcher on duty in Marianna, Florida, that night was a crippled man by the name of Red Williams. Red heard Sheriff McDaniel on the radio all the way over in Pensacola and said, "Sheriff, bring it home."

He did. Lord have mercy, he never took the pedal off the floor. Approximately 150 miles and eighty minutes later, Sheriff McDaniel was sitting in Greenwood where Deputy Bevis had been murdered. It would prove to be a horrible night.

Jackson County Fire and Rescue had already experienced a very busy night. Captain Robby Brown had left the station at 4:30 p.m. and didn't return until 9 p.m. Capt. Brown updated EMT David Selman when he arrived for the evening shift. Others on duty were EMT Paul Hatcher and Paramedics Marcus Basford and R. D. Selman. They were watching a football game when line three (non-emergency line) rang. R. D. answered the call, and it didn't take long for the rest of the medics to realize something really bad had happened.

"A deputy has been shot?" they heard him ask the caller. He hung up the phone and quickly advised Captain Brown that it was the sheriff's dispatcher, Hayes Baggett, on the phone advising there was a possibility a deputy had been shot on a traffic call, and they needed to move out "10-18" lights and siren. Baggett was an excellent dispatcher. He had rescue headed to the scene prior to confirmation that Deputy Bevis was shot. The rescue unit was given the directions, about a mile or two west of Greenwood on Hwy 162. Captain Brown drove, Basford sat in the passenger seat, and Selman sat in the back of Rescue One.

Dispatcher Baggett called Rescue to find out how close they were and for them to move as fast as they could; it was confirmed there was an officer down. As they turned left on Hwy 162, Basford advised Selman to have the trauma box and portable oxygen units ready. As the rescue unit topped the hill, they could see the flashing lights of three deputy cruisers ahead. Arriving on the scene, they found Deputy Bevis lying face up on the north side of the highway. His car was parked on the south side of the road, facing Greenwood. At first glance, it became painfully obvious that the officer was dead.

Investigator Dennis and Donnie Branch were on scene and coordinating efforts via their radios regarding the apprehension of the suspects. Jackson County Fire and Rescue covered Deputy Bevis's body and waited for the Florida Department of Law Enforcement Crime Lab to arrive to process the scene.

They closed off all roads that they possibly could. Shortly after Investigator Dennis put out the bolo for the suspect vehicle, another sheriff's investigator, Paul Dudley, met the car on Bumpnose Road, and the pursuit began. The El Camino veered off onto Christoff Ferry Road at a high rate of speed and ran off the road into a ditch where the suspects fled into the woods.

Around 10:30 p.m., a little down the road from where they fled, Edward Cotton surrendered to Florida Highway Patrol Troopers, Robert See, Marvin Wagner, Newt King, and Jackson County Deputy Sgt. Wayne Morris. Cotton informed them that Brown had fled from where they had been hiding. Sgt. Morris transported Edward Cotton to Jackson County Jail.

While the search was underway for Brown off Bumpnose Road, Sheriff McDaniel would arrive at the scene on Hwy 162 to find Deputy Bevis's car door still open as his lights continued to flash. The murder scene would remain this way until the Florida Department of

Law Enforcement Crime Lab completed the processing task. Sheriff McDaniel began immediately to try to get further air search assistance. Searchers almost became stationary around 3:30 a.m. since it seemed as though Brown was criss-crossing through the area and the dogs were beginning to tire.

John P. McDaniel would leave the scene long enough to lose a piece of his heart. He had to inform Mr. and Mrs. Hubert Bevis of Sneads that their son would never return home. James Lee and Susan Bevis would not see their father alive again.

At dawn, things were in full swing again as the Leon County helicopter was joined by the FHP airplane, and a new pack of dogs hit the trail. Manpower was provided by local law enforcement agencies as well as those from surrounding areas, Game and Fish Commission, and the Beverage Department. The manhunt continued for Brown, who was considered to be armed and dangerous.

By 7:20 a.m., Leon County's helicopter was running low on fuel and headed to the airport to re-fuel. Florida Highway Patrol plane spotted a black male running along an old logging road fence line; the subject's clothing matched the description of the clothes Brown was wearing. FHP Trooper See, Trooper Wagner, and John McDaniel went in off Milton Plantation Road. They had guns drawn and kept telling Brown to come out with his hands in the air. McDaniel stated, "Honest to God, I wanted to shoot him..."

Several officers from the Jackson County Sheriff Department and Florida Department of Agriculture Investigator Mike Spiers were present when McDaniel and Troopers See and Wagner brought Brown over the fence and took him into custody. Part of his clothes and shoes were taken into custody at that point. Deputies Booth and Spiers took Brown to the Jackson County Jail. States Attorney, Bill Wright, transferred Brown to

Gadsden County Jail "for his own safekeeping." Both Sheriff McDaniel and Gadsden County Sheriff Woodham agreed to the transfer as well as Judge Hatcher and the public defender.

Later Friday night, a hallow-eyed John McDaniel would go home to try and rest after being up for more than 36 hours. Rest would not come easy for a long time as a part of his family was gone. He would go to bed with prayers of peace, comfort, and protection for all the citizens of Jackson County.

***

On Monday, April 8, Sheriff McDaniel would be part of a five-mile motor procession giving a final salute to Jackson-9, Sgt. James Bevis, whose family and hundreds of friends and colleagues, including Lt. Governor Wayne Mixon, paid their respects at the National Guard Armory in Jackson County. Afterward, a procession of cars, bumper to bumper, headed down Hwy 90 toward the Lovedale community. Flashing blue and red lights twinkled against a cloudless horizon as they followed James Bevis to his final resting place.

***

On Tuesday, April 9, Sheriff McDaniel continued to pull together all possible volunteers and departmental staff to search the west side of Bumpnose Road. Prior searches on the north and east side failed to yield the .357 service revolver of murdered Deputy Bevis. The area where Brown and Cotton first fled from pursuing officers after the shooting was of prime interest. At 10:24 a.m., the searchers' perseverance paid off. The .357 Magnum was found approximately thirty feet from the road by volunteer, Robert Williams. The location was about 7/10 of a mile from Christoff Ferry Road and approximately three miles from County Road 162. The gun was very important in the case against Brown and Cotton, and it placed the weapon in the area the suspect, Brown, was found.

A preliminary hearing was held in Jackson County on April 19. The grand jury decided that enough evidence was shown for an indictment on Morris Brown and his co-defendant Edward Cotton.

At arraignment, a list of charges was read: first degree murder, attempted first degree murder, robbery with a firearm, robbery, escape with a firearm.

A plea of not guilty was entered by the defense attorney Virgil Mayo, public defender, on April 26. In July, the right to a speedy trial was waived. In August, a change of venue was requested.

The trial was held in Bay County with Judge Warren Edwards presiding. Prosecuting was States Attorney Jim Appleman and Assistant States Attorney Bill Wright, and Defending was Public Defender Virgil Mayo.

On the stand, Morris Brown denied everything that happened that night and said he was nowhere around or with Edward Lee Cotton on the night in question.

Investigator John Dennis testified of knowing Morris Brown for most of his life as Brown had been in trouble since the age of ten years old. He also testified regarding the evidence found at the scene of the robbery, at the scene of the murder, and at the scene of the captures. There were many pieces of evidence brought into this case. Some of the most important linking Brown to the night in question were 1) Brown's fingerprints were on the hood of Sgt. Bevis's patrol car 2) Brown's footprints were found on each side of Sgt. Bevis body where he had straddled him 3) Brown's fingerprints were found on the .357 service revolver belonging to Sgt. Bevis.

One of the most damning moments in the trial for Morris Brown was the testimony of Edward Lee Cotton. According to Cotton, he and Brown robbed the Jr. Food Store in Malone on April fourth. Morris carried the weapon and fired a shot at the customer who walked in during the robbery. Later, when they were being stopped by Sgt. Bevis, Cotton said that Brown wanted him to run and not stop. When Sgt. Bevis had the two men up against the patrol car, after his last radio transmission with the dispatcher, the officer asked Morris Brown to step around the car beside Cotton. Brown suggested to Cotton that they jump the officer. Cotton said no. While the officer was putting the cuffs on Cotton, Brown made his move and overtook him. Cotton said that Brown and Bevis fought all over the road, with Cotton at one point trying to break them up. Cotton was scared of Brown and decided to run from the scene. At that time, he heard a gunshot. He stopped and turned around and saw Brown straddling the officer, and he heard the officer say, "Please don't shoot me. I have two children. Please don't shoot me." At that time Cotton said he shut his eyes for a moment and turned to run and heard two more gun shots. He turned back around and Morris Brown was coming toward him telling him to get in the car. They were spotted a few moments later on Bumpnose Road. They hid after wrecking the car, and Cotton kept asking Brown to give up. He even told Brown that he was turning himself in. Brown told him "I'm going to jail for life anyway." Brown told Cotton to give him time to get away. A few minutes later, Cotton came out and surrendered.

The medical examiner, Dr. Sybers, said that the first gunshot wound entered the victim's wrist, leaving him in shock and partially paralyzed. The next two gunshots were to the head, one entering point blank at the temple and the one entering point blank in between the upper lip and nose. Both bullets lodged in the brain and either one could have killed him instantly.

The defense tried to keep Brown's past criminal history from the jury. Brown was first arrested at the age of ten, was put in Dozier School for Boys at the age of fourteen where he tried to escape, and was moved to the county jail for one year. Later, he was arrested for an armed robbery (with a knife) in Gadsden County, where he was sentenced to eighteen months in prison. He was out on parole at the time of the Bevis murder.

After deliberation, the jury came back with a verdict of guilty on all five counts and recommended life in prison without the possibility of parole for 25 years on the charge of first degree murder. On the charge of attempted first degree murder, the sentence was recommended to ten years in prison. On the charge of robbery with a firearm, the recommendation was to sentence him to life in prison. On the charge of robbery, the recommendation was to sentence him to thirty years. On the charge of escape with a firearm, the recommendation was to sentence him to life in prison.

On April 4, during the sentencing of Morris Brown, Judge Edwards found mitigating circumstances that caused him to go against the jury's recommendation of life in prison for the charge of first degree murder and let all other recommendations stand. Judge Edwards chose to sentence Morris Brown to death for the charge of first degree murder, due to the mitigating circumstances of Morris's lack of remorse and the fact that after shooting Sgt. Bevis in the arm, he could have escaped and left him there, but he chose to shoot a man with a bullet proof vest on, who was begging for his life, twice in the head. He found the killing of Sgt. Bevis to be premeditated, heinous, atrocious, and cruel.

On May 12, 1988, on appeal, the Court of Appeal found that after reviewing the case that the conviction would stand, but they would overturn the judge's sentence to death and go with the jury's recommendation of life imprisonment. This finding was largely attributed to the defense stating that Edward Cotton's testimony was a big part of the case, and they felt that he was trying to minimize his own involvement. They also contended that due to the fact that this was spontaneous and that Sgt. Bevis died instantly from the gunshots to the head, he did not suffer, which was not heinous, atrocious, or cruel.

Cotton and Brown were both convicted on life sentences and are still in prison today.

Johnny Mac shared the story behind Deputy James Bevis. "A native of Jackson County, Bevis was a Vietnam veteran. He saw true battle in Vietnam. He proved himself there, and he proved himself here in Jackson County. James Bevis was a conscientious, quiet, and understanding man. He never was one to over-react and make a situation worse than it already was. He would come in and take away from a bad situation with a calming influence. He volunteered to oversee the Jr. Deputies Program, taking care of 45 young people in that group—taking them on field trips and picnics. He was an active member of the Marianna National Guard.

James and his wife had divorced. James had two little special needs children. Their eighty-year-old grandmother was trying to raise those children so James could work and provide for them. The mother never came back or had anything to do with them. It was Mrs. Bevis, James Bevis's mother, that raised the children. His son would later get a job out at the rest area on Interstate 10. His daughter was never able to obtain gainful employment."

Johnny Mac lost contact with the children over the years. It was bad enough that James Bevis was taken from this world but to leave two innocent children that were special needs children and to leave them with their eighty-year-old grandmother to take care of them...It was unreal and always weighed heavily on John's heart. Her husband, Mr. Bevis, was in WWII and had a leg blown off by a bouncing betty—a thing that would come up about three or four feet high and explode. She tried to take care of him and the children the best she could.

***

One month and four days after Deputy Bevis was senselessly murdered, Sheriff McDaniel still grieved for the loss of one of the family. He would question himself over and over regarding how the tragic loss could have been prevented, coming up with few answers.

Shortly before 4 a.m. on May 13, 1985, John's phone rang. He answered the phone with trepidation, still fearing the worst even though he prayed nightly for protection over his home and work families and the community. John knew God was in control. It just took time to heal from such a tragic loss as they had all suffered in losing James.

John groggily put the phone receiver to his ear. "Hello."

"Daddy, it's time. I'm headed to the hospital," Machelle said excitedly over the phone.

"Baby girl, I'm headed to Tallahassee." John dropped the phone, and out the door he went. His daughter was in labor. John, coming from Marianna, almost beat Machelle to the hospital in Tallahassee.

A little later that morning, John McDaniel was holding the sweetest and most precious little girl he had seen since he held his own little Machelle. His first grandchild, Stephanie Meghan Hill, lit up the whole room.

In light of the most recent loss and this most blessed event, John was reminded of the biblical scripture found in Job.

"And said, Naked came I out of my mother's womb, and naked shall I return thither: the Lord gave, and the Lord hath taken away; blessed be the name of the Lord." (Job 1:21) *King James Version.*

CHAPTER 43
Murders Continue

Investigators with the Jackson County Sheriff's Department were working hard to determine the identity of a man found dead under a bridge on Bumpnose Road at approximately 9:00 a.m. on Tuesday, June 18, 1985. Investigator Farrell Taylor and Deputy Walter Davis were the first to arrive on scene at Charles White Bridge where it crossed Wadell Mill Creek after a member of Burgess Logging Company reported the dead man.

Sheriff McDaniel initially reported that the body appeared to have been dropped over the side of the bridge into some bushes below. Investigators found drops of blood along the bridge and a larger pool of blood near the location they believe the man was dropped.

Officer Quinton Hollis would respond to a Kelson Avenue residence in Marianna to take a missing person's report from a Mrs. Kelley at approximately 12:30 p.m. on Tuesday. Richard Kelley was last seen on Monday night, June 17, around 8:00 p.m., reportedly drinking.

Chief Investigator Dennis would later release the dead man's identity as 26-year-old Richard Lewis Kelley of 802 Kelson Avenue in Marianna. Kelley died of multiple gunshot wounds to his head, chest, and arm.

The department investigators would comb the area in search of a weapon as well as following up on leads and conducting multiple interviews for years to come.

It would take some time, but the case was closed by the arrest of Ricky Joseph Enyart. Enyart was sentenced on November 30, 2007, to twenty years for the second degree murder of Richard Lewis Kelley.

CHAPTER 44
War on Drugs

When John McDaniel first ran for sheriff, he made a promise to the citizens of Jackson County that he never backed away from: "I hate drugs. Over ninety percent of those in jail are there because of drugs. If I don't do anything else as your sheriff, I'm going to give the dopers hell."

Sheriff McDaniel did declare war on drugs. Jackson County, being 943 square miles with a lot of rural area, was constantly faced with the problem of people who would get out in the woods and plant marijuana on other people's property.

Johnny Mac faced a few stumbling blocks along the way. Early on in his administration, he hired a man from the Escambia County State Attorney's Office—William F. (Buddy) Deates. He came very highly recommended, so Johnny hired him and placed him in charge of the drug unit. Within a short period of time, there appeared to be problems. Often, Buddy would set up deals and send the other units up on the main highways to wait and then call the units back, stating the deal fell through. Drug dealers didn't show up. This became a pattern. Then 1000 pounds of marijuana was missing from evidence. FDLE showed up at the sheriff's office to question Deates. McDaniel advised his staff to let FDLE handle the investigation. He wanted no innuendos of improprietary behavior and would not tolerate corruption in his department. Buddy Deates was indicted and placed in Calhoun County Jail. Shortly after this incident, Lt. Dennis would become major and later chief deputy for the department.

As far as initial resources went, they had Florida Department of Law Enforcement willing to do some flying for the department. They couldn't seem to get in line fast enough to make that work, so Johnny Mac decided they would invest in their own solution.

They utilized drug money gained from seizures and hired Deputy Cowboy Morris, who later became a lieutenant for the department as their very first pilot. He flew for the department for years. He was an outstanding pilot because he didn't know any fear. There wasn't anything that Wayne couldn't do. They used Buddy Bannerman's airplane, a 1959 Cessna 172, and they put a lot of hours on that plane.

In 1985, Sheriff McDaniel hired the first female narcotics officer at Jackson County Sheriff's Department. Rebecca Dodson was the first female drug officer he hired. He had no problem hiring a female. "She did a great job," Johnny said. "We gave them hell. I just had to rein her in on occasion."

Chief Deputy Dennis was put in charge of Officer Dodson. He went to Johnny Mac on several occasions stating, "She's going to cause me to go to the hospital on a stretcher….She just gets in the car with any drug dealer and goes with them to get the drugs."

Anytime Chief Deputy Dennis would caution Dodson about this behavior, she would just laugh and say, "Now, Chief, how else are you going to get the ones at the top, the ones that will make a difference? We have to follow the drugs."

The narcotics group did a great job then, and they still do today.

***

December 1985

As it worked out after the beginning of John P. McDaniel III's second term as sheriff, some felt it was too political for the Christmas program to be called The McDaniel Christmas Program, so they changed the name. It still functioned the same—just under a different name.

This hurt Johnny Mac, but if they felt it was too political, it didn't matter in the end so long as the program still helped all the children in need.

John sold his home in Indian Springs and bought a house on Club Drive in the Subdivision of Meadowview just a few miles north of Marianna. He and his son, Little John, would live there for a few years to come.

CHAPTER 45
A Calmer Frontier:
1986-1987

Coming off the heels of one of the worst years John P. McDaniel had seen as sheriff, 1986-87 was proving to be better. Burglaries and robberies were down, violent crimes were down, drug activity was lower than it had ever been, and his department was growing with the needs of the county.

The department lost a great investigator in Donnie Branch, who left for a better-paying position with Florida Department of Law Enforcement.

Johnny Mac was still faced with the jail issues and an inadequate patrol fleet. The regional jail concept was not looking like a viable option. There were too many legality issues involving transport, inmate custody, control across county lines, staffing, and the division of financial responsibilities for this concept to be a solution. The counties could not agree upon a site location as whichever counties did not house the new facility would experience an eroding authority.

The jail was still presenting a huge problem. Once again, failing inspection reports from the old dinosaur of a facility were presenting impending closure by the feds. It was simply beyond repair and could no longer be brought up to code. Johnny Mac came up with a new design for a split-level jail which would enhance the sight and sound requirement of DOC by requiring fewer staff. Initial concept was a 200-capacity jail. The county still could not afford to build the facility.

John P. McDaniel and Commissioner Ernie Padget began going from town to town and speaking at town hall meetings. They were requesting the imposing of a one percent sales tax for the building of a new jail. The imposition would only last until the $5 million building cost could be raised. The sales tax for the criminal justice facility would appear on the upcoming ballot in the Jackson County Presidential preference primary on March 8, 1988.

***

Johnny Mac had always had a love for music. He enjoyed listening and singing. He sang to his granddaughter, Meghan, just as he had done with her mom when she was his little girl. At the lowest times in his life, the music seemed faded, but in mid-1987, the music became a little stronger in his life.

While working a case in Blountstown, Florida, with the Calhoun County Sheriff's Office, Sheriff McDaniel kept seeing this nurse coming up and down the hallway. Johnny Mac thought she was the prettiest woman he had ever seen. He asked questions and found out her name was Verlie Diane King.

Johnny got her phone number and called her. He found out she was a divorcee. Johnny said to himself, "Well I'm going to impress the hell out of her. I'm going to pick her up and carry her to the Elks Club."

Johnny was a long-standing member of the Elks Club and thought he would take her there, get a drink or two, have a nice meal, and dance for a while.

Well, he took Verlie there, and they sat down. Johnny asked, "Verlie, could I get you a drink?"

"No, just a Coca-Cola."

Johnny had no problem with that and ordered their drinks. As he was bringing their drinks to the table, he stopped by the jukebox and dropped a few coins in. Soon, the sweet country tunes began floating through the air.

"Would you like to dance?" Johnny asked.

"No, I don't listen to contemporary music."

"Okay."

Then Verlie said, "I think you need to know something about me. I was married to a preacher."

Johnny Mac thought to himself, "Oh, Jesus Christ. I've really, really impressed the hell out of this woman."

Well, she was a phlebotomist for the Calhoun County Hospital, and she ran the lab down there.

Johnny was simply enchanted by Verlie. They began dating. She brought music back into his life. She played the organ and piano as well as Liberace.

One Sunday afternoon, Johnny, Verlie, Machelle, and Little Meghan were out riding—no particular destination in mind, just enjoying the country roads of Jackson County. All of a sudden, *POW, POW, POW*. They had arrived upon poachers shooting out of season, and they were inadvertently shooting at the car. John was as mad as a bull being waved a red flag.

"Jackson one to dispatch. Get an officer out here now and find these poachers and put their butts in jail."

That was the end of that.

CHAPTER 46

By Water, Land, or Air

Jackson County had a small child on Chipola River that drowned. The sheriff's department got the call. There were two or three little boys playing in the water and one went under and drowned. Mr. Bud Timmons who used to be the game warden in Jackson County previously trained a bunch of people in scuba diving and recovery groups. He was now retired. There wasn't anyone around that could put on scuba gear and recover that young boy's body.

Johnny talked to the family and had to tell them that the little guy had drowned and that they didn't have anybody that could go get him. It was a helpless feeling for Johnny to know that he couldn't perform a service that someone needed.

Then finally, they got with John Pforte, Lina Parrish, and one or two others that had been students of Bud Timmons. They found the little boy and recovered the body.

This bothered Johnny, so he made up his mind. There was a dive shop in Dothan, Alabama. He went there and to talk about a dive team. He came back and asked for volunteers from the department for divers to go and recover bodies, etc. He received several volunteers for the team. Ricky Cloud, Rusty Booth, Dee Booth, Jeff Johnson, and Johnny would become certified as well. They attended classes, going over to Vortex Springs, the Jetties in Panama City, and a sunken ship for their training. They became certified divers and a few went on and became recovery divers.

From time to time, they had to go and recover bodies. They sent the dive team to Elba, Alabama, once when a man and his son had drowned in a river. They dove and dove and dove and never could find them.

About three days later, they were found about five miles further down the river.

Then they got a call from Nashville, Georgia. Supposedly, a black boy had killed a girl and thrown her in a river into a slew (back water) with zero visibility. Johnny recalled, "They dove in water that you couldn't see six inches in front of your face. You could get on the bottom and run your hands across and things would just run out in front of your face. It was so cold Ricky Cloud had gotten cramps and was just squalling like a panther." Johnny grabbed him to get him up on the bank. "You could feel the knots in the back of his legs. It was so, so cold down there. They had gotten some fat liter stumps and built a big fire. When members of the dive team came out of the water with their wetsuits on and walked close to the fire, you could see the steam coming off them."

Another rescue effort was on the Chattahoochee River. A subject had drowned. The dive team went and found that victim. This started the Jackson County Sheriff's Office dive team. They went wherever they were needed.

Johnny found a way to resolve not only the needs on the water but also in the air. Every time he trained a pilot they would leave for more money. Johnny stated, "We couldn't pay very much and our pilot, Cowboy, went back to Morris Timber Company. We had several others that became pilots, but as soon as we trained them, they would leave for more money."

John said, "Bullshit with this. If anybody else is gonna learn to fly; it's gonna be me because I'm gonna stay here and ain't going nowhere."

Well, Johnny met with Mr. Harold Foran, owner of Chipola Aviation. Foran sent him to Sowell Aviation in Panama City. Johnny went through ground school there. Before he took his final test, his instructor said, "Sheriff

McDaniel, you still don't know the front from the back of an airplane. The thing for you to do is go back and get with Mr. Foran and learn to become a pilot. Learn to fly and learn a little bit about a plane before you come back here and take your test."

So that is what Johnny did. Mr. Ray Kirkland was actually the outstanding instructor who taught Johnny that an airplane up in the air with a strong enough head wind could fly backward if it was trimmed out just right and the power reduced enough. Johnny did that with Mr. Kirkland there with him.

Harold Foran did all the inspections of the license, and Mr. Godfrey Lawrence, a dear friend to Johnny, was licensed and would fly with him. Johnny was grateful to everyone that had a hand in helping him learn to fly. He wasn't that good at it, but he really enjoyed it.

Johnny ended up buying an old airplane. He made it available to the sheriff's office and didn't charge the county a dime. Mr. Godfrey handled any mechanical repairs necessary. They used the plane to fly around and do whatever was needed in the county. They were successful in using it to spot dope fields, etc. Sometimes they would rent a better plane from Mr. Foran. That's how Johnny got into the flying business.

"Later on, the department used helicopters. Robert Wiggins trained our pilots but they too, once trained, would leave the department for more money."

They couldn't afford to keep training and losing pilots.

The more Johnny Mac thought about the expenses lost in training and re-training, he came up with a solution as he always did. He got his helicopter license so he knew the department would never be in a bind. He wasn't going anywhere unless the people voted him out of office. The government gave them helicopters to use. They were just responsible for the maintenance.

Whatever had to be done, he made sure he was qualified so the county wouldn't get caught in a pinch. On the land or in the water or in the air, Johnny was the sheriff for whatever needed to be done.

CHAPTER 47

A Year for Innovative Ideas:
1988

March 8, 1988, arrived. The Jackson County Presidential preference primary also presented a Yes or No vote for a one percent sales tax for the building of a criminal justice facility. John P. McDaniel and Commissioner Ernie Padgett had hit the road and attended every town and city meeting in the county at least once to explain and ask for support of the sales tax.

The people of Jackson County delivered. No precinct was lost. With a grand total of 5963 voting Yes and 1814 voting No, the sales tax passed with 74% of the vote.

County Manager, Leon Foster, would end up being a financial genius. The tax was limited to the jail only. He invested the money, and the interest rate alone would later allow for the purchase and renovation of a new sheriff's office on top of the building of a new jail.

New cars and salary increases were among the things that Sheriff McDaniel requested in his upcoming budget. The Jackson County commissioners met with the sheriff and Jim Williams, administrative director for the sheriff's department, in a July of 1988 budget workshop.

Johnny Mac asked the county to include in the budget salary increases for his department employees, new cars for the department, and additional deputy and investigator positions. He elaborated that his department was having a high turn-over problem because of the low starting salaries for deputies and correctional officers. His department was still working with old highway patrol cars which resulted in high maintenance costs for the county.

County administrator, Ernie Padgett, told the commission he had researched the possibility of leasing patrol cars. However, he said that over a three-year period, it would cost the county $47,000 more to lease than to purchase the cars outright.

The Commission agreed to the purchase of nine new patrol cars and an increase of deputy salaries up to $14,500 as well as an increase in salaries for other positions. However, the commissioners stated the county could not afford to budget any new positions because of the above increases.

McDaniel appreciated the wins and could live without the new positions for the time being.

***

Johnny Mac decided he was going to get in better shape, so he started riding his bicycle. Well, one Monday morning before work, John was riding back from the store; he was coming down the hill too fast, hit a hole, and wrecked the bicycle. He had scrapes from head to toe.

He went to work on Monday, but by Tuesday, he was really sore. Every Tuesday morning, they had a meeting at the jail. Sammy Efurd was in charge of the jail and worked hard to get the plumbing among other deficits repaired. No matter what they did, they continued to receive poor inspections. Johnny planned to discuss the upcoming jail which would be built with the tax money. He hobbled behind the podium and what did he find? A pair of bicycle training wheels. He tossed them to the back of the room and vowed to get Sammy back for his practical jokes.

CHAPTER 48
Justice at Last

In July of 1988, Johnny was sitting in his office when he received a call from Ronnie Cornelius with FDLE in Tallahassee. He said, "Was your daddy the mayor of the city of Malone?"

John replied, "Yes."

They started talking. As it worked out, they had a fellow with information that was trying to work a deal to get off of death row.

His name was Ottis Toole. He said he would tell them about a murder that took place up in the panhandle of Florida if they would not give him the electric chair on another case he was involved in. He would also turn state's evidence against Henry Lee Lucas.

Well, they made the agreement and formed a task force. REA out of Graceville allowed them to use their office over in Bonifay. They worked from there for quite some time and were able to solve four cases in the tri-county area of Jackson, Washington, and Holmes Counties where Lucas and Toole had committed murders.

Among the Florida murders they were charged with include:

- December 16, 1980, murder of John P. McDaniel Jr. of Malone
- February 10, 1981, murder of Jerilyn Murphy Peoples of Caryville
- March 25, 1981, murder of Brenda Jo Burton of Bonifay
- April 9, 1981, murder of Mary Ruby McCrary of Chipley

The killing spree of Lucas and Toole lasted a little over three and a half months in the panhandle area of

Florida. Ottis Toole gave sworn testimony under oath, providing details of the crimes he and Henry Lee Lucas had committed. Of course, they had received national fame for being serial killers and killing more than 350 people. It was unknown how many people they actually killed, but based upon the details they provided and the evidence in the cases, there was no doubt they were a part of the four cases in the panhandle.

On March 9, 1989, Sheriff McDaniel went with the FDLE Special Agent Supervisor M. R. Cornelius and Special Agent Joe Mitchell to the Department of Corrections State Prison, Ellis 1 Unit, located in Huntsville, Texas, for the purpose of interviewing Henry Lee Lucas. He refused to talk to FDLE without his lawyer being present. FDLE said there was nothing they could do. McDaniel stated that Lucas had refused to talk to FDLE, not to him. He went to the warden and explained why he needed to talk to him. He requested that the warden let Lucas know that it was John's father that was murdered, and that John's son needed answers too as he was very close to his granddaddy and to ask Lucas if he would talk to John.

Lucas agreed.

Johnny can still see Lucas sitting there, talking to him to this day. Johnny told him he had a son and wanted to try and satisfy the questions that haunted him about his granddaddy.

Lucas said, "Well, I can tell you who killed your daddy."

Johnny asked, "Okay, tell me who killed my daddy."

Lucas replied, "The hands of death."

"Who are the hands of death?"

"That's…that's just some bad people."

Lucas continued talking, hedging around questions. He admitted he was there but stated he was outside on the telephone when they killed Johnny's daddy.

That was not true, and John knew that he was lying. Lucas talked about all kind of things that he would not have known had he not been there in the store and a participant in the murder.

With the information provided by Ottis Toole and all the evidence gained by law enforcement, investigators were able to put it together.

Ottis Toole told investigators that they had gone in that station and got out and pumped some gas into the car that they were driving. He said there was a little boy and a little girl in the back seat of the car.

John recalled the statement given by Toole. "They went in. It was after midnight. The store had blocked the cooler so you couldn't get beer…because the county had a rule you couldn't sell alcohol after midnight. Well, Ottis Toole told us they took the bar out so they could get the beer. They set it on the counter, pumped the gas, and then didn't have the money to pay for the gas.

"My dad challenged the men, telling them they had to pay for the gas and put the beer back. The men exchanged words. My dad stepped around the counter where the men stood. He grabbed the beer and put it back in the cooler. That's when he was jumped.

"Ottis Toole was wrestling with my dad, and Henry Lucas was trying to help. Ottis Toole said, 'You know on that man's left arm, he didn't have a hand. He was beating the hell out of us with that ole nub.' He said, 'That's when Lucas dropped back and shot him.'

"I said, 'He did what?'

"Toole repeated, 'He dropped back and shot him right above the right ear.'"

On May 4, 1989, FDLE provided a press release which stated:

Authorities from several North Florida jurisdictions today released information concerning grand jury

217

indictments for Ottis Elwood Toole and Henry Lee Lucas on four counts of first degree murder. Toole, age 42, and Lucas, age 52, have been previously convicted of multiple, unrelated homicides across the nation and are currently incarcerated in Florida and Texas prisons, respectively.

The crimes which led to the current indictments involved four homicides which occurred in the Northwest Florida counties of Jackson, Washington, and Holmes between December 1980 and April 1981. Officials from the Jackson County, Washington County, and Holmes County Sheriffs' Offices worked the investigation in cooperation with the Florida Department of Law Enforcement and the State Attorney's Office for the 14th Judicial Circuit. The participating agencies formed a task force in March of 1988 to focus on the four homicides after a significant break in one of the investigations led investigators to believe that the cases were connected.

Henry M. "Mickey" Watson, special agent in charge for the Florida Department of Law Enforcement's Northwest region said, "This investigation has been a solid effort by all of the departments involved. By these indictments, the communities involved can begin to put the personal tragedies of these senseless acts behind them and rest with the assurance that the individuals responsible for these crimes are no longer free to endanger anyone else."

The first alleged victim of Toole and Lucas was John P. McDaniel Jr., the father of Jackson County Sheriff John P. McDaniel III, who was found murdered on December 15, 1980, in Jackson County.

The other three victims were:

• February 10, 1981, murder of Jerilyn Murphy Peoples of Caryville

• March 25, 1981, murder of Brenda Jo Burton of Bonifay

- *April 9, 1981, murder of Mary Ruby McCrary of Chipley*

State Attorney Jim Applemen, whose circuit includes the four homicides, said, "We will move forward to prosecute both Toole and Lucas on all counts of first degree murder. Extradition proceedings will be initiated with the Governor's office immediately to bring Lucas to Florida to stand trial without unnecessary delay."

Ottis Elwood Toole was sentenced to life in prison for four Florida murders. He died in prison in Raiford, Florida, on September 15, 1996. Cause of death was Cirrhosis. He was 49.

Co-defendant, Henry Lee Lucas, who confessed to hundreds of murders, was sent to Texas because Florida was unable to afford his massive legal expenses. He was convicted on eleven murder convictions spanning from 1960-1983. His death penalty was commuted to life imprisonment. Lucas died in prison on March 13, 2001, of heart failure at the age of 64.

CHAPTER 49

Feuding in Rural Jackson County Ends in Shooting

On August 5, 1988, the Jackson County Sheriff's Department received a call at 11:35 p.m. from the Johnson family in the St. Rose Community. The Johnson family reported a disturbance between themselves and their neighbors across the road, the Collins's.

Sheriff's deputies arrived at the scene shortly after midnight. After spending almost an hour calming down those involved and sending them to their respective homes, the deputies left but notified dispatch that they would remain in the area to make sure everything remained calm.

However, at 2:31 a.m., a second call was received from the Johnsons reporting a disturbance in front of their home. While the deputies were en route to the call, a third call was made to report a shooting.

At about the same time, Lt. Wayne Morris, en route to the scene, reported hearing several gunshots. Lt. Morris was the first officer to arrive on scene.

Moments later, the deputies arrived and found Madison Collins dead in the roadway and then Herman Collins was found wounded but still alive. Herman died shortly after the officers' arrival. The deputies also discovered Lawrence Collins wounded. While Jackson County fire and rescue was transporting Lawrence, he died. In addition, deputies found Laughton Collins to have been shot in the shoulder. He was transported by fire and rescue to Jackson Hospital and later transferred to a Dothan hospital.

Also transported were Robert Johnson Jr., who had been shot in the side and hit over the head with a shotgun, and Carolyn Collins, who had been shot in the buttocks.

Since the incident involved a triple homicide with three others wounded, a major investigation would be required by the sheriff's department. Sheriff McDaniel requested the assistance of Florida Department of Law Enforcement, the Federal Bureau of Investigations, and the state attorney's office.

Sheriff McDaniel gave a press conference on Monday morning, August 8, stating that the early morning Saturday shootout was the culmination of a history of problems between the Collins and Johnson families. He stated that Collins had moved to the St. Rose Community, located in the southeast section of Jackson County, almost two years prior from Polk County. They were self-employed, having their own independent trucking business. They purchased land which formed an "L" shape around the Johnson property. McDaniel elaborated that the problems arose between six months and one year before when an eighteen-year-old female family member of the Collins's left home, and when she returned, she moved in with one of the Johnson family members. He had tried on numerous occasions to counsel with both parties, advising them to let it go before someone got killed.

It was also noted that the Collins girl had miscarried a child approximately one week prior to the shootings. It was on Tuesday prior to the shooting, when the child was buried, that law enforcement officials noted tension between the families.

Almost four months after the shootout, the grand jury, handed down a "No True Bill' which meant no one would be indicted in the case. The Grand Jury noted that Florida law states, "If a person is attacked in his own home or on his own premises, he has no duty to retreat and has the lawful right to stand his ground and meet force, even to the extent of using force likely to cause death or great bodily harm." The case was marked as justifiable homicide.

CHAPTER 50
Tragedy Strikes

The tragedy began to unfold shortly before 6:00 a.m. on Monday, August 15, 1988, when the Jackson County patrol car driven by Lt. Larry Dean Garrett, apparently overheated. Garrett pulled the car, which was transporting five prisoners, off the interstate on I-10 near Live Oak, Florida. He pulled into the emergency lane "well off the road," according to a state trooper who investigated the accident.

While Garret was waiting for the car to cool down, he allowed two of the inmates, Randy L. Facemyer and James Sapp to stand, hand cuffed together, beside the vehicle. Garret, according to witnesses, stood behind the two men.

A short time later, a tractor trailer rig driven by Willie James Collins, 38, of Houston, Texas, crossed into the emergency lane and struck the rear of the patrol vehicle. Troopers said the truck struck the car, dragging it 554 feet.

The three inmates died instantly. Included among the dead were a Marianna native, Tommy Sorey, who along with four other inmates, who was being transported to the receiving and medical center at Lake Butler Correctional Facility. Sorey was to begin serving a prison sentence for violation of community control. Andrew Allen, 19, a Miami resident was to begin serving an eighteen-month term for battery on a district school board employee. Allen was sitting in the back seat of the car with Sorey. Terry L. Sullivan, who was sitting in the front seat, had been sentenced for battery on a correctional officer.

The force of the impact forced the two men in the back seat through the steel cage in front of them. The crash mangled the car to such an extent investigating

225

troopers were unable to tell how many bodies were in the car. Trooper Bud Smith said, "In my 23 years on patrol, I've never seen such a mess."

Three wreckers were used to remove the car from the undercarriage of the truck. Two were used to lift the truck, while the third pulled the car out.

Troopers speculate that Garrett, Facemyer, and Sapp were apparently hit by the rear door of the patrol car when it was struck.

Both Garrett and Sapp said all they could remember was hearing a loud explosion. Troopers stated Collins never applied his breaks before the collision. He was traveling 70 -75 miles per hour when he struck the patrol car.

Sapp, an Altha resident who was being held on grand theft auto charges and the only person to escape injuries, reported he went to the aid of Garrett after the wreck. Sapp stated, "I heard Lt. Garrett calling for help, so I drug Randy over to the Lt. to see if I could help."

Lt. Garrett gave Sapp the handcuff key and asked him not to run. Still stunned by the accident, Sapp took the handcuffs off and began to flag down traffic. When emergency aid did arrive, Sapp assisted, holding glucose bags and doing whatever he could to help.

After Sapp arrived at the Suwannee jail, he gave officials the key to the handcuffs. Medical personnel wanted to fly Garrett and Facemyer to medical facilities in Gainesville, but bad weather forced then to transport via ambulance.

The State troopers notified Sheriff McDaniel of the tragic event. Johnny Mac immediately headed to Alachua General Hospital where Lt. Garrett underwent surgery on Monday evening for treatment of multiple fractures. Johnny was waiting for him in his room when he returned from surgery. The six-year veteran of the sheriff's department suffered a broken pelvis, broken right leg, broken right foot, and dislocated left elbow. Facemyer suffered a broken leg which required surgery.

John McDaniel would return to Jackson County and inspect the wreckages. According to Johnny Mac, the overheating issue was one of the problems he had been faced with because of the age of the fleet used by his department. Hopefully, since the Jackson County Commission had agreed to budget for the replacement of one-third of his fleet with new cars, it would help resolve those types of problems.

CHAPTER 51

John P. McDaniel III
Bids for Third Term

Tuesday night, September 6, 1988, saw a few new faces on the ballots. The sheriff's race had three contenders: the incumbent John P. McDaniel, Harrell Glisson, and R. G. Russell. The county judge seat had incumbent Woodrow W. Hatcher up against John D. Simpson.

Two incumbents would retain their constitutional offices with large margins of victory in Tuesday's Jackson County Democratic Primary.

County Judge Woodrow W. Hatcher won by a landslide over challenger John Simpson carrying 81.5 percent of the local vote. "I'm very gratified," Hatcher said following the tabulation of votes. "I believe what the citizens of Jackson County are looking for in a judge is one who is going to ensure that the case load is up-to-date and all the citizens of the county are treated with fairness. This is done with a touch of courtesy." Judge Hatcher had already served three terms in office, a stint that has involved almost 50,000 cases.

In a highly-publicized Jackson County sheriff's race, incumbent John P. McDaniel carried 67.4 percent of the county vote to retain his office. McDaniel overcame strong challenges from Harrell Glisson and R. G. Russell to secure a third term in office. McDaniel had 8,156 total votes while Glisson finished second in the balloting with 2,158, Russell had 1,785 votes. When the final results were in, John McDaniel said, "I'm very humble to all the people of Jackson County. I'm glad to have run a race with people like Glisson and Russell. Campaigning aside, I'm ready to go to work tomorrow and get out of politics and focus entirely on the job."

CHAPTER 52

Bringing New Bride Home
to House of Horrors

Johnny McDaniel and Verlie King continued dating throughout the year of 1988. She stood behind him during his campaign for sheriff. By November, he popped the question and...she said "Yes." They were married on November 5, 1988, in a simple ceremony performed by Minister L. C. McDaniel. Both of John's children, Machelle and Little John, were present for the union.

John asked her if she would like to go to the mountains he loved for their honeymoon. She was delighted with the idea.

John talked to Chief Parmer, who was chief of police at Marianna Police Department at that time and asked him to look after things while he was on his honeymoon.

Well, they went to the mountains and played in the leaves and enjoyed the nature God had created. Johnny called the sheriff's office and checked in each night, telling them where they were in case they needed him.

Well, when they headed back, they got as far as Eufaula, Alabama, when Verlie said she had to go to the bathroom. Johnny told her it was another hour and a half before they reached home and that he could stop at one of the local service stations.

She said with a grin, "No, don't worry about it. I can hold it 'til we get home."

They kept driving, and she kept grinning and crossing her legs and holding it. They finally got to the house and Johnny quickly unlocked the door so she could go inside to the bathroom. She went inside to complete darkness. There were no lights!

Johnny said, "God almighty, the electricity is off!"

Verlie went down the darkened hallway and discovered there were no commode seats on the commodes.

Johnny laughed. "That sorry bunch of damn deputies of mine—some of them sorry friends of mine..." Johnny thought that Sammy Efurd, Jimmy Grant, and Lavaughn Parmer had something to do with it?

The practical jokers had the water turned off, the lights turned off, and the bed linens were short-sheeted.

Johnny spent the next hour getting everything hooked back up and getting the seats back on the commodes. Verlie found humor in it after a while and laughed herself silly. There was corn in the bed. Johnny recalled, "We had one helluva time cleaning it all up."

Well, they finally got it all cleaned up and got it to where they could go to sleep. They were exhausted. It was going to be so nice to have peace and quiet and just sleep.

Chirp, chirp, chirp... Chirp, chirp, chirp...

Johnny looked at Verlie, and she looked at him. Johnny shook his head. "It was *crickets*. Those guys must have put a thousand crickets in that house. You couldn't lie down without them rubbing their legs together and chirping all over that house."

John and Verlie thought they would never catch enough crickets to get them out of the house so it was quiet enough they could go to sleep. The loud chirping melody had them laughing until they were crying.

That was the damn craziest night in the world, and everybody denied it. Jimmy Grant, Sammy Efurd, and Chief Parmer all. But, Johnny had somebody come to him and snitch them all out.

Johnny just said okay and waited.

He didn't have to wait long. Parmer had bought a trailer for him and his wife, Mrs. Glenda, to use for their vacation. He had it all fixed up. Johnny caught the trailer sitting outside his home one day with no one at home. He went and bought about five hundred crickets and poured them in that motor home.

Sammy's wife was Mrs. Martha. Mrs. Martha was so sweet Johnny wouldn't do anything to her, but he got Sammy back in other ways and Jimmy Grant when he got married too.

And don't sell Cowboy short. Cowboy Morris, another one of Johnny Mac's deputies, knew what was going on too. He always knew what was going on.

CHAPTER 53
"Things Like This Don't Happen Here"

John McDaniel began the year 1989 with his new bride of two months and the start of his third term in office as sheriff. He was still working out the jail issues with plans being formalized for the new facility.

On Sunday, January 22, 1989, the local paper, Jackson County *Floridan* splashed the following headline: "Law Officials Refute Arrest Rumors." The staff of the Jackson County *Floridan* and several law enforcement agencies were inundated with phone calls from persons wanting to know about the arrests of prominent businessmen for drug trafficking.

The Drug Enforcement Agency in Panama City refuted a rumor running rampant around Jackson County that Sheriff Johnny McDaniel and local businessmen Bob Pforte, J. D. Swearingen, Herman Laramore, and several others had been arrested or were being investigated for drug involvement. The DEA spokesperson denied any knowledge of any such investigation or arrests, further stating Sheriff McDaniel was one of the finest local law enforcement people they worked with. They also went on to say that no prominent person named in the alleged investigation had been arrested, and they questioned the reliability of the source as well as stating the newspaper should find something else to report because this was just petty gossip.

Officials with the Federal Bureau of Investigation office in Panama City also denied any knowledge of the sheriff or anyone named in the rumor being arrested for drugs or on any other charge. John Peck, press secretary for Governor Bob Martinez, stated no action had been taken against Sheriff McDaniel.

Sheriff McDaniel was outraged that anyone would spread such a malicious rumor about himself and other Jackson County citizens.

"This is so frivolous it is unbelievable. Someone with an ax to grind started it, and it's so juicy it spread like wildfire." John worked hard to keep Jackson County free of drugs and was hurt that someone would spread such rumors about his honesty.

Attorney Herman Laramore stated the stories were "ridiculous." Pforte said it was just a rumor that had been going around the county for a couple of months. He said that the old saying "Great minds talk about ideas, average minds talk about things, and small minds talk about people" summed it up pretty well.

Local businessman J. D. Swearingen said he hadn't heard a word of the rumor and didn't care anyway because anyone who doesn't have the courage to accuse a man openly to his face, wasn't worth worrying about. He added that he sailed his own ship and that "mine is wide open."

Even though he was hurt, Sheriff McDaniel put this behind him and continued to focus helping the citizens of Jackson County.

John and Verlie spent a quiet night at home on Saturday night, January 28, 1989. They were getting ready for "Super Bowl Sunday." They planned to watch the game after church. When John went to bed on Saturday night, he had no idea of the evil lurking in Northwest Jackson County in the small town of Graceville, Florida.

John received the call shortly after 2:30 p.m. on Sunday, informing him that tragedy had struck in Graceville. Two young neighborhood girls, approximately ten years old, discovered two ski masks and jewelry lying outside the Highway 2 home of Robert and Kathryn McRae. The young girls were going to see if the McRaes' grandchildren were still there. One of the girls went to open the door and the other pulled her back. The duo knew that something was wrong and ran across the street to neighbor Josh "Sonny" Campbell who was a former Graceville High School football coach. The girls were so frightened that they opened Coach Campbell's front door and ran straight in his house.

A member of the Campbell family notified law enforcement, who discovered the bodies of Robert and Kathryn shortly after arriving at the twelve-acre McRae estate.

Graceville Police Department received the call and a Graceville police officer along with the couple's son, Finley McRae, had to force a door open to gain access to the two-story mansion. John McDaniel arrived quickly. The McRaes were found lying face down in the kitchen of their spacious home, approximately four feet apart.

The two ski masks were recovered as well as an expensive ring. Initially, law enforcement felt that robbery was the motive behind the deaths; however, further investigations would cast a shadow of doubt on that theory. Sheriff McDaniel instructed the scene to be secured and contacted Florida Department of Law Enforcement. He requested FDLE immediately send their crime lab to process the scene.

The only item they found to be missing in a home full of expensive items was Mrs. McRae's ring. The ring had been custom made for Kathryn several years earlier and was described as White gold with approximately eleven diamonds total—one diamond in the middle with one smaller diamond on each side, and four smaller diamonds on each side of the top row. The ring was identical from both sides. It was a size 5 ½ with unknown karot weights of both diamonds and gold.

The medical examiner's report would show that the couple died from single gunshot wounds to the back of the head. A spent cartridge was located at the home and was taken into evidence by FDLE to be examined by technicians in Tallahassee. The FDLE Crime Lab personnel would remain on site collecting evidence for the next twenty-four hours. On Tuesday, John McDaniel would pay his respects at the First Baptist Church of Graceville.

Robert McRae was a partner in Rex Lumber Company before it was sold for a reported $10 million. He also owned a sawmill in Bristol. He was a former member of the Gulf Power Company board of directors and served on the board of trustees for the Baptist Bible Institute. The McRaes had one daughter, two sons, and twelve grandchildren. All who knew Kathryn stated her love was her grandchildren.

John McDaniel left no stone unturned in his efforts to solve the slaying of the prominent Graceville Couple. At 4 p.m., lawmen searched the bottom of the two-acre pond on the west side of the mansion, looking for evidence.

It was believed that the McRaes were killed when they returned at 9:00 p.m. from a dinner outing in Dothan, Alabama.

Chief Deputy John Dennis stated there was nothing that went "undone." Graceville police officers and Jackson County deputies pulled double shifts to make up for the loss of manpower for the investigative force impaneled by Sheriff McDaniel.

Another strain on the Jackson County Sheriff's Department was guarding the McRae mansion. The crime scene remained sealed off so investigators could retrieve additional evidence as needed. This required around the clock security.

On Thursday, February 2, Sheriff McDaniel released additional information regarding the McRae murders. Graceville Police Chief Bruce Ward and John reinvestigated the crime scene and did a crime stoppers re-enactment at the McRae mansion.

This led to the department making contact with a man who saw a car leaving the McRae home late on Saturday night. The man was passing by the home on Hwy 2 when the grandeur of the house caught his eye. Lights were on inside the home, and he slowed down to admire the mansion. He noticed a car with its lights on. He remembered this because the car only had one headlight.

John P. McDaniel's heart was broken. The tranquility of the small town of Graceville had been shattered. The community residents were afraid and living behind locked doors. Graceville was the kind of town where people didn't lock their doors at night. They had felt safe from big city crime. "Things like this don't happen here…"

***

In 2017, 28 years later, the murders of Robert F. McRae, 72, and his wife, Kathryn, 70, remain unsolved. According to the Bureau of Alcohol, Tobacco, and Firearms, the type of bullet casing found at the home was unusual, at least in rural Florida—a 124 grain, 9mm, Israeli T.Z.Z. cartridge. Not many run-of-the-mill burglars use this type of ammo—an Uzi-type firearm. Robert, a wealthy executive, often carried large sums of cash. It is believed the killers took cash from his wallet, as well as Kathryn's diamond ring, leaving other valuables behind.

During the course of the investigation, another case was linked to the McRae murders by the Florida Department of Law Enforcement, Georgia Bureau of Investigation, and the FBI.

On October, 15, 1989, two hundred miles north of Graceville, Florida, in Tuscaloosa, Alabama, Acie

Worthy, 67, and his wife, Carolyn, 54, met the same fate as Robert and Kathryn McRae. As they returned home from church that Sunday evening, gunmen ambushed the couple in their driveway. The killers then dragged Acie and Carolyn into the residence and set it on fire. Like Robert and Kathryn McRae, the Worthy family was wealthy. They were in the process of building a 10,000-square foot house and had been living in a rental home. Acie had fought in World War II and served as an officer for Bessemer Veterans of Foreign Wars, while Carolyn was the director of the Lakeview Baptist Church choir. The killer stole jewelry and cash from the Alabama couple, but left other valuable items.

The bullets used in the crime were 124 grain, 9mm, Israeli T.Z.A. cartridges.

Detectives report to have unreleased incontrovertible evidence the four murders were committed by the same people, eliminating the possibility of "contract" killers.

CHAPTER 54
More Homicides

John continued in his attempts to solve the McRae murders with little success. They chased every lead to a dead end. Evidence submitted to the lab took some time to yield results. There were no hits on what had been submitted.

Johnny thought about the needs of the county and decided to purchase a van. FDLE was very good, but they covered all of northern Florida so there was often a delay in response time. Little by little, Johnny Mac stocked the van with supplies and equipment necessary to work any crime scene. He felt this would speed the process up and maybe yield success in charging the offenders. The resources would soon be utilized.

On Saturday, March 11, 1989, another murder occurred. Roger Allen Alday was stabbed several times with a knife in Cypress during an altercation with William Andrew Robinson. Chief Deputy Dennis along with Deputies Jeff Johnson and Ken Tate conducted the investigation. At first, Alday was walking around mad because he had been cut. He was transported to the hospital and was pronounced dead on Sunday afternoon. The stab wound to the leg cut the femoral artery. On Sunday, Robinson was arrested for aggravated battery and placed in the Jackson County jail. The next day a murder complaint was filed against Robinson.

***

On Friday night, September 29, 1989, a popular local club was kicking it up with a large number of patrons. Deputies made their usual patrol of the area west of Two Egg in Northeastern Jackson County, seeing nothing amiss at the Dreamland Inn.

Benjamin Mack and Willie B. Hearns were found dead in the early morning hours on Saturday inside the popular night spot. Both men died of a single gunshot wound. Jackson County had another double homicide.

Deputies and investigators questioned anyone and everyone they could find that were at the club on Friday night as well as surrounding neighbors. Very little information was forthcoming. Rumors flew rampant that it was a "Miami Hit" for a drug deal that had gone bad. No evidence could tie any suspect or suspects to the murders and no motive could be proven. The case remains unsolved.

CHAPTER 55
The Beginning of the End

On Thursday night, December 13, 1990, Johnny Mac got off work a little later than usual. He stayed late to help staff sort some of the donations received for the Christmas project.

As John was cleaning up, Little John stopped by to visit his dad. John prepared him a plate.

Johnny Mac and his boy visited for a while. Johnny tried to get Little John to stay, but at about seven o'clock, Little John said he had to go because he had to be at Bonifay, Florida, in the morning at six o'clock to pick up another driver to take him over to Geneva, Alabama, to pick up another log truck.

John P. McDaniel's son, John, was driving a log truck for a fellow from over in Bascom. Little John had stayed on the road with Shelton Trucking for several years before that. He had bought a house and fixed it up. He had long days but was home every night and off on weekends which gave him time for the things he enjoyed like fishing and hunting.

On Friday Morning, December 14, 1990, Johnny Mac got up, got dressed, and ate breakfast before venturing off to work. It was a very cold December morning.

On his way to work, Johnny had to travel slowly as the fog was so thick, visibility was minimal. Johnny arrived at his office, which was located in the courthouse, shortly before 7 a.m. He began going through his messages and returning calls before switching gears and delving into the departmental budget. He was engrossed in the numbers when dispatch transferred a call to his private line at approximately 8 a.m.

"Sheriff McDaniel."

"This is Sheriff Doug Whittle with the Geneva County Sheriff's Department in Alabama. Sheriff McDaniel, do you have a son named John?"

"Yes sir."

"Your son has been involved in a wreck in Geneva County Alabama."

Well, you can imagine what went through Johnny Mac's mind.

Sheriff Whittle said, "Your son is okay, but... we have a fatality of an eight-year-old girl who was a passenger in the vehicle. The driver sustained injuries but will be okay."

"God almighty! Tell me what I need to do." Johnny Mac's heart was racing.

"Your son is up here, and he's coming unglued....he can't function; he can't speak; he can't do anything; he's just all to pieces. I need you here." Sheriff Whittle advised.

"Where are you, and I'll be there as quick as I can."

"Hartford, Alabama. Hwy 123 and 167."

Johhny Mac left his office consumed with fear. He prayed hard as he traveled over to the Peanut Road just north of Cottondale and took Hwy 2 out of Graceville over to Hwy 79 north. He continued north on Hwy 79 until it crossed the Florida/Alabama state line turning into Alabama Hwy 167. He continued north a short distance before arriving upon a sea of blue lights in Hartford, Alabama.

When Johnny Mac got to John, he was backed up against the hood of a patrol car trembling and shaking violently.

"What happened son?" Johnny asked Little John as he put an arm around his shoulders.

Little John was totally unresponsive. His normally twinkling blue eyes stared dully out from his colorless face, staring ahead in the distance...seeing nothing.

"Son, answer me..." Johnny gently shook his son. All he could do was shake.

The other driver, whom Little John was taking to pick up a truck, stepped over to Johnny Mac and said, "John was driving, and we were driving along the highway talking when this girl came across the highway in front of us. She pulled straight across, never slowing up. We were going slow because of the fog, but she just came across right in front of us. We hit the car, and that little girl was looking up at us. It cut that car in two and threw her out."

Geneva County sheriff's office and Hartford Police Department along with the Alabama State troopers worked the accident. They took Little John to the hospital and had blood tests performed. No alcohol or controlled substances were found in Little John's system. Alabama State troopers worked the accident and found no fault with Little John. Due to extreme fog, which limited visibility, the passenger car had traveled into the highway in the path of oncoming traffic. Neither vehicle was speeding. It was an accident—an unfortunate incident that happens unexpectedly and unintentionally.

The beautiful little eight-year-old girl was Carrie Elizabeth Justice. She was the daughter of Joe and Sandra Justice of Hartford, Alabama. Carrie was a third grader at Hartford Elementary School. Born on August 17, 1982, Carrie left on angel wings much too soon. She left behind her family consisting of loving parents; two sisters, Michelle and Anna Justice; a brother, Timothy Michael Justice; grandparents, Allen and Stella McCullough and Eldon and Eloise Justice.

On Monday, December 17, 1990, eight days before Christmas, little Carrie was laid to rest at Pondtown United Methodist Church Cemetery in Hartford, Alabama.

Days later, Johnny Mac was finally about to get his son to talk. Bless his heart, he said, "Daddy, she looked like Meghan." (Meghan is his niece, John P. McDaniel III's granddaughter). She looked up at me…"

It took Johnny Mac four to five months before he could get his son John to drive a vehicle again. He was a total basket case. He had always drunk beer after he became of age, but after that accident he began to drink heavy. Little John carried with him a guilt complex about the wreck that was not rational. The authorities had deemed he was not at fault. But, his heart was so tender he couldn't live with even accidentally causing the little girl's death. It ate him up. That was the beginning of John P. McDaniel IV's end.

CHAPTER 56
More Endings

John McDaniel spent much of the first part of 1991 overseeing the new jail project, the demands of running a sheriff's department, and trying to pull Little John out of a dark depression. It left little time for his wife, Verlie, and their young marriage of three years.

Verlie received a better job offer, running a lab in Brewton Alabama. She wanted John to quit his job and go with her. She took the job, but the long-distance relationship didn't work. John and Verlie ended their marriage as friends on October 10, 1991, so she could pursue her career and John could continue his as sheriff of Jackson County.

Verlie's family was wonderful. John loved her momma and daddy, adored her aunt, and admired how her son grew up to be a great young man.

She was a staunch Christian in every sense of the word. Her daily walk in life was always that of a true believer, and she led by example. Verlie would later end up marrying Glenn Culver, a very nice man. She eventually got another job traveling with another company and they bought John's Uncle Wilson's old house down south of Marianna.

John and Verlie remained friends over the years.

CHAPTER 57
No Peace on Earth in the Little Community of Cypress

The City of Marianna held its annual Christmas Parade in Jackson County, Florida, on Monday night, December 9, 1991. Thousands of residents lined U.S. Highway 90 as the procession moved through the downtown area. The hour-long event featured floats, marching bands, and, of course, an appearance by Santa Clause himself.

Rain and colder weather would be moving into the area shortly after the parade came to a close at 7 p.m. A beautiful, blonde-haired 25-year-old young lady and her precious five-year-old daughter bundled up against the winter cold as they left the parade intent on grabbing some fast food before going home to the little community of Cypress, just a few miles east of Marianna.

She was Teresa Carmichael Hall and the little angel was Tiffany. Teresa's brother, who was handicapped and lived in a DCF facility near Sneads (just east of Cypress) stopped his sister and niece and wanted to go home with them. Teresa had to work the next morning, so it wasn't possible for her to bring her brother home with her. He wasn't happy, but she promised to get him soon and bring him to stay.

Teresa was married to Brian Hall. They had experienced some problems as couples often do and had just got back together. Teresa and Tiffany had moved back in with Brian to the family home on Village Avenue in Cypress on Sunday, the day before the parade. They were looking forward to celebrating Christmas as a family.

Brian, Teresa, and Tiffany attended church services at Cypress Baptist Church on Sunday.

Bryan had left for work out of town in Quitman, Georgia, early on Monday morning. He was a carpet layer.

Teresa and Tiffany ate their fast food after they arrived home in Cypress. Brian called shortly before 8:30 p.m. and spoke to his wife after they arrived home from the parade. Cold was setting in, and the heavy rains had begun.

Teresa had lived in the Cypress area all her life. The railroad tracks ran right by her home. She was in charge of the nursery at Cypress Baptist Church. When the train stopped in Cypress to switch over, the church provided food to those drifters jumping off who were homeless and without food and clothing. Teresa would take home-made lemonade out to the conductors.

She worked at New Beginnings, a children's clothing store in Marianna, and Tiffany attended Golson Elementary School.

Tuesday morning, December 10, 1991, came and went. Teresa Hall didn't show up for work at New Beginnings in Marianna. The owner's daughter contacted Teresa's father-in-law, Dudley Hall, inquiring why Teresa wasn't at work.

Teresa's father had passed away, and her mother, Charlotte Mitchell, remarried Angus Mitchell. They both lived in Sneads, Florida.

If Teresa was supposed to be somewhere, she was there on time or she called. Dudley Hall called Golson Elementary School to see if his granddaughter, Tiffany, was present and discovered she was absent. He then drove to his daughter-in-law's home.

In the meantime, Angus Mitchell had been contacted as well. He drove to the home and the sight he found made him nauseous. He left but could make it no further than the stop sign up the road before he became violently ill.

250

Dudley Hall arrived a few minutes after Angus and found the door of the Cypress home ajar, entered, and discovered his daughter-in law and granddaughter's bodies. Upon arrival, Hall said he noticed the door had been kicked in. The metal latch was underneath the door. Once inside, he saw the body of his "grandbaby" lying on the floor, covered in dried blood, not far from her mom's brutalized body lying in a pool of dried blood. He didn't know at that time that Angus had just been there and left to notify authorities as well.

At 2:30 p.m. on Tuesday, December 10, Sheriff McDaniel was notified of the brutal slayings of the Cypress mom and her little girl. The sheriff was in Tampa at an FDLE training school when the murders were discovered. He left immediately upon notification.

There were signs of forced entry into the home and the house's telephone line had been snatched out of the outer wall. Inside the home, there was damage in the kitchen and the door frame had been split. The kitchen door jamb was cracked and the metal latch on the door jamb broken off and lying on the floor.

Sheriff McDaniel, Major John Dennis, and all five of Jackson County Sheriff's Department investigators worked the crime scene around the clock.

It was a gruesome scene. Teresa had defense wounds on her arms and hands where she had fought her attacker who had gained entrance through the kitchen door. The first blow between Teresa's eyes probably killed her, but the assailant continued to beat her from head to toe.

There was evidence to suggest that Tiffany was picked up by her heals and her head bashed on the door frame. The evil monster then stepped on the precious five-year-old's head.

Both were found fully dressed on the kitchen floor in casual clothes.

On Tuesday night, Sheriff McDaniel and investigators took nineteen statements from neighbors and family. The medical examiner's report showed that Teresa and Tiffany Hall died from repeated blows to the head and face and neither was sexually assaulted.

FDLE came in and did the blood spatter. Seventy-nine items of physical evidence as well as the evidence from the medical examiner were submitted and tested. None of the physical evidence submitted was a match to any subject in the crime data base.

On Friday, December 13, 1991, Teresa and Tiffany Hall's funeral was held at the Cypress Baptist Church. John P. McDaniel, along with his son Little John and Major John Dennis, rode together to the funeral. Little John sat in the back seat sobbing uncontrollably. No one could console him. Early that Friday morning was the one-year anniversary of when Little John's semi-truck killed an eight-year-old little girl. He had never been able to get the images out of his head or to stop blaming himself.

In addition to those inside the small church, over 200 mourners stood outside for the service as there was no room inside. The mom and daughter were laid to rest side by side in the church's cemetery, less than a mile from where they were brutally and senselessly murdered.

Sheriff McDaniel and Major Dennis would return to the investigators who were still working the investigation on Friday and all day on Saturday. Ten auxiliary deputies assisted in pulling security on the Hall home and searching the grounds.

McDaniel, Dennis, Jackson County Sheriff's Office investigators, the Florida Department of Law Enforcement, and ten auxiliary deputies worked non-stop from Tuesday afternoon to midnight Saturday night. No interviews reached the stage of interrogation.

Sheriff McDaniel told them to go home and get some rest on Sunday and come back Monday morning with a fresh and alert mind.

Along with Major Dennis, the five investigators were Capt. Widner, Lt. Birge, Lt. Rabon, and Sgt. Roberts. Johnny Mac knew that these officers had children and families of their own, and two or three were about the same age as Tiffany. They were running on raw emotions and concern. He needed them to rest and come back with a new set of eyes.

Over the next few months, rumors began to fly rampant as often happens in a small community. Subjects whose names were linked to the incident approached the sheriff's department and requested polygraphs to clear them. They asked, and Johnny Mac saw that they were performed, each taking two-three hours.

Teresa's car was in the driveway of her home after the murders. There was no evidence of any items taken from the home. It rained hard and heavy on Monday night after the parade. Any evidence of another vehicle entering or leaving the residence would have been washed away.

A sheet of plywood was placed over where the kitchen door had fit. Little Tiffany's two tricycles sat on the back porch, and Teresa's flowers hung at the front door.

The senseless murders wrenched at John's heart. They left no stone unturned, interviewing all neighbors, school friends, other friends, fellow co-workers… anyone who would have known her or known of her travels. Many stated Teresa hadn't said anything about anyone bothering her. Teresa was active at Cypress Baptist Church and was known as a good wife and mother.

Police confirmed that Brian Hall was in Quitman, Georgia, working as a carpet layer on Monday and Tuesday until he was notified of the deaths and brought home.

Sheriff McDaniel put out a plea for videotapes or photographs of the Green Street and Lafayette Street areas of the Christmas Parade. A man did come forward and volunteer a video tape. It was reviewed in detail.

A cold, rainy December night when there should have been peace on earth and goodwill to all, the complete opposite occurred. December 10, 1991, ended tragically for a precious and utterly defenseless five-year old girl and her beautiful mother. The murders of Teresa Hall and Tiffany Hall still remain unsolved to this day.

CHAPTER 58

Serving the Community from the Inside Out

John McDaniel entered his tenth year in office as sheriff seeing some light at the end of the tunnel with regards to the jail issues which had plagued his entire administration.

They would now be able to serve the community from the inside out with a new jail and sheriff's office. The Jackson County Correctional Facility was completed with a holding capacity of 300 inmates. In the summer of 1992, inmates were moved from the old jail located behind the Jackson County Courthouse to the new facility located on Penn Avenue.

The jail went from being a burden on the county and tax payers to totally funding itself. Due to the insight of those involved, the capacity of 300 inmates allowed for the county to rent out bed space to the Federal Marshall's etc. This generated revenue for the county and covered most of the cost of operating the jail. The design of the jail alone allowed for the sight and sound requirement imposed by Department of Corrections to be met with minimal staffing changes.

On July 10, 1992, John P. McDaniel and County Manager Leon Foster and the Board of County Commissioners were able to negotiate the purchase of the old Coca Cola plant on Hwy 90 in Marianna for $250,000.

The site contained 6.325 acres with a total building area of 27,028 square feet which was built in 1965. After renovations were complete, the building was ready for occupancy.

The new Jackson County Sheriff's Department located at 4012 Lafayette Street in Marianna was ready to house staff. This included having the sheriff, investigations, patrol, dispatch, and warrants all under one roof at one central location.

This was one of Johnny Mac's dreams that had become reality. It meant better service for all the citizens of Jackson County. Prior to this, the department was spread out in various offices on different floors of the courthouse as well as dispatch being in the front of the old jail down the street from the courthouse. It had taken years of hard work and innovative thinking to reach this point.

Johnny Mac continued improving the sheriff's department with the purchase of additional diving equipment, certifying more divers, the purchase of a helicopter, an airplane, and a boat as well as new radio equipment.

Each investment enhanced the sheriff's department's ability to meet any need the community faced.

In his personal life, Johnny Mac remained single. He devoted much time in trying to help his son who was battling with alcohol and depression and helping to care for Papa (his step-father Lawrence Russell Owens).

Papa wasn't doing well and was in and out of the hospital for some time in 1993.

One day, Jeannette Barber, Johnny Mac's cousin, called and told him she had a friend that worked with her at the bank. She wanted to fix Johnny up with the nice and pretty lady. Her name was Mellie. Johnny was really excited about this and got her number and called her for a date.

Then Johnny's papa, Russell Owens, got real sick. He was in the hospital, and Johnny ended up calling Mellie to cancel the date. He told her that Papa was in the hospital, and he had to sit with him.

Well, she thought Johnny was telling a fib. The next time Johnny called her back, she said, "No, you don't want to go with me. You're too busy for me." Well,

Johnny was sad because things kind of ended on a sour note.

Johnny continued helping his mom, Ruth, and caring for Papa. Papa was not getting any better. On April 5, 1993, Russell Lawrence Owens left this world on angel wings. He was buried at Marvin Chapel Freewill Baptist Church.

That same day Johnny kept thinking about Mellie. He called her again and told her Papa had passed away. Johnny's cousin, Jeannette, had called her and told her that he was telling her the truth and that his Papa had died.

So, Mellie came down to Johnny's Momma Ruth's house and got right in the kitchen with all the family. They did the cooking and taking care of Momma Ruth. Ruth wanted Johnny and Mellie to go down to the lake house and check the water because the weather reports were predicting a hard freeze that night.

Well, Mellie was there, so Johnny asked her if she would like to ride down there with him. It just so happened there was a harvest moon that night.

The Harvest Moon tends to be larger and more colorful than other moons of the year. The Harvest Moon gets its name from the extra light it gives farmers—in times before electricity they had even longer to harvest their crops.

Johnny and Mellie drove down to the lake and got out of the car. Johnny recalled, "Looking out across the pasture behind them was the biggest moon you had ever seen in your life. Everything was illuminated in a magical glow." That set things off for Johnny and Mellie and they began dating.

Johnny was still trying to help Little John. It had gotten to the point where he had to be placed in inpatient treatment for alcohol. Little John hated his dad for having him committed for treatment.

He purchased a dry-cleaning business for Little John to run. Little John was dating a wonderful young lady by the name of Carole.

On April 2, 1994, John Perry McDaniel IV married Carole Dee Smith in a ceremony at Cottondale Baptist Church, performed by Minister Jack H. Brock.

Little John was such a handsome 28-year old groom, looking much like his dad at that age. Carole looked like an angel as she walked down the aisle toward her soon to be husband.

John P. McDaniel III was John IV's best man. Things were better. The music was back in Johnny Mac's life. Little John was doing well and had a beautiful, sweet wife that adored him. Johnny was dating Mellie, a woman as beautiful inside as she was out.

Carole did her very best to help Little John overcome his drinking problems. Things were good for a while, but by the first part of December every year, Little John would become inconsolable. He would contact the family members of Carrie Elizabeth Justice every year just to check on them.

He told his wife, Carole, that he wondered every day what type of life little Carrie would have had—her first date, first experience driving a car, her graduation from high school, etc. He couldn't let it go.

Little John kept on drinking and drinking and drinking. His wife, such a wonderful little lady, did all she could to straighten him out, but it wouldn't be enough.

Little John and Carole purchased Johnny's old home in Meadowview from the people who bought it from Johnny Mac earlier. Between 85-86 Johnny Mac bought a farm on Hwy 72 in Marianna.

CHAPTER 59
Campaign of 1996:
Fighting the Rumors

John P. McDaniel began campaigning for his fifth term in office just as he always had, listening to the people and their needs. "Every time you campaign you get out and work with the public. That is where many of your answers lie."

The September primary election would see a face-off between the two democratic candidates: the incumbent sheriff and Dudley Hall.

As is the case with most political campaigns, many things are tossed out there in the face of adversity. Whether the opponent facilitates or truly believes the rumors running rampant or not, only the individual actually knows.

Just as the 1996 campaign for Jackson County sheriff was heating up, vicious rumors surfaced. The rumors concerned the incumbent sheriff's son, John and his having pertinent knowledge surrounding the Teresa and Tiffany Hall murders in Cypress five years earlier.

The source of the rumors was undetermined, and no prior evidence existed in the investigative files regarding John IV.

All of this surfaced when Dudley Hall, the father-in-law to Teresa Hall and grandfather to Tiffany Hall, entered the sheriff's race in 1996.

Johnny Mac privately felt like a piece of his heart had been ripped out. Jackson County was his heart. His children and family were the essence of his soul.

In January of 1989, he had publicly addressed rumors which surfaced during the end of his 1988 campaign. Those rumors were regarding allegations that he and several prominent business men had been arrested or were being investigated for illegal drug activities. The rumor mill had gone too far this time. He refused to acknowledge the ludicrous information.

Johnny Mac's son was off limits. Little John had been unable to come to terms with the fatal accident from December of 1990. When Little John first heard the rumors of his supposed knowledge surrounding the murders in Cypress, he dove head first back into the bottom of a bottle. His tender heart could not handle the mere idea of people thinking he had knowledge regarding a crime so atrocious.

Johnny Mac continued his campaign for sheriff, winning the first primary election on September 3. McDaniel carried every precinct winning the first primary with a grand total of 8,482 to Dudley's 3,669.

John would face Republican candidate W. Isaac "Bill" Bishop in the general election on November 5.

John was joined by his mother, Ruth Owens, at the Jackson County Sheriff's Office to listen to the returns on November 5.

For the fifth term, Democratic John P. McDaniel would be serving Jackson County as sheriff. McDaniel received 11,547 to Republican Bishop's 4,099. John P. McDaniel carried every precinct with a total of 73.9 percent of the vote.

There were some other significant elections at the polls that year. Hands on experience as well as management skills counted with voters in the race for Jackson County clerk of circuit court. Voters put Dale Rabon Guthrie into office as the first woman to be elected to the position. She brought seventeen years of working in the clerk's office to the table, with a portion of that time as administrative assistant to the retiring clerk, Daun Crews.

Bascom resident and Democratic candidate Jamey Westbrook won the State Representative District 7 seat against Republican opponent Mark Anderson.

Another local resident, Allen Boyd, won the U.S. Congressional seat in the House of Representatives.

Marianna resident and former assistant state attorney, Bill Wright, won as the new Circuit 14, group 4 judge.

State Attorney Jim Appleman won his bid for re-election with 63.2 percent of the vote.

Sheriff McDaniel saw Appleman and Wright frequently as his officers prepared criminal cases for Appleman to oversee and Wright to judge.

CHAPTER 60

Fifth Term in Office:
Positive Changes Personally and Professionally

Sheriff McDaniel started his fifth term as sheriff of Jackson County in January of 1997. He continued working every lead possible in the unsolved double homicide cases from prior years.

He never stopped searching for ways to improve the department and better serve the citizens of Jackson County. The Lake Seminole project was renewed with the Corp of Engineers in 1998.

Johnny Mac requested funds for a dedication plaque for the Jackson County Sheriff's Facility which was completed back in 1993 and never dedicated.

Johnny continued making progress within the department. On April 14, at a regular meeting of the Jackson County board of commissioners, Sheriff McDaniel presented a request for a budget amendment in the amount of $21,982.00 to upgrade the computer system at the sheriff's office as well as $2,500 from the contraband fund to be given to five county high schools for Project Graduation. Both requests were approved and carried unanimously.

By June of 1998, Johnny Mac requested and received approval to renew the Drug Control and System Improvement Formula Grant Program.

By December of 1998, Sheriff McDaniel requested and received a budget increase of $49,970.00 due to a traffic grant received from Florida Department of Transportation. Jackson County had the highest traffic fatality rate per capita due to high rates of speed in 1998. Grant money was used to purchase equipment to establish a two-person traffic unit in Jackson County.

March 9, 1999 saw another request for a budget amendment by Sheriff McDaniel in the amount of $27,379.78. This was the Federal Cops Fast Grant. The grant covered seventy-five percent of the cost for the addition of two new officers to the county for three years. And the Corp of Engineers Lake Seminole Contract was again approved for another year.

In April of 1999, Sheriff McDaniel presented a request for matching grant fund for the purchase of C.R.I.M.E.S. Imaging System in the amount of $7,375.00 to be paid from the contraband forfeiture fund. Approval was granted. He also requested approval for participation in the FY-2000 Federal Drug Control and System Improvement Program as sub-grantee. Again approval was granted.

Johnny and Mellie had been dating for six years. They were both ready for a lifetime commitment to each other. On April 4, 1999, Mellie Estelle Edenfield became Mellie McDaniel. They were married by Jeannette Kosciw at Johnny's Uncle Don Grant's home at 4861 Davis Drive in Marianna. Mellie was beaming with a tiny spray of baby's breath in her curly blonde hair above white pearl teardrop earrings. She clutched her bouquet of pink and white carnations with one hand as she grasped Johnny's hand with the other.

Johnny and Mellie returned from their honeymoon to make their home at "North Fork" just outside the city limits of Marianna.

Sheriff McDaniel also requested and received $21,250.00 for the grant for Domestic/Sexual Violence Victims Advocate expenses during the FY 98-99.

Johnny Mac never stopped researching and applying for grants which would enhance the department's ability to better serve Jackson County. He built up a large resource network. In a regular meeting of the board of county commissioners on May 25, 1999, Sheriff

McDaniel requested board approval for submitting a school resource grant application which would add five additional school resource officers. Sheriff McDaniel advised that the Jackson County school board had agreed to pay the twenty-five percent match required of this grant for the first three years. At the end of the three years, the school board and the commission would need to look at funding those positions. Again, approval was granted.

By June 8, 1999, Sheriff McDaniel presented to the board a report on the Drug Task Force Grant and the direct impact on the supply and demand of drugs within the county and advised the board of the Jackson County Drug Task Force VI Grant which he had applied for as well. If approved this would be the drug task force's sixth year in operation within the county. He stated the grant of $58,656.00 would come from the Anti-Drug Abuse Act funds. The additional twenty-five percent required as match funds would come from the Jackson County Drug Task Force project-generated income.

Johnny Mac also presented a request for criminal justice technical books to be purchased in the amount of $1,800.00, using funds from the contraband fund. The books would be used by the Jackson Academy of Applied Technology. Both requests received unanimous approval from the board.

On August 10, 1999, Sheriff McDaniel presented a request to purchase a Piper Super Cub fixed-wing aircraft though the Bureau of Federal Property Assistance for a cost of $1,500.00 to be paid from the contraband forfeiture fund. Unanimous approval was granted.

By September of 1999, the sheriff's department aviation would be hit with several high-dollar costs. Flight instruction check ride expenditures totaled $120.00, and this was paid from the contraband forfeiture fund. A crankshaft was needed for the Piper Cub aircraft which cost $3,500.00 and was also paid from the contraband forfeiture fund. But repairs on the N325JC helicopter in the amount of $9,644.02 had to be paid from the sheriff's aviation fund.

By November of 1999, Sheriff McDaniel requested a budget amendment for $95,886.00 for the FY 99-2000. The Jackson County Sheriff's Department added two additional deputies full time to work narcotic investigations.

CHAPTER 61
2000 Election Year

The year 2000 opened with no closures or arrests in the double homicide cases still unsolved in Jackson County. Investigators continued to work every possible lead to the end. The open cases weighed heavy on Johnny Mac's heart.

By April, Sheriff McDaniel had worked up the Edward Byrne State and Local Law Enforcement Assistance Formula Block grant for State FY 2001 in the amount of $58,656.00, which the commission approved unanimously. Sheriff McDaniel also requested approval for the contract with the U.S. Army Corps of Engineers for Law Enforcement Services on Lake Seminole in the amount of $12,292.00 which was also approved by the commission.

On May 23, at a regular meeting of the board of county commissioners, Sheriff McDaniel presented a report regarding the activity of the Jackson County drug task force. Checks were received in the amounts of $208,293.03 and $82,860.40.

Sheriff McDaniel presented for approval the Jackson County Drug Task Force VII grant for the purpose of combating drugs within the county. This would be the drug task force's seventh year in operation within the county. Again, the $58,656.00 would come from the Anti-Drug Abuse Act funds and the additional twenty-five percent required as match funds would come from Jackson County drug task force project-generated income. Unanimous approval was gained.

McDaniel continued the year of 2000 campaigning for re-election to the office of sheriff. The first primary election in September was closely approaching. The incumbent sheriff would face Pelvo White, Jr. for the position of Jackson County sheriff on September 5, 2000.

In an overwhelming show of voter support on Tuesday night, September 5, Sheriff John P. McDaniel was returned to office to serve his sixth consecutive term as the county's top law enforcement official. McDaniel received 76.8 percent of the vote with 9,260 ballots cast his way. Challenger Pelvo White, Jr. received 2,786 votes for 23.1 percent.

On October 10, 2000, Sheriff McDaniel made a request for $600.00 to be expended from the contraband forfeiture fund to the Florida Sheriff's Association Law Enforcement Memorial. The Memorial consisted of a name wall to honor the deputies and other sheriff's office personnel of Florida who had given their lives in the line of duty. At this time, Jackson County had six officers of the Jackson County Sheriff's Department known to have been killed in the line of duty. The commission granted unanimous approval.

In January of 2002, a young man had just graduated from the police academy at Okaloosa Walton Training Center. He took his test for certification in Tallahassee, passed, and went home to Ponce de Leon in Walton County. He printed off his resumes and hit the interstate. His first exit was Holmes County. They had no officer openings. His next exit was Washington County. They had no openings. His next exit was Jackson County. The captain on duty, Earl Cloud, asked if he had a resume he could leave. While the young man fished for his resume, Capt. Cloud asked, "What's your name" and "Where are you from?"

"Billy Dozier, sir." Billy extended his hand.

"Do you play basketball?" Capt. Cloud asked.

"Everyone does," Billy said with a smile. He had been asked this many times as he was a pretty tall fellow.

About this time, a jolly looking man in a blue jumpsuit came strolling through. Capt. Cloud told him you might want to talk to this young man here.

Billy Dozier followed the man in the blue jumpsuit down a corridor into a side office.

The man in the blue suit was very nice and asked Billy several questions: where are you from, where have you worked, any military background, how long have you been certified?

Billy was told there was one rule. "Don't screw my dispatchers."

And the last question really threw Billy. "Can you shuck corn?"

Billy answered all the questions, advised he was happily married so he wouldn't bother the dispatchers, and said yes, he could shuck corn.

"You're hired."

Billy was so excited. He started to work that night, January 20, 2002, as a deputy with the Jackson County Sheriff's Department. He didn't realize until he was leaving the office that the jolly man in the blue jumpsuit was John P. McDaniel, the sheriff of Jackson County.

Billy was determined to make the sheriff proud of giving him a chance. He rode four nights with his assigned field training officer, Sgt. Rusty Booth, before an incident occurred and they had a suspect run from them on foot. Billy chased him down and caught him. Tim Hinson, the Lt., gave him the nickname of flash. Within six months, Billy became a member of the SWAT team and brought his excellent marksmanship skills to the team.

A couple of years after being hired, Billy was working a case in the north end of the county which was reported as a black male with a white female on her hands and knees with a dog leash around her neck. Billy arrived on scene and found tracks. Sheriff McDaniel showed up and unscrewed the antennae from his car and circled foot prints in the dirt for him to take pictures of as evidence. It was going to rain before the investigators arrived and the evidence would be gone. They completed the investigation and Billy went to an auto salvage yard the next day and bought an antenna off of a junked vehicle to keep in his patrol car.

CHAPTER 62

Sixth Term in Office
(Greatest Loss of All):
January 2001-December 2004

John McDaniel began his sixth term in office much like those in the past. At the end of this term, he would have been sheriff for twenty-four years.

He continued building a department the citizens could be proud of. He fought for every grant dollar he could find to meet the needs of a growing county.

Sheriff McDaniel continued his fight against drugs and turned the confiscated funds into equipment and tools to better protect the community.

By 2004, John III's son had become very sick. Little John had developed a problem with alcohol.

A few years earlier, Little John was having difficulty running his laundry, Cavalier Cleaners. He got to drinking so heavily while he was working, he blacked out. Johnny Mac again had him committed for treatment.

Another time, Little John just kept on and on and on and fell out in his own yard, drunk. Johnny had a deputy pick him up and take him to alcohol rehab in Panama City.

Johnny and his son talked. Little John loved his daddy, and Johnny loved him, but Little John resented his father interfering and it caused problems between father and son.

Little John became a victim of cirrhosis of the liver. Johnny took him to Shans Teaching Hospital, and did everything we could to try and save our son, but nothing worked.

The saddest moment in Johnny Mac's life happened the last few precious minutes that Little John was alive. Johnny stayed with him at the hospital in Tallahassee. Little John's wife, Carole, never left his side

Once, while Little John sat on a portable commode, he looked at his father and said, "Daddy, I didn't want to die this way."

With tears in his eyes, Johnny said, "Son, I'm sorry."

A few minutes later, while back in bed, he said, "Daddy, I didn't want to die," and he cried.

Johnny choked on tears. "John, son, you done killed yourself. I can't help you. There ain't nothing I can do."

He got worse and worse.

Johnny was sitting there holding one hand and Carol was holding the other one when Little John drew his last breath on June 22, 2004. He fought to the end, taking that last breath.

Johnny brushed his son's cheek and reached up and gently closed his eyes. The music stopped for Johnny that day. A piece of his heart was gone forever.

When Johnny reflects back on Little John, the memories turn to water. He stated he didn't know if it was a good thing or not for families to be there when their loved ones draw that last breath, but to have to reach up and close their eyes.

John recalled, "It will never, never, never leave you. You will think about it every time somebody dies. I think about reaching up and closing John's eyes. It haunts me to this day."

John has the ability to look at the positive things in life and not dwell on the negative. That is the only way he has been able to cope with life and his unwavering belief in Jesus Christ as his Savior. His belief that God was with him gave him strength all the way along.

CHAPTER 63
Campaigning for
Seventh Term in Office

Just days before John lost his son, he announced his intentions to run for sheriff in the upcoming election.

Sheriff McDaniel had made application earlier in the year for an EMPA grant for Project Operation Agriwaves. This grant would supply new repeaters and consoles in dispatch, a vital communication center for officers in providing assistance to citizens. The grant in the amount of $176,289 was originally not awarded to Jackson County. The agency that was awarded the funding for 2004 turned it down, making Jackson County eligible for the funding. Communications International advised that they could still provide the equipment at the prices originally quoted with a projected completion date of August 14, 2006.

John McDaniel hit the campaign trail late in the year 2004 due to the loss of his son. He still presented the same beliefs and values as he did the first time he ran for the office of sheriff in 1980—that being a sheriff was everything to everybody.

The 26,474 registered voters would have the opportunity to shape the future of their county by going to the polls in sweltering heat and humidity to cast their ballots in the Florida primary election.

Incumbent Jackson County Sheriff John P. "Johnny Mac" McDaniel easily defeated his Democratic opponent, Dudley J. Hall, in the Tuesday night primary on August 31, 2004. McDaniel seized 7,583 votes with Hall capturing 3,213. Sheriff John P. McDaniel carried 70.25% of the vote in the August primary. He would now face the Republican challenger, William Nelson, in the November general election.

Sheriff McDaniel spent election night at the Jackson County Sheriff's Office with family, friends, and staff, watching the results on TV and listening to radio results. The sheriff gave credit for his first-round win to a "team effort," involving family, friends, and employees.

John had a new mission to fill if elected sheriff for the next four years. He reflected that every week of his life in office, he had family members come to him with problems involving loved ones suffering from addiction to alcohol and/or drugs. He wanted to be able to help them. There were no long-term programs in the area which provided for involuntary commitment. He wanted to develop a program that would provide six months to a year to keep those needing help from self-destructing. This mission came from the deepest part of Johnny Mac's heart because of his son's addiction.

On Tuesday night, November 2, 2004, Jackson County Sheriff John P. McDaniel won a seventh consecutive term in office, easily defeating his challenger. This began Johnny Mac's silver anniversary year as the top law enforcement official of the county. McDaniel gathered 14,004 votes to Nelson's 5,247. Incumbent Sheriff McDaniel carried 72.75% of the vote.

The 2004 election saw a few other changes. Long-term state attorney, Jim Appleman retired. This created one of the hottest and closest political races in the area for the State Attorney of the Fourteenth Judicial Circuit. "Sister" Martha Blackmon Milligan won Jackson County by just 325 votes, but Steve Meadows overcame the deficit by winning the rest of the district and replacing Appleman.

In the presidential election, Florida helped to push President Bush over the top. Bush was the popular choice in Jackson County in 2004.

CHAPTER 64
Seventh Term Begins
25ᵗʰ Year as Sheriff

Sheriff McDaniel had several priorities on his agenda for his seventh term as sheriff. He planned to establish a civil service type of status for his employees, which meant most deputies and other workers in his department would be protected from being fired in an "at the pleasure of" house cleaning if a new sheriff came into office. He planned to work with the medical community and law enforcement to establish a means of ordering mandatory long-term treatment for substance abusers who have demonstrated self-destructive tendencies or a threat to the safety of others. McDaniel also planned to use the newest advances in DNA evidence-gathering techniques in an attempt to solve cold cases. He would continue searching out grant monies available in an effort to advance training of officers, provide additional equipment, and put more officers on the streets.

He spent much of 2005 working toward those priorities. There was some time for play even during work. The Charlie Daniels Band came into town. One of the band members ended up in a little trouble and Charlie wanted to see the sheriff. Johnny took Mellie with him so she could meet the singer.

Another huge loss came for Johnny in 2006.

His mother, Ruth Grant Owens, left on angel wings, February 18, 2006. Ruth was born on April 10, 1919, and passed two months before her 87ᵗʰ birthday.

She had always been Johnny's rock. After his daddy left, his momma had no job and no income coming in. Ruth managed to get a job working at the peanut mill and then got a job with Florida State Department of Labor, where she worked until the mid-'50s and was laid off.

Ruth went to work at the peanut mill again until the state hired back. She worked for 33 years with the Department of Labor until she retired.

Ruth would get in from work after five o'clock in the evening and try to cook dinner for the children. She had an old kerosene stove. It had an oven that didn't work and four kerosene burners, but she managed to provide her kids with hot meals growing up. Through the years, she was always there for all of her children. She raised them to be God fearing, loving and patient, and to never give up no matter what life threw at you. She didn't send her children to church. She sat in the pew next to them and worshipped with them.

Momma Ruth would gather her children around like a bunch of little bitties and wrap her arms or wings around them, cry with them, pray with them, and work her heart out for them.

Momma Ruth was by herself after her husband died in 1994. She moved over to Davis Drive to be next to Uncle Don and Aunt Eleanor.

Johnny could see his momma being lonely there by herself, so he would get up every morning and go to town and get a biscuit, bacon, egg, and cheese or egg McMuffin. He had a key to the house and would open the door and go in and holler, "Momma, get up. I'm here."

She would say I'll be there in a minute. Johnny would fix her a cup of coffee and lay her breakfast out. She would come and sit in the same spot every morning. Johnny told her he just wanted to make sure she had breakfast every morning.

She said, "You ain't in no hurry. Sit down over there. Sit down. Tell me what's going on."

Johnny said, "It was her way of having company. Momma Ruth enjoyed that."

Johnny did that for thirteen years. He carried her breakfast, and whatever she wanted done, he saw to it that it was done. If he didn't get it done, his brother Wayne would, and if he didn't, her daughters or daughters-in-law would get it done.

So Momma Ruth pretty well ruled the roost, but she did it with love. She used to call Doris or Helen and say, "I think it wouldn't hurt ya'll to come out here and help me with something." She was kind of diplomatic in what she would say. She would call and say "That dad gum pump out there is acting up. You gotta come do something with it."

Johnny recalled, "Well, Lord have mercy, I would work on pumps and her swimming pool. She didn't swim in it, but she liked it. It didn't matter what it was; you dropped what you were doing to take care of momma."

Johnny never had any regrets with the loss of his momma because he knew she was with Jesus.

A slow smile eased across Johnny's face as he recalled. "There were two times in our lives when we were all going to be with momma. That was the Fourth of July, when we celebrated Grandma and Granddaddy Grant's wedding anniversary and Easter Sunday at Marvin Chapel Freewill Baptist Church. You were going to bring yourself and all of your family that you could muster and sit on momma's pew."

"She wanted to fill that pew up. And if Johnny heard his momma sing, "I Come to the Garden Alone," one time, he heard it a million times. He just wished he could hear her sing it again...wishes he had recorded her singing it."

Ruth was laid to rest next to her husband Lawrence Russell Owens at Marvin Chapel Freewill Baptist Church. Johnny was lost without his mother. For 65 years, she had been there for him no matter what he did right or wrong. "How do you say goodbye to that? The answer is, you don't. You brush back the tears because you know she is with Jesus and thank God for blessing you with a wonderful mother and simply say, 'Until we meet again.'"

On June 13, 2006, Sheriff McDaniel came up with a proposal to put before the board of county commissioners. Every summer, the sheriff's department fought everything from drug activity, underage drinking, to excessive littering at several of the parks and landings in Jackson County. Johnny Mac wanted to provide extra security at Spring Creek Park, Turner's Landing, and Magnolia Bridge Landing. The projected cost would be twenty dollars per hour for an employee for each eight-hour shift. In 2006, Sheriff McDaniel estimated the cost to provide security from June 17 through September 4 to be $12,960. Johnny Mac's proposal was met with board approval. The county would see a huge reduction in crime and littering in these areas by fall of 2006.

Sheriff McDaniel never lost focus on the unsolved homicides in Jackson County. He wanted more than anything to bring the killers to justice and to provide closure for the families. Angel Maturino Resendiz had been interviewed twice previously as one of the many suspects in the brutal slayings of Teresa Hall and her five-year-old daughter Tiffany whose bodies were discovered on December 10, 1991.

Resendiz, also known as the "Railroad Killer," was set to die by lethal injection in Texas on Tuesday night, June 27, 2006. Sheriff McDaniel sent Jackson County Sheriff's Office Major John Dennis to Texas to interview the killer one last time prior to his execution in hopes of clearing the unsolved murders.

Major Dennis had kept a picture of five-year-old Tiffany Hall and her mother Teresa in a book-style calendar on his desktop since their bodies were discovered in 1991. He handled that picture almost every work day of his life since then, moving it forward month by month and year by year on the calendars each time he flipped a page.

Resendiz was developed as a suspect in the case because he had been imprisoned at the federal prison in Marianna and was released in 1991, shortly before the Hall Murders. Some circumstances in the Halls' deaths matched other murders attributed to Resendiz. For instance, the Hall home was located not far from the railroad tracks that run through the Cypress community. Resendiz earned the "railroad killer" nickname because some of his victims lived near train tracks and because he was known for traveling by rail.

Sheriff McDaniel held a press conference at 2:00 p.m. on June 28, 2006, regarding the results of the Dennis interview with Resendiz. Major Dennis was escorted back to interview Resendiz and spent approximately two hours with him. Resendiz described the area around the Halls' home in great detail. Resendiz remembered it being cold on the night of the murders and said he rode the trains between Tallahassee and Pensacola around the time of the deaths. Major Dennis showed him line-ups twice with six adult females and six children. Resendiz picked Teresa and Tiffany up quickly, stating he believed he recognized those people, having seen them several times when the train stopped in Cypress. Teresa would take lemonade out to the conductor when the train stopped. The local Old Cypress Church gave clothes and food to homeless people. Those rail jumpers on board all knew which areas provided food and clothing. But Resendiz said he had no memory of killing Teresa and Tiffany Hall.

Major Dennis asked Resendiz if he went into the house and killed or hurt them in any way. Resendiz did not confess to the crimes. He told Dennis that he often awoke with blood on his clothes some mornings during his cross-country killing spree but could not remember what happened the night before. Dennis asked Resendiz if he wore gloves. Resendiz replied no.

Major Dennis stated on his way back from the interview that he received a call from prison personnel saying Resendiz wanted to tell him something. Resendiz got on the phone and confessed that he had lied to Dennis and that he did, in fact, wear gloves.

After the Halls were murdered, fingerprints were lifted from the crime scene and compared at one time to Resendiz's prints. The prints did not match. During this phone call, Resendiz mentioned that it was raining the night he was in Cypress.

Major Dennis stated that Resendiz showed no remorse, except for in acknowledging the death of Tiffany. He stated that he hoped that he didn't murder a child. Resendiz's DNA was sent to Florida Department of Law Enforcement for processing.

Resendiz was convicted and executed for the rape-slaying of Claudia Benton, a Houston-area physician killed in her home a week before Christmas in 1998. Resendiz had been linked to eight slayings in Texas, two each in Illinois and Florida, and one each in Kentucky, California, and Georgia. He was executed on June 27, 2006, in Huntsville, Texas. Nothing came from the Dennis/Resendiz interview to stay the execution.

The crime scene from the cold rainy night in Cypress left behind DNA, 17 unidentified prints—including the killer's fingerprints on the door facing going in where the door was kicked in—and a palm print on the door. Resendiz's DNA nor his fingerprints yielded a match to the crime scene.

During the course of the Hall investigation, a black male who was a meter reader who worked for REA stated that he went to the Hall home on Village Road on the morning of the night they were murdered. His purpose was to read the meter with an electronic device. He

280

alleged that he observed two white males standing in her yard, one he allegedly identified as Wayne Mears (a neighbor and acquaintance), and the other unknown white male was shorter with curly hair. The REA worker advised he said "Good Morning" and they both looked the other way. The REA worker assisted with a photo composite of the white male with Mears. Major Dennis stated he put the composite in the local *Floridan* paper, the *Democrat* in Tallahassee, and the Bay County paper, asking anyone to identify the unknown white male. No one ever came forward to identify the unknown male. The Hall case remains unsolved.

***

In December of 2006, Johnny Mac decided to surprise his wife, Mellie. She had never seen snow, so he took her to the mountains. She played in the snow for hours, lying on the ground, moving her arms and legs up and down, making snow angels, and giggling like a little girl.

Mellie also had a beautiful voice. She and Johnnie had a karaoke machine and would gather around the fireplace and sing on the weekends. One time, Johnny snuck the recorder on without her knowing and recorded her singing, but when she caught him, she made him turn it off. She never realized how beautiful she sang.

CHAPTER 65
Horrible Afternoon of
January 30, 2007

January 30, 2007, started out like most mornings at the McDaniel household. Johnny's wife, Mellie, loved to feed the birds and would sit out back in the mornings, drink her coffee, and watch the birds play and sing. She and Johnny sat bundled up against the cold and talked before they both headed off to work.

Around 4:15 p.m., CPL Billy Dozier headed to work at the Jackson County Sheriff's Department. He lived in Campbellton in the north part of the county and took Highway 73 to work every day. He passed by the sheriff's home between 4:15 and 4:30 p.m. and noted nothing unusual in the area. Billy was the supervisor for the night shift on that night. Sgt. Quinton Hollis was off that day, and the Lt. was working a basketball game at Chipola College. Mike Altman was a new hire and was returning from eight days off. It was his first day back and his first day working the night shift from 5:00 p.m. until 1:30 a.m. Once CPL Dozier went 10-8 (in service), dispatch notified him he had a subject waiting at the sheriff's office to see him. CPL Dozier headed that way, giving out the deputy zone assignments for the shift. He gave Deputy Mike Altman B-Zone, which was the Campbellton, Cottondale, and Graceville area of the county. This would normally have been Billy's zone, but since he was acting supervisor for the shift, the supervisor had to remain center.

That afternoon, Mellie had left the office a few minutes early to go by and pick up some stuff she was going to cook for their granddaughter, Erika, for a school project. They both had Nextel cell phones that you could talk on, using push to talk/direct connect features by just keying the button. Mellie finished her shopping and was headed home when she called Johnny. "Where are you at and what are you doing?"

"I'm doing just exactly what you told me to do. I'm going to Winn Dixie to pick up those feeders for the birds," Johnny replied with a smile.

Mellie laughed. "That's what you're supposed to be doing."

"What are you doing?"

"I'm just about at the house. I'm going to cook some stuff for Erika....Oh my goodness, somebody has killed one of our deer."

"What?"

"Somebody struck a deer and killed it right here on the corner of our property."

"I'll move it when I get home."

"I just turned in and somebody is turning in behind me."

She approached the house, driving the 100 yards down the driveway. They lived right off a main highway, so it wasn't uncommon for somebody to pull in and want to sell something, ask directions, etc. They lived in a very safe area. Johnny didn't think anything about it.

John recalled, "I mean who would want to harm Mellie? She had never harmed anyone or anything and loved everybody."

"Just stay in the car, roll up your window, and tell them to go away. We don't want it; we're not interested," Johnny instructed Mellie.

"Okay."

"Just stay with me. Don't get off the phone."

"Okay."

Johnny didn't hear anything and didn't hear anything, so he called Mellie on the radio and said, "Where are you at?"

Still, nothing. Johnny tried her again.

In a minute, Johnny heard Mellie scream over the phone's radio—a blood curdling and agonizing scream.

Johnny hollered, "MELLIE! MELLIE!" He turned around right in the middle of the road on Highway 90 in downtown Marianna—right in front of the post office—slinging everything everywhere in the vehicle.

He had a hand-held radio and was trying to put the blue light up on the dash and talk on the radio at the same time.

At 4:49 p.m., Johnny couldn't get Mellie to answer him back, so he called dispatch. "Get somebody out to my house immediately. Mellie just screamed into the radio. I don't know what's going on….I can't get her to answer me back. Get some help out there."

He put the radio and phone down, but they slid away as he was going in and out of traffic, making them impossible for him to reach.

Deputy Mike Altman wasn't two miles away from Mellie when he heard the request over the radio. He told dispatch, "I'll take the call….I'm right here at her house. I'm about to pull in the driveway. 10-97 (arrived on scene)"

Deputy Altman then requested a 10-28 (registration information) for Michigan tag 2894J. Immediately following this transmission was the sound of someone attempting to transmit twice and then a third broken transmission by Deputy Altman. "Get off of me. Get off of me."

That's the last thing they heard him say. The next radio transmission was another broken transmission of a gurgling sound.

At 4:50 p.m., CPL Billy Dozier advised that he was en route to the residence. He left the sheriff's office and headed east on Highway 90 to take 73 north to the sheriff's residence.

At 4:50 p.m., Captain Joey Rabon had just pulled into the parking lot of a local grocery store in his department-issued white Ford Expedition. The minute he heard the radio request for assistance by the sheriff, Captain Rabon activated his lights and siren and proceeded west on Highway 90 toward Highway 73. A few minutes later in the area of McDonald's, Captain Rabon encountered Sheriff McDaniel traveling west on Highway 90 at a high rate of speed in his white Chevrolet Tahoe.

Sheriff McDaniel turned right off of Highway 90 onto Highway 73 north. Capt. Rabon followed closely behind Sheriff McDaniel.

At the intersection of Hwy 90 and Hwy 73, CPL Dozier yielded to Sheriff McDaniel and Capt. Joey Rabon, falling in behind them, heading up Highway 73 north.

McDaniel, Rabon, and Dozier, in that order, arrived at Sheriff McDaniel's residence on Highway 73. They proceeded down the driveway at a high rate of speed to the rear of residence.

Sheriff McDaniel stopped his Tahoe in front of an older tan-colored Ford Crown Victoria that was parked facing northwest and to the rear of Mrs. McDaniel's Lincoln Town Car. Rabon stopped his vehicle on the left and a short distance ahead of Sheriff McDaniel's vehicle. Dozier stopped his patrol car on the right and a short distance behind Sheriff McDaniel's vehicle.

Johnny went to grab his gun and couldn't find it as he was flying up the drive. He had forgotten that he had the grandchildren with him over the weekend the week before, so his pistol had been put in a case in the back of the Tahoe.

Sheriff McDaniel, defenseless without a weapon, exited his Tahoe and ran toward the front of the vehicle. At approximately the same time, Dozer exited his vehicle. As Dozier exited, he observed an unknown subject wearing camouflage running from the area where Mrs. McDaniel's Lincoln was parked. The subject ran toward the driver's side of the older tan Ford Crown Victoria. Prior to reaching the Crown Vic, the subject stopped and extended his hand down toward his leg. Dozier surmised that the subject was possibly reaching for an ankle gun.

Dozier moved from the side of his patrol car to the rear to take cover. He then took up a position on the right side of a large pecan tree situated forward and to the right of his vehicle. As Dozier was moving to the pecan tree, he drew his weapon.

At approximately the same time, Dozier heard a gunshot and observed Sheriff McDaniel drop down. Dozier believed at the time that Sheriff McDaniel had been shot, so he fired at the subject, subsequently identified as Lionel Jay Sands, whom he believed had shot Sheriff McDaniel. Dozier continued firing until the subject fell to the ground. It was at this point that Dozier realized there was a second subject, subsequently identified as Daniel Ray Brown, in the area. The second subject had a gun and was pointing it in the area he had last seen Sheriff McDaniel. Dozier fired at the second subject and continued to do so until the subject fell to the ground.

As Sheriff McDaniel had run around in front of his vehicle, Lionel Sands had run out at him, facing point blank, and fired. It had missed Johnny Mac and went in the hood of his truck, to his right side. Johnny had dropped to his left and rolled around to take cover behind the Tahoe.

Dozier moved up to the area where the suspect vehicle was parked. Captain Rabon covered Dozier as he checked the subjects. The first subject, Lionel Sands, appeared to be dead. Sands had very thick, whitish-colored make-up on and looked like a villain from an Old Batman movie. The second subject wore a suit and had a ponytail with a hat and rubber gloves on—Daniel Brown; although wounded, he was alive and moving and trying to get up.

Dozier with cover by Rabon, approached the second subject, kicking the .22 weapon away from him. When Sheriff McDaniel got to Brown, he was down but kept trying to get up and was wrestling violently with Dozier.

Captain Rabon kept ordering him to stay down, stay down. Johnny Mac yelled, "He's fixing to!" He reached over and popped the hell out of him, trying to make him stay down. At that point, not even realizing what he was doing, Johnny wondered, "Where's Mellie?" He dropped down beside Brown and said, "Where's my wife? Where's my wife?" Dozier secured Brown with handcuffs.

Dozier then directed his attention to the residence. He observed the doors leading from the house out to an attached deck appeared to be ajar. Dozier continued scanning the area and observed Deputy Altman lying on his back in front of Mrs. McDaniel's vehicle Dozier hollered for Rabon to cover him and moved to where Altman lay near the lattice and flowers. Upon arriving in that area, Dozier observed Mrs. McDaniel lying beside Deputy Altman. Mike Altman's hat was off. Dozier saw the burnt holes in his shirt and his pale white face. Dozier turned to Mellie next to him, also on her back, and noted her ripped pantyhose where she had been drug across the pavement. Dozier checked Altman and Mrs. McDaniel for signs of life and found no pulse for either.

Johnny Mac had jumped up and found his wife, lying face up. She had been shot in the back-left side of the head. Altman was lying there beside her, shot once in the face and twice in the back. They could have reached out and touched one another.

Johnny jumped on top of both of them and screamed, "NO, NO, NO!"

Johnny was holding Mellie in his arms and crying. Dozier heard a noise from inside the residence at the base of the window. Dozier yelled at Rabon, "Help me get the sheriff out of here. There may be another suspect inside the house!"

They had to physically pull him away and make him leave. They got him in his truck and told him to drive it up to the end of the drive up by the road.

Rabon and Dozier went in the residence through the open sliding glass door. There was a long rifle sitting in the corner of the living room. There were too many weapons in the home. Both Rabon and Dozier decided it was not tactically safe to proceed. They needed to exit and wait for back up. They had no way of knowing how many suspects there were or if any were in the residence.

They had ordered Johnny Mac to leave the immediate area. Well, he'd left, but then he walked right back to the house.

When Dozier and Rabon exited the residence, Johnny Mac was back demanding to know, "Where the hell is the ambulance?"

Johnny thought about Tara, Mellie's daughter, thinking, "God, don't let her drive up here and see her momma lying there like this...please."

At 5:01 p.m., the call for an ambulance was received and dispatched. One ambulance arrived at 5:06 and a second arrived nineteen minutes later.

Dozier lifted Deputy Altman over his shoulder and carried him to the ambulance.

Captain Earl Cloud and Dozier gently lifted Mellie, cradling her in their arms and placed her in the ambulance.

At 5:15 p.m. Deputy Harold Michael Altman had no respiratory rate and no pulse.

At 5:18 p.m. Mellie McDaniel had no respiratory rate and no pulse.

At 5:25 p.m. Daniel Ray Brown had no respiratory rate and no pulse.

At 5:25 p.m. Lionel Jay Sands had no respiratory rate and no pulse.

The SWAT Team and other deputies and officers had arrived. A subsequent search of the house was completed and everything was clear. The noise which was heard turned out to be the air conditioner handler going off. The SWAT team kicked the back doors of the house open and went in the house and threw tear gas up in the attic. There wasn't anyone else there. Only two people were involved in the murders—just Sands and Brown—and both of them were dead from gunshot wounds received during the shootout.

FDLE and deputies had stopped everybody out at the road because they didn't want to contaminate the crime scene.

They told Johnny Mac that Mellie's daughter was there. Johnny ran to Tara, and she went to her knees. It hurt her so bad. She said, "Tell me Johnny. Why did they stop me...?"

Johnny said, "Baby, your momma was shot and the officers didn't want you up here in the middle of it to see such a bad thing."

It tore her to pieces. Johnny and Tara went to the hospital, and they were informed that Mellie was DOA as was Deputy Mike Altman.

Both suspects had been wearing disguises. Lionel Sands was bald headed and had a wig on with heavy make-up and a mustache. Brown looked like the fellow on the Blue's Brothers with an old hat and dark sunglasses and a suit with a tie.

The Michigan license plate (2894J) attached to Sands's vehicle was found to be placed directly on top of a Florida license plate (T382ZZ) that was subsequently determined to be registered to Sands.

An inventory record of the rear passenger area of Lionel Sands's vehicle revealed a tan-colored vinyl-sided brief case that contained numerous letters possibly authored by Sands, duct tape, latex gloves, and black plastic trash bags. A large container of bleach and a large container of vinegar were on the floorboard behind the front driver's seat. Next to the bleach was a large brick. Sands's wallet was recovered from the front driver's side floor board. A black hard-sided briefcase was recovered from the truck of Sands's vehicle. The briefcase contained several boxes of .22 caliber cartridges, one box of .38 caliber cartridges, two black "Flex Cuffs, a handcuff key, several opaque latex gloves, and an opaque plastic shopping bag.

***

On the afternoon of June 9, 2001, Gail Sands, a native of Louisiana, was found dead at the bottom of a shallow, mucky, rain-filled swimming pool behind her home. Across her back rested a sixteen-foot aluminum ladder. When police questioned Gail's husband, Lionel Sands, he claimed he left his wife early that day to clear brush on the couple's 120-acre farm in rural Jackson County, Florida. Lionel Sands was accompanied by his friend Daniel Brown, a handyman and three-time convicted felon. Lionel Sands claimed his wife, Gail, accidentally drowned in the swimming pool of their Birchwood Road home in Grand Ridge, Florida. Police believe he killed his wife for her life insurance money.

Lionel and Gail Sands married in 1981. At the time of the ceremony, Sands was still married and living with another woman. Five years after Gail's death, Sands maintained his innocence and was never charged with the crime.

The way Sands explained it, his 53-year-old wife must have slipped and fallen into the pool while trying to move a heavy ladder. His story collapsed the next day when the medical examiner noticed a round fracture in the back of Gail's skull that the M.E. believed to be caused by a hammer or similar object. Gail Sands's death, the examiner concluded, was not an accident. It was murder.

In rural Jackson County, just west of Tallahassee in northern Florida, the sheriff's office quickly focused its homicide investigation on Lionel Sands and Daniel Brown. The men were the only people known to be on the farm that day. Both told authorities they'd spent the morning working near the quarter-mile driveway leading to the Sands's farmhouse.

Both of them also said they never saw a car or a person travel down the gravel road toward the house. Further, the Sands's kept several trained attack dogs—Rottweilers and Bull Mastiffs—fenced in the three-acre yard surrounding their home. The dogs were roaming the yard when Sands discovered his wife's body.

Despite strong circumstantial evidence tying Sands and Brown to the crime, prosecutors were never able to build a convincing case against the men. The suspects repeatedly stated that they were within eyesight of each other at all times and were innocent of the crime. Five years later, the Jackson County sheriff had yet to arrest anyone in connection with the murder.

In early March of 2006, Gail's elderly mother and two sisters were subpoenaed to appear in a Florida federal court. Unbeknownst to them, Gail Sands held several life-insurance policies that totaled more than $400,000, with her husband named as the primary beneficiary. With the murder still classified as an "open investigation," and with Lionel Sands the main suspect in

Gail's killing, none of the insurance companies were willing to pay out.

On March 7, 2006, AXA Equitable Life Insurance Company pushed the issue and filed suit, demanding the federal court rule on whether Sands or his wife's mother and sisters receive the $228,345 in insurance proceeds AXA held in her name.

The lawyers in the case had no idea what they would uncover, nor could they—or anyone—foresee the mayhem that would transpire when a cornered Lionel Sands launched a desperate attempt to clear himself of his wife's murder in an attempt to collect insurance monies.

Tallahassee headquarters of FDLE had taken over the inquiry into Gail Sands's death in 2002.

Nine months after his wife's death, Sands attempted to throw off investigators. At a Republican fundraising event in 2002, he cornered then-Governor Jeb Bush to complain that the sheriff was trying to frame him. In April of that year, Sands met with an agent with the Florida Department of Law Enforcement (FDLE).

For seventy minutes, he spun a tale of conspiracy stemming from the day in 1993 when he was arrested for kidnapping a former coworker. Angered by what he considered to be false charges by the Jackson County sheriff, Sands sought consolation with a local Bible study group. It's there that he met the thrice-convicted felon, Dan Brown.

Sands reportedly told the FDLE agent regarding his two-year stint in Bible study that for the first year he was there, his contempt for the sheriff was so bad that they were praying for him ten times a day.

Although the murder investigation remained an "open case" with the Jackson County Sheriff's Office, FDLE closed its file in late 2003. The lawyers involved in the case eventually went to Marianna to meet with the sheriff department's homicide unit. Sheriff deputies revealed items not made part of the FDLE file, including Gail's autopsy report, morgue photos, and a video of the crime scene in which Sands explained to the police his version of how Gail fell into the pool.

Lawyers became optimistic that Gail's family could prove, in an insurance lawsuit, that Lionel Sands murdered his wife. This was the equivalent of a wrongful death suit—no criminal charges would be filed, but it would hit Sands financially by denying him access to the pricey life-insurance policies.

Further investigation into Lionel Sands's background revealed Sands had been married three times. Though he claimed to have no children, the attorneys found he'd fathered a son with his first wife but abandoned the family and never paid child support. The marriage ended after Sands reportedly beat his ex-wife and threatened to harm their son.

Sands's second marriage also ended violently, according to police reports; his then-wife filed a restraining order against him in October 1981, months after he'd already married Gail in the fake ceremony.

Lionel Sands showed up to his court-ordered deposition in late August and suspiciously could no longer produce the ladder in question. He claimed the sheriff's office hauled it away during a follow-up search of his property—an assertion refuted by law officials.

Yet there remained one last piece of the puzzle. For 38 years, Gail had kept a diary, and now—like the missing ladder—all seven volumes of the journals had disappeared.

Sands never mentioned the diaries to the police. Sands at first denied their existence but later acknowledged giving the diaries to Donna Campbell, a friend of Gail's to whom he had grown close in recent years.

Campbell lived in Dothan, Alabama, an hour drive from the Sands's Florida farm. Donna Campbell was found dead in her home. After not hearing from his mother for several days, her son broke into her home to find her naked body lying in a pool of blood in the bathroom. Police reports indicate the room having the strong odor of bleach. The medical examiner ruled that the 55-year-old woman suffered a stroke and hit her head as she fell to the floor. Gail's diaries were nowhere to be found. To this day, their location remains a mystery.

The case was finally scheduled for trial in early January of 2007. The judge postponed the trial to Monday, January 29, 2007.

On January 16, Sands filed a motion to dismiss his claims to his wife's life-insurance policy. Nine days later, on January 25, the judge granted Sands's motion to dismiss the case and ordered that Sands pay Gail's family court costs to the tune of $30,000.

With the trial set for Jan 29th, the insurance company wanted the federal judge to decide who should get the insurance money because the Jackson County Sheriff's Office named Lionel Sands as the primary suspect in the insured's death. Florida law says a person can't collect on an insurance policy if the person participated in the killing.

On Tuesday, January 30, 2007, the day after his re-scheduled trial was set to begin, Lionel Sands loaded his beige Crown Victoria with bleach, duct tape, plastic handcuffs, and latex gloves. He wore camouflage fatigues and combat boots and was disguised with a wig, heavy make-up, and a fake moustache.

Brown was sloppily dressed like the fellow from the Blues Brothers in a dark suit, tie, and hat. Sands carried on his person a .38-caliber Smith & Wesson revolver and another .38-caliber Taurus pistol. Brown had a .22-caliber handgun.

295

At approximately 4:45 p.m., the duo pulled up behind Mellie McDaniel on her way home from the grocery store. Mellie happened to be on her cell phone at the time, talking to her husband. She told her husband that a Crown Victoria followed her into the driveway of their home. At first, she thought the men were salesmen. Then the sheriff heard his wife scream.

At 4:49 Sheriff McDaniel radioed all officers in the area to respond to his residence. Deputy Mike Altman arrived two minutes later and called in the stolen license plates on Sands's vehicle. Moments later, the deputy's voice again came on the radio. He could be heard shouting "Get off me!"

At 4:53 Sheriff McDaniel, Deputy Joey Rabon and Deputy Billy Dozier arrived at the scene to see Sands duck behind the Crown Victoria. Sands drew his gun from behind the car and began firing at the officers. Dozens of shots rang out over the next few minutes.

When the smoke cleared, Sands lay dead with bullets puncturing his leg, underarm, neck, and stomach. Brown was shot twice in the stomach and died minutes later.

The sheriff found his wife, Mellie, and Deputy Altman's bodies lying side-by-side in front of Mellie's vehicle. Sands had shot the sheriff's wife in the back of the head, execution-style, as she knelt in the driveway. Deputy Mike Altman was shot in the face. When that facial shot did not kill him, Sands cold-bloodedly fired two more slugs in his back.

More than 100 law enforcement officers eventually settled upon the sheriff's home, that bitterly cold Tuesday evening in January. Officers canvassed the nearby wooded area for what they thought might be a third gunman. No such person was ever found. All evidence is indicative that Sands and Brown acted alone.

Inside Sands's Crown Victoria, officers found unsigned letters that Sands apparently planned to force the sheriff and his wife to sign. One of the letters was addressed to Gail's mother in St. Louis and written to appear as though it came from the sheriff. The note exonerated Sands of any and all wrongdoing in his wife's death.

Another letter, forged to appear as if written by Mellie McDaniel, alleges that her husband was involved in an outlandish scheme in which federal agents, state attorneys, and other government officials were assisting a criminal organization in distributing drugs and stolen goods. The letter states Sands was framed for Gail's death because he had uncovered the conspiracy.

On January 31, 2007, at 12:35 a.m., a search warrant was served on Lionel Sands's residence at 6295 Birchwood Road, Marianna, Florida. Additional copies of the unsigned letters were located in the bedroom office. More zip ties, latex gloves, ammunition, files, and a box containing police reports were taken into evidence as a result of the search.

Based upon investigative reports, Lionel Sands visited Mr. Neal's Wig Shop in Tallahassee on August 23, 2005. He was inquiring about a wig and moustache. The fitting process was completed, and Sands returned to pick up the hairpiece and moustache on October 25, 2005. Sands returned several times for subsequent adjustments and fittings.

Based upon investigative reports, a few weeks prior to the assault, Sands checked out a book from the Marianna Public Library, a novel titled The Hostage *by W.E.B Griffin; the book is about the kidnapping of a diplomat's wife and the murder of her husband. This was right before he filed the motion to dismiss his claims to his deceased wife's life insurance policies.*

***

The State Attorney's Office, 14th Judicial Circuit of Florida and the Florida Department of Law Enforcement were requested to investigate this horrific case. On September 24, 2007, this case was closed as resolved with use of force justified.

CHAPTER 66
A Day of Mourning:
February 3, 2007

John P. McDaniel III recalled the days following the loss of his beloved Mellie as that of living a nightmare. "You keep thinking you're going to wake up and everything be like it was before."

Thousands attended Mellie McDaniel's funeral. The site of a grieving husband, children, and grandchildren kissing their loved one goodbye for the final time was a sight that wrenched the hearts of all in attendance.

Fifty-one-year-old Mellie lay peacefully, wearing all white as her life was celebrated on Saturday morning, February 3, 2007, at Christian Center Church.

Rev. Jack Hollis said the Bible speaks to every condition and situation that humanity may encounter, and he chose Isaiah chapter 60, verses 18 to 21 that he felt fit how Mellie met her death. As Rev. Hollis read the scripture, he substituted Mellie's name because of her faith in Jesus Christ and that she was immediately in God's presence when the life went out of her.

"Violence shall no more be heard in Mellie's land, wasting nor destruction within her borders, but she shalt call her walls salvation, and her gates praise."

Rev. Hollis praised Mellie's work as a victim's advocate with the Florida Department of Children and Families and her character as a wife and mother and said she was "known most of all as an exceptional grandmother."

The family requested that Mellie McDaniel's funeral be short because a funeral for Deputy Altman was scheduled for later that afternoon in Freeport, Florida.

Funeral directors estimated that more than 1,500 people attended the funeral at the church just north of Marianna. Close to 2,000 came to her visitation.

The sight of hundreds of law enforcement officers was a good indicator of how much the law enforcement community was grieving the loss of one of their own.

Law enforcement vehicles also lined the eighteen-mile route to the Edenfield Family Cemetery near Altha, their lights flashing, keeping other traffic still as Mellie was taken to her final resting place.

The procession left Altha, Florida, and headed to Freeport, Florida, for the services of 42-year-old Deputy Mike Altman.

In Freeport, Florida, miles and miles of cars with red, white, and blue flashing lights were greeted by hundreds of people standing alongside Florida Highway 20.

More than 1,000 people attended Altman's funeral Saturday afternoon with at least 250 representatives from the Jackson County Sheriff's Office, including Sheriff John P. McDaniel who had just laid his wife to rest.

Rev. Helms said, "Altman was one of the kindest people you would ever meet. He was genuine and had a deep love of people and helping them any way he could."

Rev. Richard Butch Helms said he wouldn't be able to heal the wounds created by their loved one's passing, but that God would. Law enforcement was something that Altman had wanted to do much of his life. It came as no surprise to those that knew and loved him that Mike would give his life for someone else. He did not die in vain. He moved on to help others in heaven.

Johnny Mac said what took seven minutes for madmen to rip from us in the flesh will forever remain with us lovingly in spirit, in our hearts, and in our memories. Johnny prayed for guidance and the ability to do for Mellie's children and grandchildren as she would have wanted him to do in her place.

Johnny took a short trip back to the mountains where he and Mellie had laughed and played in the snow just a month earlier. He felt closer to her even though there was still a huge hole in his heart that would never be filled.

John said, "Often traumatic events remain ingrained in our hearts forever. The loss of loved ones throughout our lifetime cannot be avoided. It is our faith in God that keeps us moving forward in a positive direction."

CHAPTER 67
A Time for Change

On July 17, 2007, after seven terms of serving as sheriff to the people of Jackson County Florida, John P. McDaniel III announced he would not be seeking another term as sheriff. His last day in office would be November 4, 2008.

During the latter part of 2007, Phyllis Scott became ill. Phyllis was Johnny's first true love and the mother of his children. Phyllis required 24-hour care, and Johnny went to Blountstown every week to visit her and provide whatever she needed. They were able to talk, make amends, and be true friends again after so many years.

On November 16, 2007, at 65-years old, Phyllis left on angel wings to be with their son, Little John. She was laid to rest at the Alford City Cemetery. She left behind many who loved and adored her, including John, her daughter, Machelle, and her granddaughter, Meghan. Johnny held her hand when she drew her last breath.

On March 27, 2008, at a public fund raiser, John "Johnny Mac" McDaniel officially announced his candidacy for the District Five seat in the Florida House of Representatives.

Johnny Mac began his campaign for the House of Representatives on the platform of providing the conservative leadership needed in Tallahassee by strengthening the schools, curbing illegal immigration, defending the second amendment, and preserving traditional marriage. He would face Republican Brad Drake for the District Five seat which encompassed Jackson, Holmes, Okaloosa, Walton, and Washington Counties.

A month prior to the November primary, John announced that he would be leaving his post as sheriff at midnight on the night of November 4, 2008.

He requested Governor Charlie Crist to authorize the winner of the sheriff's race to take over immediately.

November 4, 2008, quickly approached. Voters went to the polls to select the candidates of their choice in both local and state elections.

The District Five State Representative Seat was a hard-fought battle. Republican Brad Drake defeated Democrat John P. "Johnny Mac" McDaniel III. Drake carried 59.6%. Johnny Mac carried his home county of Jackson and sister county of Washington, but they were not enough to overcome the defeat in the largest county of Okaloosa.

The local sheriff's race in Jackson County saw a face-off between Democrat Lou Roberts (prior Marianna Police Chief) and Republican Jim Peacock. Roberts took 57.8%to Peacock's 36.3%.

The McDaniel administration had officially ended after twenty-eight years. Jackson County Sheriff Lou Roberts inherited an extremely efficient and competent department.

CHAPTER 68
"The Rest of the Story"

John McDaniel needed some time to think and prepare for his retirement. After losing his bid for the District Five representative seat, he knew his days had to be filled with something meaningful. He was still grieving the loss of his wife and the mental exhaustion from the civil suit and legal battles that followed left him totally spent.

John decided to take another trip to the mountains to reflect and find himself again. He was faced with a major lifestyle change after years of trying to be everything to everybody.

During his absence, the results of the civil suit relating to the murder of his wife at the hands of Lionel Sands in January of 2007 had been made public with no verification or input from him. The results were publicized in such a manner as to allude to the fact that John McDaniel had received and kept all of the settlements and insurance funds paid due to the 2007 tragedy.

John McDaniel is a very private man when it comes to personal matters, but he shared the rest of the story.

Below is the full perspective of the net financial outcome to the four families that were traumatized and forever damaged by the tragic event—the Sands Family, the Altman Family, Mellie's Family, and the McDaniel Family.

The Altman Estate received $647,000 from the workman's compensation policy/state law officer policy.

The Sands/Heaps Estate received money for the three policies on Gail Sands—$600,000. (Some and perhaps all three policies were double indemnity. Total payments could have been $800,000).

The McDaniel Estate received Mellie's workman's comp policy at $110,000, and the estate value of Sands's farm & assets at $500,000. Of this, $540,000 was deeded and transferred from McDaniel to Crumpler/Edenfield Estate (Mellie's Children).

The Sands/Heaps Estate, which is the family of Gail Sands who was allegedly murdered by her husband in their swimming pool, received insurance settlement payments for three policies—$200,000, $100,000, and $100,000. At least one of these policies was a double indemnity policy, so the total paid was at least $500,000 and could have been as much as $800,000. They also received $50,000 from McDaniel for payment of accrued legal fees as terms for the settlement of the pending civil suit against the Sands Estate by McDaniel. Because they had received these payments and did not want to engage in a court battle over the wrongful death suit, their lawyer approached McDaniel with an offer to settle the suit by yielding all the remaining assets of Lionel Sands.

The Altman Estate, which was Deputy Mike Altman's widow and children, received payments from the workman's compensation program and from the state uniformed officer insurance benefit policy totaling $674,000. Some additional funds were realized through public donations.

The McDaniel Estate received workman's compensation benefits of $110,000 for the death of Mellie and received the assets of Lionel Sands which included the farm which was valued at $500,000. Upon receipt of these funds, John P. McDaniel immediately gifted the monies and transferred the deed to the surviving children of Mellie McDaniel. The McDaniel Estate only kept enough funds to cover funeral expenses and pay some existing family debts. All the rest of the funds were given to the children of Mellie. In total, the McDaniel Estate kept no funds after these payments were settled, and in fact, has loaned the children approximately $60,000 (which includes the $50,000 Sands settlement payment)

The Crumpler/Edenfield Estate, which is the children from Mellie from her previous marriage, received properties and funds totaling almost $600,000 in value. McDaniel is happy they have the farm and a comfortable living.

Tara is Johnny's step-daughter and her oldest child is Erika whose children are Brett, Sterling, and Waylon. He loves them like they were his own children.

CHAPTER 69
Apple of Daddy's Eye

Machelle McDaniel, John's oldest child was born May 2, 1962. She was, needless to say, the apple of her daddy's eye. When she was delivered at the hospital, the nurse that helped Phyllis was a Mrs. Hebb, a wonderful, wonderful lady. Johnny and Phyllis left the hospital with their precious baby girl a couple of days later.

They first went to Grandma at the old store. That was Johnny's grandmother and baby Machelle's great grandmother.

Phyllis was holding the baby and Grandmamma Grant unwrapped the baby's feet and got those feet and put them up to her mouth and kissed and blessed them. Johnny never, never forgot how his grandmamma kissed his baby's feet.

Now Grandma Grant loved anything and everything there was—every stray, every throw away...just everything.

John and Phyllis lived at 230 W. Lafayette Street, Marianna, across from where Pizza Hut is now when they had Machelle. They rented a house from a man named, H. H. Blount. Rent was $32.50 a month, and they had to work tooth and toenail to pay it. They had a little driveway, and right behind the house was an old makeshift car garage.

When they brought Machelle home, her mother was a high-strung woman. She had a hard time adapting to having a child in the house with them. She was worried, nervous, and upset. Johnny would take Machelle when Phyllis was upset and cradle her in his arms, sitting down in his chair. Johnny put her in his lap and swung his legs back and forth, and she would go to sleep every time.

That upset Phyllis. It upset her because Johnny was doing something that she hadn't been able to do, but it was only because she was so tense. There was nothing wrong with Phyllis, but the baby could sense it.

They got a baby bed and put it in their two-bedroom house. They set that baby bed so that whenever she cried, they could look right down the hallway. There was one bathroom and two bedrooms. The hallway wasn't twenty feet away from them. If the baby moved, they knew it, and Phyllis and Johnny took turns getting up with the baby.

Later, as Machelle got to where she could stand up, she would stand up in the baby bed and bounce up and down to get their attention. If it was in the middle of the night, she knew her daddy would come in there and get her and bring her to sleep with him and her momma.

As she got a little older, she wore beautiful little dresses. She was so pretty to her daddy and beautiful just like her momma.

Later, she wanted a sack swing, so Johnny made one out of a burlap sack filled with straw. He tied a rope around it and hung it up so Machelle could swing on it.

Well, one time when Machelle was really little, just old enough to hold on, he took her out there to swing a little bit. She would open and close her little hands when she wanted something, so Johnny took her out there to swing. He put her on the sack swing and swung her a little bit, and she went to screaming and hollering. Johnny grabbed her and picked her up. There was a wasp nest inside that sack, and they were eating up her little legs. That like to have killed Johnny.

Over the years, they left there and moved to several places before coming back in 1972. Machelle would have been nine years old. They moved to a house in Dogwood Heights.

Phyllis's momma always raised Boston Bull Pups, so there wasn't anything Johnny could do except to get one for his wife and daughter. When they were living in Lantana, Florida, they were practically broke, but Phyllis made a ham one Sunday before they left for Sunday School. When they returned, that little Boston Bull Puppy was sitting up in the middle of the table, eating the ham.

Johnny grabbed that puppy and tossed. It just broke Machelle's heart. She couldn't stand that her daddy was that mean a man. She didn't understand how broke they were and that there was nothing else for them to eat and that dog had eaten their dinner.

Machelle loved dogs. When they lived in Ft. Walton, they had them over there. When John and Phyllis came back to Marianna, they had them there too. Little John had come along by then.

Johnny recalled, "We had a tree swing that I had put up in a big ol' oak tree with a rope and a sack swing next to it. At the end of the sack swing, a rope hung down, and it would just about touch the ground. Those little ol' Boston Bull Pups would grab that rope and swing with those young'uns. They would swing from one end to the other up high, and those pups would just latch on and hold on."

In 1972, when they came back and bought the house in Dogwood Heights, Johnny's daddy had come back into their lives and helped him build a big porch off the back of their house next to his and Phyllis's bedroom. They could go out there in the afternoon, through the sliding glass doors, and just relax. It was so beautiful. That was one of the nicest houses Johnny had ever lived in, and that was where he was proud to have raised their children. Next door to them was Sid and Judy Riley with their children.

Across the road was one of the best friends Johnny had ever had in his life, Sgt. Roy Hutto with the Florida

Highway Patrol. He had two boys, Mark and Mike. It was Roy, Libby, Mark, and Mike. They would walk the neighborhoods at Christmas and sing Christmas carols.

On up the street was another dear friend, I've been friends with all my life, Gary Jackson and his children. So we had just a family affair of people in Dogwood Heights, so that is where we raised our children.

Johnny would sit in the floor in the late evening with John on one arm and Machelle on the other arm, just hugging them young'uns and watching TV. It was every night routine. After they had dinner, they watched TV, whether it be Gunsmoke, Bonanza, or Andy Griffith.

Phyllis began to get really apprehensive and had a lot of problems. She became totally unhappy with everything. She wanted a divorce. She said she couldn't stand it anymore; she had all she could take. Johnny was working all the time as chief deputy for Ronny Craven. Every time that phone would ring and something bad happened, Johnny was out the door because he thought that was what he was supposed to do.

It took a toll on their marriage because she didn't feel like she was number one or that the children were number one. She felt like the sheriff's department was number one, and she resented it. She told Johnny she wanted him to move out, so he did.

Johnny's momma had a little house down the lane from his grandma and granddaddy's old place. It was one that Mr. Tipton had lived in. Lord knows it was just a thrown-up old house, but it had a roof on it, and Johnny could live there. Johnny kept trying to work things out with Phyllis, but it just didn't work out.

Herman Laramore was Johnny's attorney at that time. He was an assistant public defender and practiced law. Herman had always been one of the best friends Johnny ever had. Bless his heart, he knew Johnny didn't have any money, so he didn't charge him and represented him anyway.

About three months after the divorce, Phyllis had a lot of problems with Little John. He had been acting up and showing out. That would have been in 1976, so he would have been 11 years old.

Phyllis called Johnny and said, "You come out to the house right now."

Johnny asked what was wrong and she said, "You just come out here right now."

Johnny said okay and headed to the house in Dogwood Heights. He got there, and she said, "I want you to take him and get him out of here right now. He's disrupted everything in this house."

Little John had already gotten his stuff and loaded it up in the car, he was ready to go. John thought, "Lord have mercy." He tried to work it out. Then Machelle said, "Daddy, I want to go too."

Johnny said, "Baby, somebody has got to stay here and look after your momma. She's just having some problems."

Machelle said, "No, Daddy, I want to go too. If John is gonna go, I want to go."

Johnny finally convinced Machelle that she needed to stay with her momma and he and Little John left, but about three or four weeks later, Phyllis called and said, "I want you to come back over here and take her and all these clothes out of here. I can't stand these children anymore. I can't cope with it."

Again, it was nothing but her nerves. She just had a nerve problem. She really loved the children. They didn't know it at that time, but she was eaten up with cancer. They knew something wasn't right.

Johnny loaded Machelle up, and he, Machelle, and Little John moved off to that ungodly old house that his mother owned.

Then Phyllis decided she was going to go live with her brother Davis, out in Arizona.

Johnny recalled, "She said she wasn't going to let us live in the house that we had lived in as a family with another woman. We would have to sell it. The young'uns could have the furniture, but the house would have to be disposed of by sale."

So, they did. When she moved to Arizona with her brother, Johnny bought another house in Dogwood Heights which was a foreclosure.

He let the young'uns pick what they wanted, but he made them work. They had to work to clean up the mess that was there. They worked like Trojans to get that house to where they could live in it. They closed in a carport and made a den out of it. Johnny made John and Machelle each a room, letting them pick their colors and carpet. They redid the kitchen, cabinets and all. The three of them made a wonderful home out of it.

We were at the house one evening and Johnny had just bought the groceries, picking up the things he had to have to fix for dinner for the young'uns.

Machelle said, "Daddy, we got to go to the grocery store."

Johnny said, "Hell, we just got back from the grocery store."

"Daddy, we got to go back to the grocery store."

"What in the hell did I forget? I know I bought the cereal ya'll want, the milk, the cheese, lima beans, all that kind of stuff…"

Then Johnny thought, "Holy mackerel; that child is trying to tell me something I ain't got sense enough to understand."

Well, they drove back to the store so Machelle could get the feminine products she needed. Johnny gave her cash money so she could go in and go shopping. That's how Machelle made her daddy grow up.

Machelle was always bossy as hell with Little John and Johnny. She would say, "Daddy, we want to do this…and we want to do that…." Johnny would just say, "Yes, ma'am." He let her be the lady of the house, and he and Little John tried their best to be the men of the house. They made it work.

Machelle turned sixteen in that house, turned of age, and graduated high school.

When she turned sixteen, Johnny was working at Peacock Motor Company selling cars. He had been able to save up enough to buy a '67 Mustang from a fellow by the name of McDonald. He had bought it new, driven it, and brought it back with a blown engine.

Johnny took that car and pulled the engine. The boys at Peacock helped him. He took the hood off of it, scrubbed it, rebuilt the engine and transmission, and redid the inside so that when Machelle turned sixteen, he handed her keys to a red '67 Mustang.

Johnny fondly remembered, "Now you talk about a young'un loving her car. She had her car. That was *her* car."

When she left Johnny, all grown up, married, and moved to Tallahassee, she still had that car—her '67 red Mustang. It had an AM/FM radio with automatic transmission and air conditioning. Very few of them had that in them.

Early one morning, she plowed right into the back end of a vehicle up at the intersection of Highway 71 south and 90 across from Gary Jackson's old service station. She bent the hood on it, but Johnny fixed it back up.

To this day, Machelle has been like a mother hen to Johnny. She has filled in as a boss lady, telling him what to do when there was a void with a woman in Johnny's life. But Johnny took it like whatever she said was usually the right thing, and he was in the wrong. So he would just say, "Yes ma'am. Yes ma'am, okay."

One time, Machelle got a little too far over in Johnny's business, and he went over to Tallahassee and said, "Come on, little lady....Let's go."

They drove down onto the interstate a little way and turned around and came back. But on the way, she was just eating on Johnny's ass, telling him the things he was doing wrong—this and that and the other. He listened, not fussing at his daughter, but they got to a point and he said, "Let me say something. You've had your say, right."

"Yes, sir," Machelle replied.

"Are you through?" he asked.

"Well, yes sir."

"Okay, let me tell you one damn thing. I'm the daddy, and you're the daughter, and you're not going to tell me anymore what I am going to do and what I'm not going to do. I've let this thing go as far as I'm going to let it go. So you better show me some respect."

Well, son, that was like Johnny had slapped her in the face. She learned a lesson that day. She grew up a lot more. So, if she has anything she wants to say today, she very *diplomatically* tells Johnny what he is going to do and what he isn't going to do.

Johnny said, "But that's Machelle. Machelle knows how to do the working her daddy bit."

Machelle had one child, Meghan, who honest to God, was cloned by her mother or vice-versa. Meghan is her mother made over. Johnny took baby pictures of Machelle and presented them to her and said look at these Christmas pictures. She said, "That's mine, but wait. I didn't have that dress."

"No, that's your daughter Meghan's dress. That's how much ya'll look alike. You couldn't even tell your own daughter from you. Bless your heart, I love you so much."

CHAPTER 70
The Apple Doesn't Fall Too Far from the Tree

Now, the apple that doesn't fall far from the tree would be Johnny Mac's son, Little John.

On the 12th day of October in 1965, God blessed Johnny and Phyllis with a baby boy. Johnny was in a dove field in Foley, Alabama, shooting doves when his wife went to the hospital and had Little John. She was as mad as fire at him about that one.

He didn't know she was going to have the baby that soon, so he went dove hunting with Ray Mixon and a few others. But it didn't take him long to drive from Pensacola, to Marianna, where Little John was born.

Well, any man wants a child he can give his name to, so when John was born, there was only one way to go... John Perry McDaniel IV.

Needless to say, Johnny would have loved to have seen it go to the fifth and the sixth, but it didn't happen that way.

Little John was born and Lord have mercy, when he got old enough to stand up in Johnny's old Dodge truck, he'd stand and his father would put his arm across Little John so if he had to put on brakes quickly, it wouldn't throw him into the dash.

As Little John got a little older, he loved to go to the dump. They had a city dump where his dad would load up the garbage once a week in the back of the truck to dispose of it. There was no waste management back in those days.

Johnny had constantly wanted his son to be the roughest, toughest, best shooting, straightest shooting little man there ever was, so he took pride in trying to make him tough as hell, which might have been a mistake.

Johnny has a picture of Little John when he was about three years old, wearing cowboy boots, blue jeans with a big buckle, a cowboy shirt, and cowboy hat. He was standing in front of a mud hole. Johnny took the picture when Little John's cousin Scott from Panama City was visiting in Gainesville. The two little boys got into that mud hole, stomping and carrying on. They ruined their cowboy boots, clothes, and all.

Annette, Scott's momma, gave Johnny hell about what he had allowed those boys to do. But Johnny wanted to let them be boys. It was Little John's birthday, and he let them do what they wanted to do.

They came to Marianna and always ended up going to the dump. Well, when Little John got old enough, he wanted to drive the truck.

Johnny said, "Jesus Christ, son, you can't even see over the steering wheel."

"I can do it. I can do it. I can drive it," Little John told his daddy.

Johnny said okay and Little John got under the wheel. The dump was over by the old airbase. Johnny would get out and come around to the side of the truck and let Little John sit there and try to drive.

That was a sight; he would look out from under the spokes on the steering wheel and try to make it down the hill. He learned to drive when he wasn't but twelve years old. Little John also liked to hunt. Johnny bought him a little .22 rifle, and they put that in the truck when we went to the dump.

They would back the truck up where the garbage was dumped, and Johnny would pick up bottles and throw them in the air for Little John to shoot. Well, Johnny had to go to a shotgun so Little John could hit them. That little rascal got to where he could hit them really well. As he got a little older, two or three years later, he would get up there in the seat of the truck when Johnny was

320

throwing the garbage out of the back, and he would take off and leave Johnny standing there.

"John, get your ass back here," Johnny yelled.

Little John would laugh and start backing up a little bit really slowly. As soon as Johnny would walk toward the truck, Little John would take off again.

"I'm gonna wear your ass out boy."

Little John would just laugh harder. It tickled him. They had a father and son wonderful time with him driving off and leaving his daddy at the garbage dump in that old truck.

Later on, Little John went thru the normal growing pains. Johnny bought him an M80 motorcycle when he was working at Peacock Motor Company. Little John was not allowed to get on the paved road with that motorcycle, but he was getting on Highway 71 south of Dogwood Heights toward Highway 90. One of the deputies stopped him, and Johnny got a call at Peacock Motor Company while he was at work, busy with a customer.

The deputy said, "Johnny Mac, you got a son named John?"

"Yes sir, I do."

"Does he have a motorcycle?"

"Oh, hell...yes he does."

"Well, I just caught him riding his motorcycle toward Highway 90."

"God almighty..."

The Deputy said, "Whoa, whoa, wait a minute....Let me tell you something. Now, he wasn't riding it on the highway. He was in the ditch riding it. He's been riding it down the ditches, jumping the culverts and just sailing over them."

"Deputy... I tell you what you do. You get his butt off that motorcycle, and you make him push it all the way back to the house, and you follow him if you don't mind. And make sure that he shuts it down."

Johnny said, "Little John pushed that motorcycle back to the house, and he knew that I would be home to deal with him as soon as I got home from work."

Little John wrote him out a note saying that he was running away from home. "Daddy, I know you will kill me when you get home, and I don't won't you to go to prison for killing me, so I'm running away from home."

Johnny had to laugh. He got Little John from the neighbors and brought him home.

Well, Little John graduated from the motorcycle to a car. Johnny found a 1972 Nova, six-cylinder standard shift car. He thought he could keep Little John slowed down in that little six-cylinder car. He had it painted bronze, all fixed up; it looked good.

"I gave it to him for his sixteenth birthday. He wouldn't have it....He had to have a damn pick-up truck."

Johnny managed to work it out and trade that Nova for a '72 Chevrolet pick-up truck.

Now, Little John tore up everything he had. Johnny had a picture of him with the gray-colored pick-up at Turner's Landing. He was on the other side of the creek headed back toward the bank when his friends took the picture. Johnny found that picture and called to him. "Get your ass in here. What in the hell is wrong with you? What was you doing with that truck out there in the middle of the damn creek?"

"Daddy, it wanted a drink of water."

"I'll kill you boy."

Well, Little John wrecked that one, and we got another one. Johnny got an old '69-'70 Chevrolet step-side pick-up from Rex Toole. Little John loved that thing. He went through several trucks before he became a grown man and left home. He lived down in Cypress for a while with his friends, Jim Dunnaway and Steve Crumper before he got married.

Johnny said, "Carole Smith McDaniel. A man has never had a daughter-in-law as good as Carole. Johnny loved her then and loves her to this day."

Well, Little John developed his problem with alcohol.

Little John and Johnny talked. They loved each other, but Little John resented the fact that his daddy was having him picked up.

He became a victim of cirrhosis of the liver. They took him to Shans Teaching Hospital and did everything they could to try and save their son, but nothing worked.

The saddest thing in Johnny's life happened the few last moments that Little John was alive. Johnny stayed at the hospital in Tallahassee with him. His wife never left his side.

Johnny was sitting there holding one hand, and Carol was holding the other one when John took his last breath on June 22, 2004.

Johnny had to reach up and close his eyes. He fought to the end, taking that last breath.

CHAPTER 71
Precious Memories

Along the way, there have been some very special ladies in Johnny Mac's life. He has not been able to pick up and start his life again after losing Mellie. It's just not there, and not what he wants to do.

Johnny loves his daughter, Machelle, so very much as well as his precious granddaughter, Meghan. Johnny walked Meghan down the aisle, which turned out to be a white sandy beach on September 26, 2009, when she married Gary Capps, Jr.

Meghan gave birth to Kaden John Capps on September 7, 2012, and Kyler Ray Capps on December 28, 2016. Johnny loves his two great grandsons very much. They each are a big part of his life, and his heart.

It is great to have a life like Johnny has had, to be blessed with the wonderful people who may have visited for a brief period and been unable to stay. He can't say enough about the wonderful ladies that have been a part of his life. He thanks each and every one of them for everything that they have done with and for him during those periods of time. He loves every one of them in his heart to this day.

At his 50th class reunion somebody said, "Johnny, how many times you been married?"

"I don't know. How many times you been married?"

His classmate said, "I ain't been married but one time."

Johnny said, "Well, you just told me you ain't man enough to make but one woman love you, and I made five love me!"

As it stands now, Johnny has two in spirit and three exes. "They are still all my friends, and they are all good Christian Women."

On Christmas Eve, December 24, 2014, Johnny Mac went to be by Machelle's side. Machelle was married to Leon County Sheriff Larry Campbell on July 4, 2006. They married in the Cayman Islands and chose that date as it was Machelle's great grandparents', Laura Belle and James W. Grant's, wedding anniversary date at well.

Leon County's longtime sheriff, Larry Campbell, known for his tough exterior, tender heart, and larger-than-life personality, died Wednesday, December 24, 2014 at Tallahassee Memorial HealthCare.

Campbell, 72, had been battling cancer off and on since 2007 when doctors found a tumor on his right lung. He successfully underwent surgery, but the cancer returned in 2013, prompting more surgery along with chemotherapy and radiation.

Campbell transitioned successfully from a bygone time in law enforcement to the modern age. Campbell was a former United States Marine with more than fifty years of law-enforcement experience. He dedicated his life to protecting and serving Florida, especially the Leon County Community. Johnny Mac was there for Machelle but felt a personal loss as well. He and Larry had worked together for many years, and John considered him a very good friend as well as a supreme leader in the law enforcement community.

In 2015, Machelle took her father to the actual last Frontier. They went to Alaska. Precious memories were made between daughter and father on the boat and riding the train, admiring the beautiful countryside.

CHAPTER 72

Retirement

After all the years that Johnny worked at the sheriff's department, retirement and monthly income were never the things that concerned him on a day to day basis. Needless to say, he wanted to make enough money to pay his bills and keep his family at a certain level in the community.

Those are things we all desire to do, and the people of Jackson County allowed those things to happen for Johnny Mac. With that being said, they paid him to go do things he loved to do. He loved people and doing things for people. He loved the self-satisfaction of knowing he did something for someone. He took pride in the fact that if you called him and it was important enough for you to call, he would call you back and would do everything he could to satisfy what you asked him to do for you. The satisfaction he got was self-satisfaction. It made him feel good to help people, period.

What little bit of teaching he could do, he tried to instill in other people the values he was raised with from his momma, his granddaddy, and his friends. All those people around him helped mold him. Lord have mercy, his football coach, Harry Howell, was an icon to Johnny. Charley Cox, George Riley—he could name them on and on. They were more than just coaches. They were friends. They were mentors. They were people that helped make him what he is today.

And that goes for his neighbors, grandmamma, granddaddy, brothers, sisters, coaches, teachers— Johnny loves them all. He loves the people of Jackson County, one and all. He doesn't leave a single one out.

Johnny is color blind when it comes to loving people. There is a woman he calls his black momma. She calls and checks on him, and he calls and checks on her.

Johnny called her. "Hey, momma."

She knew his momma died, and she said, "I'm your momma now."

Bless her heart. Her name is Floy Portee. Johnny love's Cookie. That's what her friends call her.

Johnny never planned for retirement. His predecessors made it available. Wonderful people helped set programs up, and Johnny is proud of what he receives.

Johnny retired the same day as a dear, dear friend of his, Earl Cloud. Earl and Johnny worked together from the Ronny Craven administration back to the John McDaniel administration. He had his own way of doing things, but Johnny always loved him and admired the way he went about doing the things he did. Earl Cloud was probably one of the best people he has ever known.

It was in the cards that Earl didn't get to live that long and enjoy his retirement. He passed away, leaving a wonderful family, and Johnny still loves them very, very much.

John Dennis was another great friend who was always there for him. He retired when the McDaniel Administration ended as well.

He loved all of his employees. They made him what he is today, what he was yesterday, and what he will be tomorrow.

Now, at retirement at first, Johnny was like a duck out of water. He just wanted to flit around everywhere. That wore off pretty quickly. He missed being involved, seeing people every day, people saying "Hey sheriff, how are you?" He loved the honor of being called sheriff.

Johnny said, "After a while, it sort of died down, and I slowed down. I'm getting a few years on me. I'll be 77 in 2017. My old joints don't work the way they are supposed to, and I don't do a whole lot of anything except working on the farm, some wood working, and making up a few of my special recipes for benefits."

He has in the past gotten miserable by being lonely, but if he gets lonely, he gets in one of his vehicles, rides up town, and goes to McDonald's, Hardee's, or Wendy's. He always runs into some of the most wonderful people in the world, so he can't get lonely too long. It's when he's at home and sits around by himself that he gets lonely. But he's glad to be above ground and so thankful to Jesus Christ for being his Savior and dying for his sins.

"Lord, have mercy, I thank him every day for everything I have, at least twice a day, including my health, my family, and the loves I've had in my life."

People…he misses the people. Misses being involved. When he sees an ambulance go by, a firetruck go by, or a deputy go by, he still wants to pick the phone up and say, "What's going on. What's going on?" But he doesn't do that because he doesn't want to disturb anyone.

Retirement is wonderful. It gives him time to do the things he wants to do. He has more to do than he can get done.

Especially at the pace he travels today. When he was young and first elected as sheriff, he would park his car up on Market Street. He could go up those steps and do the t-berry shuffle. He would get that next set of stairs which was about eight steps. He would do the same on those and go right on in the office. Now he has to hold the handrail to get up the suckers.

"Times have changed. It's all changed. Time has changed all of us. The most disappointing thing in life is I can't think of a great deal of things that have happened to me that weren't self-induced. Disappointing times was not solving some of the murders we had during the 28 years I was Sheriff in Jackson County. Not being able to go to those families and provide closures to the victims of crimes. It bothered me then, and it bothers me now. I wish I had time to get involved, have someone assigned to me, and just work, study those cases again. But you know, you see on TV, the first 48 hours. When you get past the first 48 hours, it gets harder and harder."

"When you add some years, it's even worse than that. Disappointment is in not being able to solve the most heinous crimes we had—which was murder—and not being able to provide closure to the families I loved so dearly. Those are the things that bother me to this day."

Johnny can't talk about his life without talking about every person that ever worked for him and with him. He learned from them and loved all his employees. They were family, prayed together, hurt together, and had joyous times together. Whatever it was, they were and still are family. They worked for the public. That was their job, to serve the people.

Epilogue

*In the early 1940's, this little boy, was staying with his
granddaddy as he often did.
He was outside shooting marbles in a dirt yard when an
old Model-A car pulled up.
A big, tall man with a Stetson hat pulled up to the house
and walked over to the little boy's granddaddy and
said...
"Hello there, Mr. Jim. How are you doing?"
The granddaddy spoke to him and then told the little boy
to go over and play, that he had some grown-up talk to
do.
Well, in those times, young'uns didn't sit around where
adults were, and they didn't listen to adult conversations.
As soon as the conversation was over, the little boy ran
over to his granddaddy and said, "Who was that man?"
The granddaddy was silent for a moment. Then he said,
"Son...Son, that's the HIGH SHERIFF."
The little boy asked, "What is **the high sheriff?** ... I don't
know what that is."
The granddaddy sat there for a minute longer, thinking,
and then he said,
"The high sheriff is...
EVERYTHING TO EVERYBODY."*
As that little boy, John Perry McDaniel III never forgot
that. Honest to God, that is what the sheriff's job is—
everything to everybody.

John Perry McDaniel III

DEDICATION
Commemorative Corner:
(From Those Who Know Him Best)

Upcoming are contributions from some of the people closest to John Perry McDaniel III.

Immediate family is first and then alphabetical by last name of contributor.

From the "Apple of His Eye"
Machelle McDaniel Campbell
Daughter of John P. McDaniel III

The earliest things I remember about my dad are him working, always. I watched in absolute amazement as he dug and chopped at the huge pine root in our front yard in Pensacola. He would go out and dig and dig and chop even if it was raining. It took him a couple weekends, but he never gave up. Dad loved music, so he had this old reel to reel box thing that he played Engelbert Humperdinck and many more of that era. We would lie on the floor with headsets and just listen to him for hours. There is a lot of mischief in my dad. He loved to play pranks on us or us on him. We always had some mess going. One Halloween, Dad helped us make our costumes—me a ghost and John a hobo. Dad being Dad was always hands on and took part in all things we did. Dad worked hard and long, but he played the same way. He was always a glass half full kind of man. No matter what came up in life, he could always find a way to see something good. While we did not always live in Marianna, we traveled back home often. While on the road home, if we (I) saw a dead animal on the highway, I would always ask him to call Dr. Doolittle to come help them. When we arrived at my grandparents', he always placed that call. I have no idea who he called, but as a child, I was content knowing someone was coming to the rescue.

We moved to West Palm Beach, a million miles away, but Dad made it fun for us again. We spent just about every Saturday or Sunday at the beach with him. The funny redneck came out in him again, even there. Dad liked to wear his dark dress socks with his Jesus sandals—our words and description of his sandals that looked like rubber tires on the bottom. Lord, I can still see those things. He also wore boxers, and it seemed half the time his boxers were longer than his shorts. As his children, we did have a lot of his humor, so he was picked on *a lot* by us when he practiced those traits.

We would soon move back to Marianna for the last time. I would start middle school while my brother was still in elementary school. Moving back home and my dad taking a job with the Jackson County Sheriff's Office changed everything for us. Dad worked even more and was gone more, but he was still a hands-on dad. Just not so much of the time. This move created hard times for Dad and Mom and eventually for the family. We went through several hard years then they divorced and things changed again. I moved in with Dad. John lived on and off with Mom. I know girls normally live with their mom, but Dad was at least staying in Marianna as I was starting high school soon and wanted to stay with my school friends. Dad was also very strict *but fair* about what his daughter could and could not do and when. As far as I know, I never felt like he did not listen to my view then do what he was going to do anyway. I did put him to the test several times. For a while we lived in my great grandmother's house (if you can call it that). Most of the glass panes were out, and there was only one gas heater in the living room. I think mostly they were old rental houses they had. That winter, I slept with six quilts on my bed to stay warm. Dad worked such weird hours that I would get off the school bus at my grandmother's, and he picked me up whenever he finished. The house next to ours was just about as bad, but one of the family friends was becoming a bachelor again and stayed there a short time. As luck would have things, this family friend would get in on Dad's pranks (big mistake). One Saturday morning, I found a water hose and decided to wake him up, so I put the hose on full blast and soaked him and the bed and anything else in sight. I bet he chased me a mile, and I did *run*! Dad was always cool that way. As long as you showed respect and owned up to your mistakes, things were good.

During the time, he was working for the Chevrolet dealership because he was waiting on his time to run for sheriff, my father thought it would be cool to drive a jeep with no top!!!! Well, this is not something you should do when your high school daughter has just spent hours getting ready for school—hair, makeup, etc. So, on one morning getting ready for him to drop me off at school, I took a large brown bag and cut out eye holes and wore this all the way to school. Now, you would think that most dads would be embarrassed. No, not him. He just laughed and continued to drive the damn jeep. So, another lesson learned. Once Dad was elected sheriff, things changed again. Our family grew by adding all the deputies and anyone else that might think we needed corrections in our choices. Since high school and middle school kids are not known for making the best decisions, it seemed everyone looked out for us. UGH!!!

Dad handled his children like a pro. After growing up and asking him about things and why, it all makes sense now how he could make us learn from mistakes and not push us away so that we did not talk to him about what might be going on in our world. One weekend, my girlfriends wanted to spend the night at my house. Okay, cool. If your dad is sheriff, that is usually the last place high schoolers want to be. We made our plan and all go out and agree to meet back at my house at the appropriate time. Well, I was there, but no one else showed up. About 11:30, Dad made me call their parents to make them aware they were not staying at my house. Well, that really made me popular with the girls. But lesson learned. I also thought one time it would be cool to skip classes in my senior year to go skiing. Well, I had so much fun that I took that attitude for three days in a row. Bad things happen when you never missed school three days in a row before. Lesson learned. I never skipped again and was not allowed on senior skip day. I had already used my time.

I worked at McDonald's while in high school along with most of the kids in Marianna. I had to close most nights which meant I had to go straight home after work. I was really missing going out with my friends, but as Dad said, "You have a car, and if you wanted to make it move, you would work for the gas that makes it move." So, I worked. After school and all summer too. I do not think I ever went on spring break. I worked. Back to the lesson again. I decided to run out to circle D ranch where all my friends were one night. Well, I got caught up in the activities and time flew, which meant I was late getting back to my car at Mac D's. I jumped in and tried to fire it up to speed home. No luck. It wouldn't start. About that time, Dad pulls up with my distributor cap in his hand. TROUBLE AGAIN! Dad 500 plus; Machelle 0.

I never really got into much trouble—just full of fun mischief like my dad. Dad has always been there for me as long as I am willing to listen, tell the truth, and accept the consequences of my actions. We were taught that we put our pants on one leg at a time just like everyone else. We are no better or worse than the person next to us, and you can do anything if you work hard.

"My Older Brother"
William Wayne McDaniel
Brother of John P. McDaniel III

My "Older Brother" Johnny Mac was and always will be an inspiration to my children and me. During the first 12 years of my life he was the only male example I had to look up to. He taught me a lot and between Mama, Johnny and our older sister, Iris, I received all the love and caring that a young child needed.

My mother loved us all dearly, but Johnny had a real special place in her heart, because he was always into something that made her happy. From bring home skunks and small alligators to stray dogs, he was always trying to entertain us and most specially Mama.

Johnny frequently had a disabled car in our side yard with the engine and numerous other parts on the side porch of the house. Our Uncle Caleb once said Johnny was good at taking a car apart, but not real great at putting them back together again. Mother seemed to be okay with him doing that, but when I tried it all hell broke out. I was moved to the barn to do my auto repair. When I questioned her about that she said Johnny needed the side porch to do his auto work back then and I could use the work area in the barn.

We always knew when Johnny was coming home to have lunch with the family Mother would make two Lemon pies and explain to us that one was for us, but the other one was for Johnny.

His childhood was not the "Leave it to Beaver" type; it was full of hurt and broken promises by our father. Our mother always said that we needed to be ourselves and not try and follow in anyone else footsteps. That is what my "Older Brother" did and I am very proud of him for all his accomplishments. He has suffered greatly in his personnel life and risen above it to be a leader and a kind loving person.

The reason I use the term "Old Brother" when speaking of him is because he is always introducing me to people as his "Older Brother" as a joke I hope.

Johnny will always be the best brother and friend that a younger brother can have and I will always look up to him no matter what the future brings us.

Your Younger Brother
William Wayne McDaniel

"The Baby Sister"
Lucinda Ruth Clark
"Ode to my Big Brother"

What do you say about a person that is your big brother, mentor, hero, and your friend? I would say as a big brother, he met all of the needs in my life.

As a person, he was a giver and a defender of things he felt were right—something taught to us by our mother. He is my oldest brother and in our family, when things change like a loss of a parent, he takes the reins and moves into that position as he did with me when we lost our beloved mother.

Being the baby of the family, I got to take in most things around me, and one of the reasons I chose my profession in my life was his influence.

Watching him run for sheriff, I got to learn to hate fried fish and cheese grits as that seemed to be the campaign food of choice of all politicians of Jackson County. And Mudslinging, which I never understood why people would lower themselves to the horrible standard. But my big brother rose above it and seemed to keep his honor. I, being the hot-headed baby, wanted to punch a few people out and make them understand that he gave 200% of himself to this county even as a sheriff's major for the previous sheriff, Mr. Craven.

This is a man that on holidays showed up at our mothers to celebrate whatever holiday we were celebrating but never seemed to be able to enjoy it as it seemed as soon as we sat at the dinner table, he would receive a call about something happening, and off he would go to help out with the problem so his deputies could enjoy their holidays with their families.

Once at Christmastime, while gathered at the table, my brother brought in his radio to our mother's dislike.

She had no sooner given him the speech you are gonna sit here with your family and eat and a call came in about a man who was drunk and disorderly and throwing his children's Christmas gifts in the yard, trying to destroy them. Christmas was something in our family that was sacred. We didn't get much, but we did have each other and great fellowship. He made his apologies to mother and the family and off he went, and we all knew at that table he would handle this matter so those kids had a decent Christmas. That was and still is, sheriff badge or not, the kind of person my brother is.

When I moved here to take a job so I could return home, I was employed to work with court-ordered at-risk kids in a facility. Being a counselor for many years before that, I knew that one of the things that a child needed was pride in themselves, and a lot of the kids wanted to give back to the community. It was a way they felt to make things a little right for things they had done breaking the law. I served many hats at the agency I worked for, but one of the biggest was, to me, working with their self-esteem. I went to the sheriff and discussed what I did at my job and also that some of the biggest things that caused a child in trouble when they got out from re-offending was the presence of being around law enforcement officials. He patiently listened to me and gave my proposal deep consideration. I told him I wanted to call it "The Other Side of the Law Program" as most interaction with law officials was being arrested, put in the back of a cruiser, booked, etc. He gave me a trial run on letting the children volunteer doing special projects and also encouraged some of the deputies to talk to these children one on one as they possibly had troubled teens themselves or they themselves were troubled teens. This was a success that was picked up by the next sheriff of the county after Johnny retired. It was one of the most positive tools I had in my job as there were rules to qualify to go on these outings that had to be satisfied, like their behavior at the center, their educational requirements, and their interaction with other students. Many people of Jackson County were asking us to volunteer for their organization as they watched this process. These kids just needed a chance, and also it gave the children work experience.

There were so many children in this volunteer ship and with such positive results. He tried to meet every one of them personally, and he was their hero for believing in them.

On a personal note: Today my brother watches over me and sees to it I am ok. I call him and tell him of something I want to build, and in a couple of days' time, it's built and on my front porch with a note to my "Baby Sister"—two words that have a deep special meaning to me.

In closing, these are some funny things about him. All woman seem to love him, even at 76. He's still some kid's hero who could have gone to jail but was given second and sometimes third chances by him and are now productive citizens, good fathers or mothers.

He's still my Mama's favorite—even with her in heaven—but the rest of us didn't care. He earned that place. This is a man that took a biscuit and sausage to our mother as long as I can remember when they opened a fast food place that served them in Marianna after her husband passed. You be the judge. Hero or not? I think hero.

Written by: Lucinda Ruth Clark
"The Baby"

"Memories of Johnny Mac"
Written by Mrs. Jean Foxworth
(Johnny's First Cousin)

I remember riding with Johnny on his motor scooter down to Mrs. Braxton's house. He was protective and would pick at me, warning me not to go across the limestone "dividing line" between our yards. My Momma Eleanor (Johnny's mom's sister) would send me over there invariably for some reason or another, and I felt a sense of doom coming over me, looking over my shoulder, but nothing ever happened. Johnny was always sweet-natured and never hurt me. I was just chicken-livered, and my boy cousins picked on me as most do. He was all boy. As he grew older, Johnny was always very nice and gentle. He cared for his family and was always close by and helpful to us all.

"Cousin Johnny"
Written by Rhonda Foxworth Best
Johnny's Second Cousin

My fondest memories of Johnny Mac are his kind heart. He has always cared so much for his family and goes the extra mile to have family reunions so that we can spend time together and look at family pictures and tell wonderful memories of our loved ones. He is also a very good cook!

Love you, Johnny,
Rhonda Foxworth Best

Hayes Baggett
Chief of Police - Marianna, Florida
"Tribute to Sheriff John P. McDaniel III"

It is my honor to be given an opportunity to share my thoughts about my former boss, mentor, and most of all, my friend, Sheriff John P. McDaniel III. I have known Sheriff McDaniel for approximately 43 years, and I must say he is one of the few true statesmen left in the world today. I count myself to be truly blessed to have had the opportunity to observe him over the years and learn from his example.

Johnny Mac, as he is known to everyone, has been a family friend long before he was Sheriff McDaniel. I remember, as a small child, his efforts and dedication to disabled children through his work with the Shriner's Organization—an effort he still is passionate about today. Once he was elected sheriff, he hired my mom (Gerry Baggett) to be part of the sheriff's office administrative staff, a position she still holds today. In 1983, Johnny Mac gave me my first job in law enforcement as a communications officer; this not only launched my career, but more importantly, it provided me with the opportunity to learn from someone who always put the people he served first.

I have learned many lessons from Sheriff McDaniel over the years. Did he sit down and have me write them all down and quiz me later? No, he provided the example for me to follow. He was always on the side of doing right; in life, doing right is not always the easy or popular choice, but it is the one he always made. He upheld the law as he was sworn to do, and he did it to the letter of the law. That being said, he also understood that not all who do wrong are hardened criminals—sometimes good people make poor choices. He always tried to help put the wayward on the right path again, all without ever

345

undermining the job his deputies did. He always took the time to not only talk to the parties involved, but he spoke with his deputy to explain the overall situation and explain his reasons for intervening. Many young deputies have been taught the lesson of empathy and the importance of making the difference in a person's life by Sheriff McDaniel.

In thinking of all the lessons learned from Johnny Mac, there are several big ones, but to me, the small ones say it all. One practice I adhere to today without fail is to return all messages left for me. I learned this lesson and its importance from John P. McDaniel III. If you called Sheriff McDaniel, he always returned your call. While he may not have always given the answer the caller was seeking, he never shunned a call in the effort to avoid a situation. He took the time to talk to anyone and everyone and explain the situation. This practice may not seem like much, but to the person who wanted to talk to the sheriff, it meant everything. Small practices make great men. John P. McDaniel III is a great man.

Sheriff McDaniel has been mentor and role model to not only me but many young law enforcement officers. While he may no longer serve in an official capacity, he still acts as a mentor to many. To this day, I can pick up the phone and call him, and he is always willing to listen and give his advice and reassurance on a decision I have made. Just as with anyone else, he may or may not tell me what I want to hear, but I know without a doubt his words will be what he believes is the right course of action, and they will be from his heart. I owe my career path to two great men—one being John P. McDaniel III. This is where I gained my desire to serve and help people and my community. Mere words cannot express my gratitude.

Again, thank you for the opportunity to say a few words about my friend and express my sincere thanks to him for the opportunity to work and learn from the best!

Chief Hayes Baggett

Larry Birge
Investigator
Jackson County Sheriff's Office

I first met Sheriff McDaniel at a Florida Sheriff's Association meeting in Jacksonville, Florida, in 1985. I was hired by Sheriff McDaniel so I could get back toward home as my parents were both in grave condition. The sheriff told me to come on when I got ready.

I finished my tour of duty with Daytona Beach Police Department before moving to Jackson County. I reported to work two or three weeks later. I came to work for Sheriff McDaniel and was honored that he thought enough of family to hire me to get closer to my parents. I was not used to hearing a sheriff out at night answering calls just like other deputies. Sheriff McDaniel backed up his officers in the field.

I learned that Sheriff McDaniel's father was murdered and eventually his case was resolved. I could not imagine what he was going through, the pain of losing a parent in that manner. I watched him over the years, and it appeared the more stress that was placed on him, the more resolve he had.

One of his deputies was murdered on duty in 1985, and later, another deputy and his wife. Still the pain was on his face without him saying anything.

Sheriff McDaniel always treated everyone with respect. Watching him over the years taught me to be even more respectful toward the public and fellow teammates. How do you honor someone like Sheriff McDaniel except to say he was a great boss and friend. I still pray for folks I work with and say a prayer of peace for Sheriff McDaniel, especially after all he has gone through. The term "Semper Fi" fits Sheriff McDaniel. I am honored to call Sheriff McDaniel my friend.

Larry Birge

Leroy Boone
Former Deputy Sheriff
1979 to Present—Sales with Rahal-Miller

I met Johnny Mac in 1973 when we were both hired at the Jackson County Sheriff's Department by then Sheriff Ronnie Craven. Johnny Mac was the chief administrator. His outgoing personality made me feel comfortable with meeting people. He wasn't a stranger to me, just a great friend.

Later in the years, we would again work together at Rahal in sales for about one year until Johnny ran for sheriff and won by a large margin.

We continue to be friends. He went on to make a great career as sheriff of Jackson County and retired. He will always be a special friend to me because of the bond we developed in both law enforcement and in selling automobiles. He has always been a gentleman and a dear friend.

May God continue to bless you, my friend.

Leroy Boone

Donnie Branch
Deputy, Investigator, Chief Deputy, Special Agent with FDLE
Retired

I grew up in a law enforcement family. When I was fifteen years old, my daddy, J. T. Branch, was a deputy under Sheriff Craven when John P. McDaniel, III was the Chief Deputy.

By the time I turned 16 years old, I had pretty much decided my career path in life.

One night I was riding with Deputy John Mader when we were called to the old jail. Housed at the jail at that time were six (6) ACI (state) inmates. On duty was one jailer, one dispatcher, and one matron. The six inmates were all in the holding cell, some awaiting haircuts.

When the jailer, Sonny Basford, opened the door, all six jumped him. The matron hollered to notify the dispatcher, Lowell Spooner, who in turn alerted deputies and headed to the jail area with a sawed-off shotgun. Lowell leveled the gun on the inmates, and Sonny was able to get out from under them. All six of the inmates ran back in the cell with the keys. Deputy John Mader and I arrived as did Marianna Police Department. Someone yelled, "They got a knife."

About that time, Chief Deputy John P. McDaniel, III came busting through the doors. He had a pistol on his hip and took it off saying, "I'm going in to get the keys." A couple officers and deputies tried to go in with him, and he said, "No, it will create too much confusion. I got them." Once inside the cell with the six inmates, Johnny said, "I want the knife and the damn jail keys. *Now!*"

You heard the keys drop and the six backed away.

Johnny picked the keys up after they kept saying they didn't have a knife. Johnny ordered them out of the cell and on their bellies on the concrete floor. All six immediately complied.

The expression I had heard most of my sixteen-year life, "Ten Feet Tall and Bullet Proof," came to life for me that night in the form of Chief Deputy John P. McDaniel. He was not scared of *anything*!

By 1978, I became a deputy at Jackson County Sheriff's Department under Sheriff Applewhite. By September of 1981, I left and went to Sneads Police Department. I was only there for about six months when one Sunday morning, Sheriff John P. McDaniel came in looking for someone.

He asked me, "Boy, you ready to come back to the sheriff's office?"

I said. "Yes, sir."

We discussed pay, and he told me to come see him on Monday. I did and went back to the sheriff's department in April of 1982. I would leave in December of 1986 to accept an offer from FDLE (Florida Department of Law Enforcement).

During the years, I worked for Sheriff McDaniel, he never separated himself from the public. The most important thing I learned from him was that you always try to help someone. Sometimes that might mean putting them in prison to get their life straight.

He never wanted to see anyone hurt. He expected his officers to perform their duties in a manner to keep them and everyone around them safe. He was always a very big-hearted person. I've seen him pay people's electric bills and buy them groceries.

John P. McDaniel always made time to listen to his officers and the citizens of Jackson County and find a way to meet their individual needs.

Donnie Branch
Retired Law Enforcement

Michael Daniels
Lieutenant– Retired

I had a number of great learning experiences while working with Sheriff McDaniel. The Sheriff had many great ideas of how to make the Jackson County Sheriff's Office a great place to work. This was a great asset to inspire his employees to better serve & protect the citizens of Jackson County. The sheriff basically had a standing rule of operation on how to handle any call that was presented for a request for service. Whether the call seemed important to an officer or not, it was important to the caller at the moment they made the call. I do believe to this day that the ability to communicate is more times than not the initial key to calming any situation.

The sheriff also was, in my opinion, an "open door sheriff." By that I mean, the sheriff would never refuse to discuss a situation with an officer that needed guidance. After all, we worked for the sheriff who was elected to and proudly served the public he was elected to serve.

I fondly remember a quote often used by the sheriff. "Never ask an employee, co-worker, or member of the public to do anything that you haven't done or that you can't or would not do yourself."

Sheriff John P. McDaniel is simply an icon for the County of Jackson and the State of Florida, and I honestly believe that the residents of Jackson County and the State of Florida are better for him having served. I feel proud when the sheriff and I run into each other and he says, "Hello, my friend."

I hope the best for the sheriff, and I remind him often that he is missed.

Lt. Michael Daniels
Retired

John Dennis
Under Sheriff, Retired
Jackson County Sheriff's Department

I've known John McDaniel for so many years, that's it's hard to remember when we first met or when he wasn't my friend.

I started working at the Sneads Police Department in the early 70's along about the same time, Johnny Mac was Chief Deputy for Sheriff Ronnie Craven. While working at the police department, I started to get to know him because while I wasn't on the road for the police department, I was spending time at the Jackson County Sheriff's Office learning about law enforcement.

When Sheriff Craven lost the election to Sheriff Applewhite, Johnny Mac went to work at the Sneads Police Department and I went to work at the Jackson County Sheriff's Office. We maintained our friendship during those years and we would often laugh about how we swapped jobs back and forth in the early days.

When the next Sheriff's election came up, Johnny Mac made it clear that he was going to run against Sheriff Applewhite and he did and he became Sheriff of Jackson County. Before he took office, Sheriff Applewhite allowed him to come to work at the Sheriff's office to get familiar with the cases that were going on. We worked hand in hand on every case whether it was drug related, murders or burglaries. It was during this time that tragedy struck, and Sheriff McDaniel's father was murdered.

Sheriff McDaniel hired me as a deputy sheriff and we embarked on a journey that I will never forget. He became not only my boss, but probably the best friend, I've ever had. Through the years, I worked my way through the ranks from deputy, into investigations as

Chief Investigator and became the only Chief Deputy that Sheriff McDaniel had up to the time that I retired in August 2008.

Throughout the years, we saw many tragedies including direct tragedy and heartbreak to Sheriff McDaniel. But, he always went forward, leading the Jackson County Sheriff's Office and taking care of the people in Jackson County, by putting them first and working through the bad times. But we also experienced a lot of good times and did some great things. We laughed together when we could and we cried together when we had to. As the years moved on, our friendship strengthened and he became the brother I never had and a friend I will always have. I have always had the greatest respect for Sheriff McDaniel and I always will. I look forward to spending many more years with my friend.

Sheriff, thank you for the opportunity you gave me and the experience and challenges you gave me throughout my career.

Good luck in the future.

Your Friend,
John D

Rebecca Dodson
An Officer's Perspective

I first met Sheriff John P. McDaniel in the mid-'80s when he hired me as an undercover operative for the Jackson County Sheriff's Department. I had previously worked for the Bay County Sheriff's Department, Panama City Beach Police Department, and Houston County, Alabama, Sheriff's Office. Needless to say, I was young and naïve and had a bit of a wandering spirit, never staying anywhere too long.

Upon being hired, Sheriff McDaniel introduced me to only a couple of the department personnel. I was issued an alias driver's license, provided an undercover vehicle, and given a house in an adjacent county which was owned by a prison inspector. He put Chief Deputy John Dennis "in charge" of me.

I would embark upon the first of many undercover operations, the first one lasting ten months. Once when I was returning from a drug buy three counties east of Jackson with a trunk full of dope, I was stopped on I-10 doing 125 mph. I was trying to get back and turn the evidence over as I had another scheduled drug-buy two counties west of Jackson and was running late. The state trooper approached my vehicle and inquired if I knew how fast I was going. My thoughts were racing. I had a load of dope, and my license was an alias. At that time, I wasn't sure how that worked. Well, the only thing I could think of was to tell the state trooper to call Johnny Mac, Sheriff McDaniel. It took some convincing, but I finally talked the trooper into contacting the Jackson County Sheriff. The trooper returned to his vehicle and after what seemed like forever, finally came back, gave me my license, and said, "Sheriff McDaniel said I should put you under the jail...but to let you go, tell you to slow down, and see him immediately when you get back in Jackson

County." Well, I slowed myself down and saw the Sheriff shortly afterward. I had only a little "butt" left after that meeting. Johnny Mac expected his officers to be safe and enforce the law and to know that none of us were above the law.

After the culmination of another undercover operation which lasted almost a year, we did our usual round-ups, arresting the drug dealers, but one fled the area, going out to Texas. He was a pretty high-profile offender. I didn't think much about it and continued working. One night, there was a knock on my door. Gun drawn, I went to the door, relaxed, and placed my gun down, opening the door to a Florida Highway Patrolman and a Jackson County Deputy. They informed me that an informant had advised FDLE of a contract hit out on my life—the one that got away, so to speak, had initiated the contract. Well, my thoughts were "This is my home; I'm not going anywhere." This went on for a short period until Johnny Mac and John Dennis arrived. Well, you can guess the rest of this story. I got my belongings and relocated that night.

Johnny Mac became like a father figure to me, and John Dennis was like the big brother I never had. My wandering spirit would eventually take me away from Jackson County to several other sheriffs' offices in adjacent states throughout the years before I would once again return to Jackson County. No other place seemed like home. As a sheriff, Johnny Mac was genuinely concerned about his employees and the citizens of the county. We all became like one big family. We celebrated together, hurt together, and always had each other's backs.

As I reflect back on the horrific events in Johnny Mac's life that cost him the lives of his loved ones, three things keep ringing true. He never lost his faith in God, never lost his faith in people, and never ever gave up. He always kept moving forward in a positive direction.

I thank you, Johnny Mac, for the opportunities you gave me to grow and learn under your leadership and for the patience you exhibited with the young, headstrong officer you hired when you gave me a chance. I love you, Johnny Mac. Authoring your biography has truly been an honor that no words can describe.

Rebecca Dodson
www.deepsouthpublications.com

Billy Dozier
Current Friend of Johnny Mac

In January of 2002, I had the privilege of meeting and being employed by Sheriff McDaniel. The bond that he and I share few will ever know. He is the pure definition of a true friend.

Billy Dozier

On Behalf of: Wayne T. "Cowboy" Morris
Retired Lieutenant – Jackson County Sheriff's Office
Written By: Suzanne Morris Donaldson

I was born April 14, 1981 at 2:38 a.m. at Jackson Hospital. I became the final part of the trio that Johnny Mac refers to as "Cowboy's Girls." When I arrived into this world, I met most of the Jackson County Sheriff's Department at the hospital. Including the Sheriff, who happens to share a birthday with my oldest sister, April, and Duane Davis, who I share a birthday with. Today, I'm 36 years old and even though he's retired, I still call Johnny Mac *Sheriff.* Johnny Mac was the Sheriff for 28 years of my life, so even though we may have other people in that position, he'll always be *my* Sheriff.

My daddy was Lt. Wayne "Cowboy" Morris, he was the first pilot Jackson County ever had. He also helped out the neighboring counties flying the *Pot Plane* as I always called it. He gave Jackson County more volunteer hours than anyone could ever keep track of. I know there were many birthdays, Thanksgivings, Christmases and other events he wasn't at because he was at work, he was the job.

He started out during the Craven administration, then worked for Morris Timber Company as an Auxiliary Officer. When Johnny Mac was elected, he went to work for him full-time until 1990. My daddy always taught me that when you do a job, you do it well, people depend on you. That's how he saw his life with the Sheriff's Department, that Johnny Mac and the people of this county depended on him to handle things, so that's what he did. Johnny Mac was always of that same school of thought. Being Sheriff was a 24 hour a day, 7 days a week job. Every day was election day. In high school I worked for Winn-Dixie, it always took him and Mrs. Mellie hours to do their shopping because everyone spoke to him and he spoke to everyone. He always felt that he owed the people of Jackson county for the job he had and he always honored that. If they wanted to speak to him, he was going to take the time to reply.

Now, growing up in a law enforcement family was a little different at times. My sisters had their teenage years with my daddy working for Johnny Mac. So, you know that saying about small towns where your parents know what you did before you got home? Yeah, that was their life. One thing I know Johnny Mac and my daddy agreed on was that kids were going to be kids. Where Johnny Mac always tried to help someone that may have just made a poor decision, Daddy did the same. Many a teenager was driven home or their parents simply called to come get them, instead of a juvenile mistake costing them later in life. As I'm several years younger than my sisters, it was different for me. I grew up playing in dispatch at the old jail, riding in the front seat of patrol cars, going to visit the Sheriff at his office and listening to a scanner. It wasn't uncommon for there to be undercover vehicles hidden in our backyard (which scared the life out of my sister, Judy, once) or for my daddy to be on a stake-out over a pot field for days and us not see him. Every other Friday, Momma and I would go to the jail and pick up Daddy's check to go grocery shopping. I'd visit with the dispatchers, play with the deputies and then sometimes we'd go over and visit Johnny Mac in his office. I'd visit with his secretary, Gerry Baggett (she used to let me go swimming in her pool) and then I'd go crawl up in his lap. He's always had a huge spot in his heart for children, whether they be related to him or not. Not only did he show that to us, but by helping with the Shriner's Club and at Christmas, with the fund his daddy helped to establish. The Sheriff and the deputies would always ask me "What's your name?" (This was a running joke.) My daddy would say, "Tell them your name." I'd stand firm and say, "I'm Cindy Suzanne Morris and I'm proud of it." That always got a chuckle. These people weren't just my daddy's co-workers, they were my family. Judy was a member of the Junior Deputy program at one time, then later in life a dispatcher. We all were involved in some way, even if it was just supporting our daddy and the Sheriff. I'm pretty sure we all were voluntold we could work a campaign cookout a few times, too. LOL

As I said before, my daddy was Jackson County's first pilot, when he was first learning how to fly the only thing that ever intimidated him was bad weather. One day he was flying over in Liberty County and a storm came up. He sat the plane down on a little landing strip. (Remember, this was the early 80s so there were no cell phones and radios didn't reach that far.) When the storm passed, he went back up and came back to Marianna to land. Johnny Mac told him that everyone had been looking for him and was worried about him in the storm. Johnny Mac said, "I told them, I'm not worried about Cowboy cause if it's bad weather, he sat that damn plane down somewhere. It might be in somebody's cow pasture, but he sat it down. When the weather clears, he'll come on in."

Their relationship wasn't always serious, they were always pulling pranks on each other. Like the time Daddy was the ring leader in getting the Sheriff arrested at the Biltmore for impersonating a police officer. They set up then Bay County Investigator Frank McKeithen once by placing an ad in the paper that he had goats for sale priced cheap. His wife finally got so tired of answering the phone and trying to explain that they didn't have any goats that she told Frank, when he got those damn goats sold to call her and she'd come back home. Through the years, anytime a joke got played on the Sheriff, he swore my daddy was somewhere involved.

When I was 16 years old, a man on the run for murder in Tennessee was staying in a house through the woods behind us. Deputies stopped by to question him about some local burglaries, as soon as they pulled up he took off running out the back door of the house he was staying at and into the woods behind ours. My daddy, who was retired by this time, was in bed asleep. My sister Judy, who lived next door to us, was working dispatch and was about to go into work. Dispatcher Tony Potter called my sister to tell her what was going on, he said, "Judy go lock your doors and come back to the phone." She of course went to question him and he stopped her. "Go lock the doors now!" At the same time the Sheriff was calling my daddy. Lord, you would have thought he was a new man. My daddy got up, got dressed and spent the entire night with the *boys*, looking. They had set up a perimeter around the block we lived in, no one was getting in or out without being checked.

The next morning, the Sheriff and Logger, Mike Daniels, asked my sister what the status of the situation was when they came on duty. Judy said, "Well, some of them think the man has gotten out of the block and had someone pick him up." They looked at Judy and Logger asked her, "What does Cowboy think?" She looked at them. "He says he's still in that block, hunkered down somewhere." They both said, "Okay, he's still in there then." Daddy always had a saying, "If I tell you a piss ant can pull a wagon, you'd better hook'em to it." Logger, who my daddy trained, and the Sheriff, being a close friend, believed anything he ever told them. That was the trust they had.

A little bit later, my sister came in from work, I went to school, my momma drove her bus and my daddy was still out. When my mom came home from running her bus route, she noticed that our door had been kicked in. She went back to the car and called my daddy. She said,

"We've got company in the house." He and about 40 deputies and a helicopter were in our yard within seconds. The dispatchers who were working at the time were freaking out on the radio because Judy had told them she was going to sleep at my parents' because they had a scanner, so no one knew if my sister was in the house with this man. I think my momma practically tore the door off of my sister's house going in to see if she was there. When my mom found her in bed asleep, she ran back out to tell them Judy was safe. After that, it all unfolded rather quickly. Judy sleepily wandered out of her house and quickly freaked out when she saw so many patrol cars and law enforcement with guns drawn toward our house. One of them grabbed my sister and put her behind a car where they had our momma. My daddy being the prideful honest man he was, well, he was mad enough he could've killed that man. After they put the guy in the patrol car, Johnny Mac came up to the scene. He asked in only the way that he can, "Now where is the young man who has caused all of this ruckus?" One of the deputies pointed him to the car, "He's over there, Sheriff," the Sheriff stuck his head in the car. He said, "Son, you obviously don't know who in the hell's house you just broke into. You are lucky you aren't dead, because that boy would've killed you." I don't think the man appreciated that very much.

When my daddy passed away in his sleep April 5, 2013 around 2:30 a.m., our current Sheriff Lou Roberts was among one of the first people there. Not long after daylight, Johnny Mac came to my momma's house, they'd had someone call him as soon as they knew he'd be up. He told so many stories while he was there. That day was filled with visitors and old friends. Both of *my* Sheriffs spoke at my daddy's funeral. Johnny Mac explained that through all of the pranks, all of the calls, out of everything that ever happened, he knew he could depend on Cowboy for anything.

I could go on forever telling stories of what happened back in the day. But the most important part is my daddy thought a lot of Johnny Mac, he was one of his best friends. He loved him like a brother and Johnny Mac loved my daddy. He took great pride in working for him and never regretted a day of it.

"If I tell you a piss ant can pull a wagon, you better hook'em to it."-Wayne "Cowboy" Morris

Jimmy Gilbert
Special Agent—FDLE
Retired

I had the opportunity to work with Sheriff John P. McDaniel many times over the years. I recall the many sacrifices and losses he suffered during his administration. He never allowed the horrific events he experienced to alter his belief in people or his desire to help anyone that he could.

When an agent with FDLE and working a drug deal out of a hotel in Marianna out by the interstate, I recall Johnny Mac calling to see if we needed anything. I jokingly replied, "Yea, I want some oysters." Within a couple of hours, there was a knock on the door. I opened the door and there stood Johnny Mac with an ice chest full of oysters.

One Thanksgiving, I was again part of a surveillance team watching drug dealers in Jackson County. It was part of the job to be away from our families. Johnny Mac cooked all of us a full Thanksgiving feast to include ham and turkey with all the sides and delivered it out to us.

One arrest in particular stands out in my mind. The subject was a paraplegic who had just sold a kilo of cocaine to an undercover agent. At that time, it was the largest undercover cocaine drug case in Jackson County. Sheriff McDaniel went over to the car where the subject sat and physically picked him up and carried him over to his patrol car and sat him in the back seat. Johnny had gotten a wheel chair earlier and had placed it in his trunk. He took the paraplegic suspect to jail, placed him in the wheelchair, and rolled him inside to booking.

Over the years, I saw Johnny Mac treat every person with respect, no matter what the situation might be. He was always very kind hearted and helpful to everyone I saw him encounter.

I consider it a privilege to have known and worked with Sheriff John P. McDaniel, but more importantly, I am thankful to call him my friend.

Bobby Haddock
Washington County Sheriff
Retired

I have had the pleasure of calling John P. McDaniel III (affectionately referred to as Johnny Mack) friend for the last 38 years. There are few men I would feel as humbled to have the opportunity to honor as my friend, Johnnie Mack.

Our law enforcement family is a strong one. I believe these roots run deep because we experience this life differently than the average man. Our days are filled with some of the worst of the worst. We have to compartmentalize the pain while passionately pursuing those who victimize our way of life. This job is never more difficult than when you yourself are the victim. When the criminal element knocks on your door, the pain in inescapable. You have a choice; succumb to it or march on.

None have had to survive more personal tragedy than my friend Johnny Mack. None have marched on more valiantly than him.

Martin Luther King said it best when he said "The ultimate measure of a man is not where he stands in moments of comfort and convenience, but where he stands at times of challenge and controversy." Johnny Mack has stood with bold confidence and demonstrated unwavering leadership at times when the strongest of men would seemingly falter. In those times, there is no greater testament to his character as a law enforcement officer, as the sheriff or as a man.

During the last three decades, Johnny Mack has consistently been an invaluable source of wisdom, encouragement, and assistance to me personally. Johnny Mack is uninterested in whether it is convenient to meet his fellow man's need. If there is a job to be done, a need to be met, or a life he can make better, he does so without a moment's pause.

When you're older, you take assessment of the important things in life. The material things fall away, the fancy words of halfhearted men are silenced, and all that matters are that a man is who he says he is and does what he says he'll do. Johnny Mac is one of the finest among these men.

Bobby Haddock
Washington County Sheriff
Retired

Woodrow W. Hatcher
Jackson County – 14th Judicial Circuit
Judge – Retired

I have known Sheriff John P. McDaniel III for over forty years personally as well as professionally. He has been a good friend.

At a time when a "person's word" is not as important as it once was, John has always been an individual who has done what he said he would do.

As sheriff, I had a chance to observe him for almost thirty years. Law enforcement is a tough profession, and if one is not careful, it will cause an individual to become harder toward individuals in general and especially to those who are perceived to have broken the rules.

In spite of many personal tragedies and years in law enforcement, John never lost his concern for others. He was tough when he needed to be but never failed to provide comfort and compassion when needed or justified. Many in law enforcement find this to be a difficult endeavor.

I wish him peace and enjoyment in his retirement.

Woodrow W. Hatcher

Jack Hollis
Founder of Christian Center Church
and Associated Ministries Inc.
Pastor

I appreciate being asked to put my two cents worth in this book. There are so many things that I cannot say in print, but a wry smile sneaks across my mouth when I think of them all. Johnny, you were a great friend and your mama was so patient (to a point)!!

My friendship with Johnny Mac was diverse and goes way back almost sixty years. I spent many hours with Johnny Mac in the '50s, and our paths went different directions for a few years, but our friendship never faltered. He went the educational and professional route while I went the other. Later his path took him to the sheriff's office and mine to the ministry.

Johnny was a good friend to have around when we were in a place we shouldn't be and a fight broke out (as in 'somebody' started one)! I remember his mother, Ruth, and both sisters well. All of us were welcome at their house anytime of the day or night! We might get thrown out before daylight, but we could still come back.

In 1957, my girlfriend was the victim of an attempted rape and was beaten badly. She escaped the man and wound up on Math Porter's front porch. She could not find me, so Math carried her to Johnny's house where Ruth doctored her and Johnny came and found me. There was no hesitation in taking her under those circumstances. That's just who they were.

Occasionally, Johnny and I and a few other friends would "confiscate" some peanuts and go to a deserted house on the river called "Cleve's Clubhouse" and boil the peanuts or maybe fry a chicken we 'picked up' along the way. It tasted terrible, but the spoils of robbery were good! We were 'borrowing' some watermelons from a farmer once, and when he disagreed with our venture and began shooting, we left pretty quick (statute of limitations has run out on these things…ha ha).

God certainly has a sense of humor calling Johnny to be sheriff and me to be a pastor, not to mention the others involved who wound up as beverage agents and deputies and ministers. It was a different time, but a wonderful one! I wish my son and grandson could have grown up in the '50s.

When Johnny's son was so sick, I would go to the hospital to see him, and Johnny was always there and would care for 'Little John' like he was a baby. It was breaking Johnny's heart but even more when he died. He was devastated, but he pressed on.

A few years later, Johnny's wife, Mellie, and a deputy were murdered at his house, and my wife, Shellie, and I immediately went there and stayed with him during the initial investigation. Since Johnny and Mellie were so loved by the community, I knew there would be an influx of people trying to get to him that night, so I opened our church to the law enforcement community, Johnny and Mellie's family, and the public. A few days later at the visitation service at our church, more than 2000 people showed up to pay respects.

Johnny honored me by asking me to do the funeral and the graveside. We had to put live monitors in our lobby, kid's church, fellowship hall, and teen room at the church as well as speakers outside for the ones who still could not get in, standing outside in the cold and wind to pay their respects.

I want to close with a statement about my friend Johnny Mac. He is not a saint nor is he perfect, but when Mellie was killed, he asked me if he could be alone in my office for a time. He went in there and stayed on his knees for a very long time, crying and praying and asking the questions we all would ask at a time like that. When he came out, he told me he had made peace with God about Mellie's death and his own life.

All of his years of growing up without a lot of things that other kids had, without his father at home, in politics and law enforcement, the death of his son, and murder of his wife—all these have formed a combination of virtues and vices in Johnny Mac which only God can understand and judge. He is deeply loyal, and the most down-to-earth public official I have ever known in my 76 years on earth. I am proud to call him friend from a time when that really meant something! God bless you Johnny Mac.

Jack Hollis
Pastor

Quinton Hollis
Jackson County Sheriff's Office
Sergeant

I can't remember a time in my life, even as a kid, when I didn't know who Johnny McDaniel was. Long before he was the sheriff, my dad told me stories about them stealing watermelons together as youngsters. He has always had a larger than life, charismatic personality that makes the average person feel like a close friend. He has always felt more like family to me.

I had an "Elect Johnny McDaniel" bumper sticker on my first vehicle in the 11th grade the first time he ran for sheriff, long before I could even vote.

In the old days, the supervisor of elections would put up a large chalk board on the sidewalk of the east side of the courthouse. They would fill in the boxes as each precinct reported in. There was always a large crowd gathered to fellowship and watch the results being posted. It was better than going to the fair for me.

When the last votes came in and the winner was announced, Johnny Mac's wife ran through the crowd and gave him a big hug. I had the privilege of being about ten feet away as they realized he had been elected Sheriff for the very first time.

One of the first calls I ever went to as a new officer with Sneads P.D. was in August of 1983. A man barricaded himself in the attic of a Sinai community home, armed with a .22 rifle and a shotgun. After he shot up an SPD cruiser, Sheriff McDaniel commandeered the patrol car and drove up to the house, rescuing all of the family members trapped inside. As he backed across the yard at full speed with a carload of victims, he managed to tear the driver's door most of the way off the car on a fence post. After a seven-hour stand-off in the sweltering

374

heat and Lord knows how many rounds fired at us, the man was successfully taken into custody.

Then came the death of Sgt. James Bevis, the first of two officers killed while he was the sheriff. That was my very first day on the job with the Marianna Police Department. April 4th, 1985, was a day that will always be a huge part of who I am. Short of funds, resources, and manpower, the sheriff handled the manhunt, investigation, funeral, and the trial that followed in a way that brought pride to our community and our law enforcement family.

I worked part-time for Sheriff McDaniel beginning in the summer of 1986, and several years later, he hired me full-time after I attended Chipola College. I attended his mother's funeral, his son's funeral, and had the honor of serving as a pallbearer at Mrs. Mellie's funeral. He has seen more tragedy in his life than anyone should have to endure, beginning with the murder of his father.

The afternoon that Mellie McDaniel and Harold "Mike" Altman were killed in the sheriff's driveway was the most surreal event that I have ever been a part of. We worked through the night and into the next day, not sure initially if we had caught all of the parties responsible. Seeing the sadness and heartbreak in his face that set in over the days that followed was tough to witness.

As far as a boss goes, I could not have asked for a better one. He chewed my butt and punished me just like a daddy would and cared for us all like his own children. We always knew that we could call on him day or night, and he would be there without fail. There was never any doubt who the boss was.

I remember one time being accused of being unprofessional by an irate motorist from Georgia. I got a little defensive and started giving him names of witnesses that could back up my side of the story. I will never forget what he said to me. He said, "I don't need to talk to

375

them. I asked you what happened and you told me. If I couldn't trust you, then you would not be working for me."

One night after he retired, we were sitting in his barn, working on airplane parts, and he told me that he had received word that threats had been made against his life. He looked over the top of his glasses and said, "All I can say is they better keep their powder dry, 'cause mine will be."

Most people call him Johnny Mac. I am among the few that had the privilege of working for him, so to me he will always be "Sheriff."

Thank you, boss, for being my friend, and remember, "Don't start nothin', and there won't be nothin.'"

Keep your powder dry, and God bless!
Quinton Hollis

Jeff Johnson
Lieutenant
Jackson County Sheriff's Department

I came to work for Sheriff John P. McDaniel on October 5, 1986. Within my first couple of months of employment, I was called to meet with the sheriff in his office. As was customary, his administrative assistant, Gerry Baggett, sent me straight back to his office as Sheriff McDaniel had an open-door policy for not only his officers but anyone needing assistance. I was sitting next to him in his office, and he was showing me his new Sig Sauer gun. As he was loading a magazine in it, it went off, shooting through the bookcase and into the stall of the bathroom next door.

Well, Gerry heard the gun go off and immediately called then Major John Dennis. She was afraid one of us had shot the other. This started off my career as a deputy at the department with a bang!

By 1987, Sheriff McDaniel had a fully formed dive team consisting of Johnny Mac, Hayes Baggett, Ricky Cloud, DeLight Booth, and myself. Once we went to Pea River looking for a little boy that had drowned during flood conditions.

By mid-1988 we had formed into a tri-states recovery team. At that time, we only had summer-type wet suits. We went to Nashville, Georgia, to assist in looking for a homicide victim who had been thrown in the water. The water was so cold at 30 degrees our bodies became numb and riddled with cramps. On the return trip, we were all cold, wet, and sad. The mission of any dive team recovery is just that—to bring a body back to some loved one who is waiting for closure.

Once, after a dive training exercise, an old country song came on the radio and Johnny Mac said, "I sure would love to dance to that song." We all chimed in, "Go

377

ahead." Johnny stopped in the middle of the road at a light, got out, and danced. I had never had a boss do anything like that. I came to realize over the years that Johnny Mac knew the toll the job took on each of his officers and would often try to lighten our hearts and spirits before we returned home to our families.

The dive team went to another recovery endeavor which lasted all day. I came to work on the night shift following a day of diving. At almost 4:00 a.m. when it was time for me to get off, I was in the deputy's room with the lights out, sitting with my feet propped up on the desk, almost asleep. The light came on, and somebody kicked my feet off the desk. It was the sheriff. He always knew where we were and what we were doing.

Years later in 2001, I was the road supervisor who responded to the alleged drowning of Gail Sands. After an autopsy was performed, it was deemed a homicide. I inherited this case later as an investigator with Gail's husband, Lionel, being a prime suspect. This event set the wheels in motion involving Lionel Sands and Brown who ultimately killed the sheriff's wife, Mellie, and Deputy Altman in 2007. On January 30, 2007, I was home sick as was Chief Deputy John Dennis. I heard the calls on the radio, got dressed, and stopped by to pick up John Dennis. When we arrived at the sheriff's home, which was roped off as a crime scene, I saw the sheriff over by the ambulance. He was devastated. Within a short period of time, when the identity of the killers was confirmed, Johnny Mac was insistent that an officer check on my family as I was the lead investigator in the Sands case. Considering his most tragic of losses, he still had the welfare of his officers and their families at heart.

That is just the kind of man and boss he was. He taught his officers to treat everyone with respect and help anyone they could along the way. Thank you for being a great boss and mentor.

Lt. Jeff Johnson
Jackson County Sheriff's Department
10/5/86 - Present

Herman Laramore
Public Defender - Attorney
Retired

I have known Johnny (Johnny Mac, as he is known to us) since Marianna High School days. His earlier education had been at Magnolia School and mine at Cherokee School. In high school, he was known as a "scrapper." Any time he went onto the football field, you could expect a fight to erupt. We became friends early on and have remained friends for over sixty years.

I have seen him through many life ventures, i.e. a laundry man, finance man, car salesman, deputy sheriff, and sheriff. I have provided him legal service on numerous occasions, and he has assisted me in law enforcement matters. Although for many years, we were on opposite sides in criminal cases (he arrested and prosecuted, and I defended), we never let our professional responsibilities interfere with our friendship. Johnny understood the justice system and always did his very best to see it work. A good example was when the men were charged with murdering his father, the court appointed me as public defender to represent them. I asked Johnny his feelings about me handling the defense. His answer was, "They are entitled to an attorney, and I would be satisfied with you handling the defense. You will do a good job." I was able to resolve the case to Johnny's and the defendants' satisfaction. This was the kind of law enforcement person he was.

Johnny would work day and night to catch a violator, and once he caught them, he would be on the phone to me saying, "He's a pretty good old boy" or "He's from a good family. Do your best to help him." Johnny never was vindictive or bitter as a law enforcement officer or in his personal life, and believe me, if anyone in this whole wide world had a right and reason to be vindictive and bitter, Johnny did. He has been dealt some bad cards in life, yet he never changed.

Most of all, he loved his family and felt he could never do enough for them, such as taking a biscuit to his mama every morning for years in spite of his hectic work schedule. To lose his mama, daddy, son, and wife is enough to break the average person, but Johnny is no average person. He is a "man's" man who loved his family, his friends, his community, and his profession. He will be remembered by law enforcement constituents, friends, and the community as one of the finest and most outstanding public servants this county has ever had.

I personally appreciate all Johnny has done for our community, but most of all, I appreciate his friendship.

Herman Laramore

Ray Lawrence
The Bond between John P. McDaniel, Ray Lawrence and Families

I don't know when we first met, nor where since it has been so long ago that I have forgotten. Of the things, I can remember, one is election night 1980. A lot of Johnny's friends—Masons, Shriners, etc.—gathered outside the courthouse on Madison Street to wait for the election returns and watch as each precinct came in and was posted on the board for everyone to see. Everything at that time was done by hand and had to first go through the Supervisor of Elections Office to be recorded before being put on a large board for the public to view.

Elections were a big part of things in those days. People from all over the county would come to the court house, bring lawn chairs, and sit and visit until everything was over. This was often the only time many of them came into town. Precincts would start coming in shortly after seven p.m. when the polls closed. Usually the last precinct would come in around ten p.m. Everyone had their favorite candidate; some even bet on the races. It was a big deal and a lot of fun.

The night of the elections, the Supervisor of Elections Office would get a total and announce a winner. They would call a winner, also notifying radio and TV stations. The night of October 4, 1980, was no exception. John P. McDaniel was announced as the winner of the sheriff's race. Ray Lawrence and a bunch of Johnny Mac supporters caught Johnny at the Court House, physically picked him up, and carried him down the courthouse steps out into the streets to be congratulated by his friends and supporters. Once in the street (which was blocked off for polling returns) the crowd went wild. It was a hard-fought election, and Johnny Mac won by 66 percent.

Many other times these two families along with other Shrine members would join together and go to Pensacola to the Shrine Temple for the service. Needless to say, the trip over on I-10 to Pensacola was always eventful. We all rented motel rooms in one place near the Shrine Temple. There were Skaf Kaf (three wheelers) which were little painted cars with lawn mower engines for us to parade in for the public.

Some would get on the little cars and race around the motel. Well, there was someone in the motel that did not appreciate a bunch of Shriners racing around the parking lot on little cars, so they called the local sheriff's department. A deputy sheriff responded and stopped the little cars from racing around the motel. As it was, the sheriff-elect was one of the drivers of the little cars, so the deputy got real angry with everyone. A Shriner there called the local sheriff and told him what was going on, so he sent the shift supervisor out. The shift supervisor was advised that one of the people getting his ass chewed out was the sheriff-elect of Jackson County, Florida.

The shift supervisor took over the situation and sent the responding deputy back on the road. The motel clerk supervisor informed all concerned that he had authorized the Shriners to do what they were doing, so everything got straightened out without any problems.

One of the Shriners from Marianna was on the balcony and had hollered to the shift supervisor, "Hey, you guys got the sheriff-elect down there that y'all are messing with." The officer saw the Shriners had permission to race the little cars. They met the sheriff-elect, and everyone had a great time with no harm done to anyone or anything.

There are many times over the past forty-plus years that these two families have stuck together during times of tragedy, death, and family losses. The bondage and friendship between the John McDaniel and Ray Lawrence families cannot be broken.

Ray Lawrence

William H. Long
Reporter - Retired
Finance Manager

I first became acquainted with the man I would later refer to only as "Sheriff" in 1985. It was at this time I became a young rookie reporter for WMBB-TV at the ripe old age of nineteen. The sheriff's office was in the courthouse then, and Gerry Baggett was the sheriff's secretary. Well, not only did he take me in, she did too. She made it possible to see him and talk to him almost anytime I needed to.

There were many occasions when reporters had interaction with law enforcement, and the sheriff always made time for us; he would contact us about events of importance to us and our viewers. He was always willing to provide an on-camera interview for our use on the evening news. But as time went on, Johnny Mac became more than just the sheriff. He became my friend, and I'm proud to say he remains so to this day.

He would at times take us with him to crime scenes, making sure we had access to as much of the crime scene as possible and then, of course, an interview with him for the news. And while on our way to those various places, he would let us help ourselves to any Coca-Cola or sweet tea that he had with him.

But as good as the sheriff was to me, he would never shoot Duane Davis (or let me shoot him) for hiding my camera equipment anytime he had a chance or for laughing at me when that freaking dog from the Chattahoochee Police grabbed me by the pant leg and tried to drag me off one day in the K-Mart shopping center!!!

But during my five years as a reporter and for the many years since then, Johnny and I have shared many stories, many laughs, and yes, even a few sad moments.

But at the end of the day, I am proud to call the Sheriff, my friend.

Enjoy your retirement years in good health. You've earned it!!!

William H. Long

Frank McKeithen
Bay County Sheriff
Retired
"The Weekend" by Frank McKeithen

When I was first appointed Sheriff of Gulf County, there was a period of time that my wife, Diane, and I lived separately during the work week. Diane was a teacher in Bay County where we had a home, so I bought a small condo in St. Joe Beach in Gulf County and would spend Monday through Friday there, coming home to Bay County on the weekends. Sometimes Diane would join me in Gulf County to spend the weekend at the beach.

During the course of my duties as sheriff in Gulf County, I often spoke with Jackson County Sheriff John "Johnny Mac" McDaniel. Johnny Mac and I had been friends for years and would sometimes get together to talk about the demands of our jobs, to share ideas, to get advice, and to give it too. Johnny Mac shared with me the fact that sometimes he felt it would do him good to "get away" for a weekend. So I offered him the use of my little condo at the beach anytime I went to my home in Bay County.

It wasn't long before Johnny Mac called me up and asked if he could use the condo that next weekend.

I had already made plans to go home and spend time with my family in Bay County, so I told him it would be fine. I knew it would be good for him to spend a little time away from the stress of his job.

I left a key for Johnny Mac, went home to Diane and the kids that weekend, and didn't give it much thought after that. On Monday, I returned to the condo and got back to work. Work, for me, meant long hours every day. I usually spent much more time working than I did staying at the condo.

A few weeks later, Diane called and told me she was coming by herself to the condo so we could spend our time together that weekend on the beach. I couldn't wait to see her that Friday. Living apart was a challenge, and we looked forward to the day she could get a job teaching in Gulf County and we could have our family all together in one spot. I couldn't wait to see her, and it seemed like the week would never end.

Finally, Friday came and there was my beautiful wife, coming to spend the weekend at the beach with me. It was going to be great.

Diane took her suitcase into the master bedroom to unpack her things. I was in the little living room, anticipating the places I was going to take her to dinner. I had planned the entire weekend with her in mind, and I couldn't wait to get started.

Then, I heard her say my name. "FRANK MC-KEI-THEN!"

When I'm in trouble, Diane says my full name in syllables. Our perfect weekend was in jeopardy. Mentally, I was running through everything I could have done wrong in the recent past and was coming up empty. I couldn't for the life of me think of anything I had done that could make her mad. But, of course, as every husband knows, that means absolutely nothing. The tone in her voice indicated a guilty verdict, so I headed to the bedroom to apologize and get the perfect weekend back on track.

Diane stands only about five foot four, but when she's ticked off, I swear she grows about two feet. It must have something to do with the fact she's a high school teacher, and a great one at that.

"What is this?" She shook it at me. "It" was a rather flimsy negligee.

"A nightgown?" I said, hoping it was just a trick question.

"I *know* that. I found it in the closet, and it's *not* mine."

My mouth dropped open.

As an investigator, my mind was a whirlwind of questions: How long had the nightgown been in the closet? Whose night gown was it? Was this a terrible practical joke? Who has been in my condo?

As a husband, I was sure of only one thing: I'm so dead.

"Frank?"

And then I remembered. Johnny Mac! Johnny Mac and the weekend he crashed at my condo while I was away in Bay County.

"It belongs to Johnny Mac," I said, relief spreading across my face.

Diane narrowed her eyes. "It's a little small for him."

This wasn't working out like I'd hoped. "No, I mean Johnny Mac used the condo a couple of weeks ago when I went home. It has to be his."

"You expect me to believe that?"

The possibility of a wonderful weekend with my wife was looking bleaker by the minute. From the look in her eyes, I might be in the dog house for the next couple of weekends.

As an investigator, I was used to dealing with evidence, witnesses, and alibis. I had to admit, the lacy evidence hanging in my closet was pretty incriminating. Since I didn't know when the evidence had been hung in the closet, I had no alibi. I needed a witness.

I held up my cell phone. "Let's fix this right now. I'm calling Johnny Mac." I looked up his number. "You'll see. He'll know who it belongs to."

And, of course, Johnny Mac wasn't answering his phone. I decided to call the sheriff's office in Jackson County. I needed to make a non-911, 911 call for help.

"Well, have him call me when you get him," I said on the phone to the secretary at the Jackson County SO. I looked over at Diane's face and added, "Yeah, you could say this is an emergency."

"He's gonna call when they find him," I said to Diane after I hung up. I was starting to sweat and wondering when Johnny Mac would call.

Turned out, my buddy didn't fail me. In short order, my phone rang. Thank God.

"Johnny Mac, hey buddy, you remember that weekend you stayed in my condo?" I asked.

"Sure do. Thanks again for letting me use it. Had a great time," Johnny Mac said.

"Yes, I believe you did." I looked over at the lacy negligee Diane had dropped on the bed. "Hey, I got a question for you. Did you by chance forget something in the closet?"

Johnny Mac paused, considering. "No, can't think of anything I've been missing."

"Something lacy?"

"Don't have too much lacy stuff, Frank." Johnny Mac sounded amused.

"A nightgown. With lace and not much else."

"Oh," Johnny Mac laughed. "Yeah, I guess we did forget that."

"Well, Diane found it."

"Real sorry to hear that, Frank." But Johnny Mac sounded like he was still smiling.

"She's right here. I'm gonna let you talk to her so you can clear it up." And I handed the phone to my wife.

I got my hopes up when Diane actually smiled at whatever Johnny Mac said. Then she started laughing and looked up at me, shaking her head. The weekend was saved.

"I can't believe you don't trust me," I said when she got off the phone, hugging her close.

"It's not you, Frank," Diane said. "It's other people I don't trust."

We went on to have a great weekend, but I learned two valuable lessons from that experience. Innocent until proven guilty applies only to our judicial system, not to marriage. And never let John "Johnny Mac" McDaniel stay in your condo without checking the closet after him.

Frank McKeithen
Bay County Sheriff
Retired

Ernie Padgett
Jackson County Commissioner and Administrator
Santa Rosa, Manatee, and Okaloosa County
Administrator

Johnnie Mac and I were both elected to office in 1980, he as sheriff and me as county commissioner. John was a pleasure and a challenge to work with. He always asked for more money than we (commissioners) thought we could give him. Actually, he asked and argued for the budget he felt strongly was needed in order to provide good law enforcement for the citizens of Jackson County. He was truly a professional law enforcement officer and was well respected throughout the state of Florida.

Sheriff McDaniel and I worked together in government for seven years, he as sheriff and I as a county commissioner and later, county administrator.

During my tenure as county administrator, Johnnie and I started the discussion to build a new county jail. Needless to say, this was a very controversial issue. The federal government was breathing down our necks because of the old, outdated jail in Marianna. They said we were in violation in many areas. The state of Florida was also on our case.

During 1987 and early 1988, Johnnie and I participated in many citizen meetings across the county. We were proposing a one-cent sales tax in order to build a new jail. At first, these community meetings were somewhat hostile. Many citizens couldn't understand building a new jail for "a bunch of criminals."

As time went by and more community meetings were held, our citizens began to understand that unless we did something to correct the jail situation, the state and federal governments would step in and make us do it.

The county put a one-cent sales tax referendum on the 1988 presidential primary ballot. The ballot stated

392

that the one-cent sales tax would end as soon as the new jail was paid for. Over 70% of the citizens in Jackson County voted in favor of the tax to build a new jail. The jail was paid for in about four years and the tax came off.

Sheriff McDaniel could have sat back and done nothing, but that wasn't Johnnie Mac. He saw the need and stepped forward in advocating for a new jail. There is no doubt that he saved taxpayers millions of dollars in legal fees as well as state and federal interference in our local affairs.

It was a pleasure working with Johnnie during the 1980s. I personally witnessed his professionalism and his desire to help people. He truly "walked tall" as our sheriff for many years.

Johnnie may have retired from being Jackson County Sheriff, but he has never retired from doing good works and helping people...and he never will.

That's who he is.

Submitted by

Ernie Padgett

Sid Riley
Local Business Owner
Neighbor, Friend

I have had the pleasure of knowing "Johnny Mac" for over forty years. During the early 1970s, John McDaniel and his family were our next-door neighbors, living in Dogwood Heights, a small subdivision located just East of Marianna. At that time, Johnny Mac was a young, ambitious lawman, serving as chief deputy under then Sheriff Ronnie Craven.

The McDaniel children were the same age as ours, and for a major portion of their childhood, they were raised together, romping through the same neighborhood and sharing those growing years.

That formed the foundation of the friendship between us that has endured through the years. I vividly recall being at a small house party at their home and standing in the kitchen talking to Johnny Mac. The subject was aviation, something which he already loved. I was already a pilot and regularly using that talent to travel in my work.

"Sid, I only have two lifetime goals that I hope to achieve. If I can only accomplish those things, I will be fulfilled and happy," he told me. "First, I want to become the Sheriff of Jackson County, and second I want to learn to fly an airplane." Little did we know at that moment that he would completely fill that wish, with a life filled with events of extreme accomplishments as a lawman, punctuated by events of extreme violence and grief. He also reached the goal of owning aircraft and spending many hours of personal pleasure as he soared the skies over his homeland.

As "the High Sheriff of Jackson County," he built an unmatchable legacy as a lawman, in the county and state wide. During his life, he has dealt with unthinkable personal pain and sacrifice. Through it all, his spirit and devotion to friends and profession remained undaunted. And they all loved and respected him in return. He made the decision to retire a few years ago but could have remained in office as long as he wanted the job.

Today, he enjoys time at his homestead on the Chipola, tinkering in his shop at his home or at the airport, being with family and grandchildren, and continuing to serve the people of our county through civic service. He is always a pleasure to be near, and our family treasures him as a friend.

Sid Riley

Louis Roberts III
Jackson County Sheriff

Approximately forty years ago, I met a man who impacted my life and my career. To many, this man is recognized as Jackson County Sheriff John P. McDaniel. To most, however, he is affectionately known as "Johnny Mac."

In January, 1977, at age 20, I began my law enforcement career under the newly elected sheriff of Jackson County, Charles Applewhite. During my late teens, I often associated with members of the local and state law enforcement community. On many occasions, I rode with local law enforcement officers. My father was very active in both the Florida Highway Patrol and the Jackson County Sheriff's Auxiliary programs. These connections allowed me the opportunity to meet and interact with Sheriff "Johnny Mac" who was serving as chief deputy under Sheriff Ronnie Craven.

There are many personal and professional tragedies Johnny Mac has gone through in his career that have shown me the strength and courage it has taken for him to weather these storms. Just prior to his taking office in 1980, his father was a homicide victim at a truck stop on the Alabama/Florida state line in northern Jackson County. On this particular night, I was the only deputy sheriff still left on duty in Jackson County. Donnie Branch, who is my chief deputy, and I were eating breakfast at the Shell Station just north of I-10. Donnie had already checked off duty when the call came in about the robbery and shooting at the truck stop. I personally knew Mr. J.P. as I often stopped and visited with him. I remember the homemade spaghetti sauce he made for me and my wife. We would discuss the events going on in his life and mine. Mr. J. P. often reminded me of my father. Both of them were very civic minded and community oriented.

As I responded to the location with Deputy Donnie Branch, I was hoping that the call as given to our dispatch center was not as reported. Unfortunately, as we arrived, we realized the magnitude of the incident which ultimately claimed the life of Mr. J. P. I watched as "Johnny Mac" dealt with this horrific situation and can only imagine the challenges he would be facing as a newly elected sheriff not yet taking office. I often wondered how I would have dealt with this type of situation if it had been my father. "Johnny Mac" and I have often reflected on how much my father reminded him of his father. He felt in many ways he still had his daddy through mine.

There were many other tragedies throughout his career that would have overwhelmed and consumed most people. He allowed me to come to work for him as a deputy sheriff in January 1981, and I had the opportunity and privilege to work not only for, but with him, for a good portion of his tenure as sheriff. He allowed me to progress as a supervisor and then investigator within the Jackson County Sheriff's Office. While at times demanding, he always led by example and expected the best from his staff. He always reminded us that not only do we serve the citizens of Jackson County, we also represent him and Jackson County as a whole. Working at the Jackson County Sheriff's Office under the direction of Johnny Mac was like working with a large extended family. While we may not have always agreed on every aspect of a case, we respected each other's viewpoint.

In 2001, the opportunity presented itself for me to seek the elected office of Chief of Police of Marianna. Having no personal political experience, with the exception of working for an elected official, I was unsure as to whether or not this was the proper career choice to

397

pursue. With sick parents, a young family, and job security as an investigator at the sheriff's office, I had serious doubts as to whether or not the risk would outweigh the benefits. I had a lot to consider in my decision, and he was very supportive and encouraging of this opportunity. The day after having successfully qualified to run for chief of police, my mother passed away and my father was sick in the hospital in Dothan, Alabama. I began to wonder if this was the path I should embark on. The day after my mother passed, Sheriff Johnny Mac and other friends came to my house to prepare my campaign kick-off, which allowed me to be able to be with my family and arrange for my mother's funeral. I will always remember the support, commitment, and compassion that was shown to me in such a trying time by such dear friends.

Over his 28 years of serving as sheriff of Jackson County, I have witnessed him overcome many personal tragedies, and through each, he became stronger and exemplified courage and respect. Although he faced many tragic events in his life, there was a personal side of Johnny Mac that was larger than life that embraced humor and showed his empathetic and compassionate side with a light-hearted wit.

As his successor to the office of sheriff of Jackson County, when facing difficult decisions, I often reflect and draw from the leadership he demonstrated to me and to the public during his tenure. I want to take the opportunity to thank him for his friendship, mentoring, and guidance.

Lou Roberts
Jackson County Sheriff

Henry Mark Sims
14th Judicial Circuit
Public Defender

Let me start out by saying that when I was contacted by Becky Dodson to contribute to her book about "The Sheriff," I was extremely honored but also a little overwhelmed. What can you say about this man that hasn't already been said? I hope that what I write at this time gives sufficient honor to Sheriff McDaniel, who I have always loved, admired, and respected.

I've known "The Sheriff," a title by which he will always be known, practically all my life. In my teenage years, I must admit, that I feared him to some degree, for he was the person who my teachers, coaches, FFA advisors, etc. threatened us with if we cut up too much at school or got caught skipping. Only one other person scared me more in those days, and that was my father!

I don't want to give the impression that I was a bad kid for nothing could be further from the truth. However, in those teenage years, we all are susceptible to lapses of good judgement that tend to get us in a certain amount of trouble. One threat from a teacher, etc., to speak to my father or Sheriff McDaniel about my conduct resulting from said lapses of judgement quickly produced the intended result, and my behavior was corrected in short order.

Later in life, my "fear," if you will, ripened into respect and admiration. When I returned from serving a two-year mission in Colombia, South America, for the Church of Jesus Christ of Latter-Day Saints, the sheriff learned in a conversation with my parents that I was home and could speak fluent Spanish. I later confirmed my ability to him in a subsequent conversation when I bumped into him in Marianna. Next thing you know, I started getting calls to come to the jail, which then was still located behind the courthouse, to translate for Spanish-speaking detainees. He offered to pay me for my services, but I declined because I enjoyed practicing the language and I considered it an honor to assist him and his deputies in any way I could.

Several years later, I attended the University of Miami School of Law in Coral Gables, Florida. Now, as I have alluded to earlier, this was not my first extended period away from home. In fact, I never really got homesick at all, except once. I had a particularly bad day my first semester and seemed like anything that could go wrong did on that particular day. I remember going back to the house where I rented a room to relax a while before getting ready to go to my last class of the day. As I entered the door and went through the living room, the lady of the house had The Sally Jesse Raphael Show playing on the television. I meandered down the hall and then I heard a voice that I recognized. I immediately turned around and saw Sheriff McDaniel on the TV! I watched the show and, of course, it was emotional because of the subject matter. Besides that, I had a feeling of homesickness that I was not accustomed to. Upon seeing Johnny Mac on TV, coupled with my recent adversities, I had the almost uncontrollable urge to pack up and go home. Luckily, I fought the feeling off and went on to class, and from then on, I never suffered from homesickness again.

When I came home from law school and went to work with Jim Appleman, who was the State Attorney at that time, my working relationship with Sheriff McDaniel enabled me to get to know him even better. We quickly became fast friends, and I am happy to say that we are still so today. During the nearly sixteen years I served as an assistant state attorney, the sheriff was always there to support me and the tough decisions I sometimes had to make. He was a true friend and a great mentor, and I learned volumes from him on the art of leadership and dealing with people, both skills of which he was a master!

Probably, the greatest lesson I have learned from Johnny Mac is the art of dealing with extreme adversity in the most positive way. I knew that he had tragically lost his father, and I was with him the night he lost his wife, Mellie. He also lost his son, John, who I knew and went to school with as a boy. Lesser men would have withered under such tribulation. But not John P. McDaniel! He marched on and still marches on, an example to us all that despite trials and tribulation, life must go on. He is always joyful when you see him, and I can honestly say that I have never heard him speak negatively about the painful things that he has suffered in his life. Rather than retreat into a shell of self-pity as most of us would, he constantly is out and about in our community upbeat about life. He cares about us, his neighbors, and if has the power to help others, he does.

John P. McDaniel is in my estimation the quintessential Jackson County man. He embodies many of the qualities that I personally strive for. I am proud to know him and even prouder to call him my friend!

Henry Mark Sims

Jimmy Standland
Retired / Classmate

Johnny Mac and I became friends when he came to school in Marianna from Magnolia. We played on the Marianna High School football team with him playing the guard position and me playing the nose guard position. We had successful winning seasons the four years we played. After high school, we were married and remained friends with our families, often getting together for cookouts, fishing, and hunting. Then Johnny moved from the area and was gone for a while. Years later, he returned to work for the Jackson County Sheriff's Department, ran for sheriff and was elected. I was then working for the state as a juvenile probation officer. I had to find a new office for my agency, and Johnny and I convinced the county to locate our office in with the sheriff's office. We worked hand in hand until I retired in 2002. We continue to be friends today. He was a great sheriff and friend.

Glenda F. Swearingen
Attorney at Law

When I think of Sheriff McDaniel, I think of strength, commitment, and substance. He served as sheriff in Jackson County, Florida, for many years. He was fondly referred to as "Johnny Mac." He was in touch with his citizenry and desired to protect the integrity in our small Southern county.

Glenda Swearingen

Guy Tunnell
Sheriff – Retired
Bay County Commissioner

When I was asked to provide a few words about my good friend, Johnny McDaniel, I was more honored than perhaps any other time I have been asked to contribute for someone. I'd like to sincerely thank those responsible for allowing me this wonderful opportunity.

At the same time, I was completely terrified! I mean, how was I going to be able to say something different than that which had already been said by some folks who'd known "Johnny Mac" since their childhood? What I can say, however, is straight from my heart.

I remember some time ago hearing a sermon on "pauses," and the pastor used our country's Pledge of Allegiance to make his point. We're all familiar with the line"...one nation, (pause) under God, (pause) indivisible..." What he was saying can be summed up as "In one's life, if something's important to them...if it's a priority...then there shouldn't be any pause!"

I've known Johnny Mack for some thirty years, and while we don't see one another or talk on the phone as often as we used to, over those many years, I've personally seen him in a number of life situations, some of the most terribly challenging and others the most joyous.

I can unequivocally say that when it came to priorities—his profession, his friends, his family, or his faith—Johnny Mac never paused. While not claiming to be perfect, he always knew what was most important in his life and committed himself to those ideals.

Though he'll probably disagree with me— strongly—I liken Johnny Mac to the fellow described in the first chapter of Psalms (chapter 1:1-3): "Blessed is the man who does not walk in the counsel of the wicked or stand in the way of sinners or sit in the seat of mockers, but his delight is in the law of the Lord, and on his law, he meditates day and night. He is like a tree planted by streams of water, which yields its fruit in season and whose leaf does not wither. Whatever he does prospers."

We've all been told that at the end of one's life, if they can count on one hand the number of true friends that they've had, then they were blessed indeed.

In my life, I've been extremely blessed to count on Johnny Mac as "one of my five."

Guy Tunnell

Joe F. Watson
Law Enforcement
Retired

In my thirty-plus years in law enforcement, I had the opportunity to meet many great officers. None of them were quite as iconic as Sheriff John P. McDaniel.

Johnny Mac unceasingly displayed enduring commitment, honesty, and integrity during his tenure as sheriff of Jackson County, Florida.

His legendary career began with his pursuit of serial killers who murdered his father and ended with the murder of his wife by ruthless murderers who intended to kill him also.

Johnny Mac's reputation for great personal sacrifice will live long after him. His undying devotion to justice and his commitment to fairness to those he served earned him an unsullied reputation as one of the greatest sheriff's ever to serve in modern law enforcement.

Joe F. Watson
Law Enforcement – Retired

PHOTOGRAPHS

John Perry McDaniel Sr. – Circa 1942

McDaniel old homeplace – eventually relocated to John III's
current property

J.W. Grant County Store – Circa 1946 (John's grandparents)

John at 3 months with his mother Ruth – January 1941

John at 2 years 1943

John at 4 with his dad, John Jr. – 1944

John with Jimmy Grant – 1948

McDaniel home place in Bascom

John's first school - Magnolia School in Oakdale – Circa 1948-50

Wayne, John, Iris and Ruth – Circa 1949

Church Johnny grew up attending – Marvin Chapel Freewill Baptist
Church – Circa 1958

Post office used by McDaniel's – Bascom – Circa 1941

Iris, Wayne and John – Circa 1947

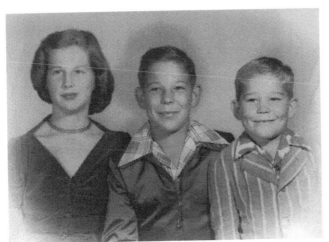

Iris, John and Wayne – Circa 1950

Grant Family Photo - Circa 1952 (Back Row: Eleanor Pearl Grant,
Iris McDaniel, Ruth McDaniel Hall, Annette, Moose LaPointe,
Ronald Eudon Grant, Wilson Grant, Jimmy Grant, Pauline Sellers
Grant, Elaine Alexander; Middle Row: Ruby Jean Collins, Virgil
Grant Collins, John Perry McDaniel III, Evelyn Owens Grant;
Marion Arthur Alexander IV, Front Row: Eleanor Joanne Collins,
William Wayne McDaniel, James William Grant, Laura Belle Davis
Grant

Johnny riding Jean and Joanne Collins on his Cushman Scooter –
1954

Johnny and Gwen Sexton - Prom 1956

Johnny – MHS Football – Circa 1958

John – Navy – Circa 1959

John – Navy Graduation, February 25, 1959

Marriage of Phyllis and John in July of 1961

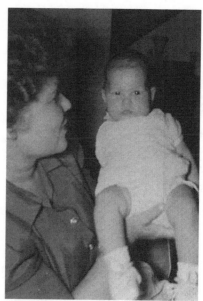

Baby Machelle and Grandma Ruth – Circa 1963

John and daughter Machelle – 1965

The four generations: John III holding baby John IV, John Jr and
John Sr. – Circa 1966

John III with son John IV – Gainsville 1968

John's mom Ruth

John's mom and her husband Lawrence Russell Owens

John's dad and his wife Helen Bender McDaniel

John and wife Linda – Campaign December 1979

Dana, Linda, Machelle and Little John – North Carolina vacation –
Circa 1979

John and Linda – Election Night – October 1980

John and daughter Machelle – Election Night – October 1980

John – First Campaign photo

John in office as sheriff for the first time

John making a traffic stop – Circa 1980

John and John Dennis – working through an investigation

Jackson County Sheriff's Office Group Photo - 1982: Back Row L to R: Claude Widner, Mike King, Rusty Booth, Louis Roberts III, Tommy Merritt, James Arthur Bevis, Eddie Ingram, Next Row: Jeff Skinner, Henry Keith, Dale Sims, Sharon Morris, Willie Nix, Frank Adams, Donnie Branch, Duane Davis. Next to Front: Ronald Grant, Doyle Hall, Billy Williams, Ann Trammell, Janet Thornton, Frances Malloy, Louie Seay, Front Row: John P. McDaniel, Gerry Baggett, Brenda Keys, Nancy Basford, Jim Williams

Sheriff McDaniel meeting with Lt. Wayne "Cowboy" Morris –
October 1983

Swearing in ceremony January 1981 – L to R: John P. McDaniel,
Duan Crews, Liz Alford, Sylvia Stephens, Betty Ford Hatcher,
and Robert L. McCrary

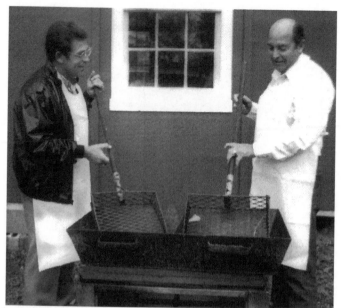

John and Marianna Chief Parmer – frying fish for benefit fund raisers

John – Back in Time Reenactment – September 1983

John and son Little John – Circa 1984

John as McGruff Crime Dog – 1984

Working a crime scene – June 1985 – L to R: Captain Gary Sullivan,
Chief Wiley George Pittman, Sheriff John McDaniel, Officer
Quinton Hollis

John and Verlie marriage – November 1988

John's new bride – Verlie – November 1988

John and James Bevis' mother at Memorial Wall – Circa 1988

First Lady visit – October 1990 – L to R: Rep. Coley; Barbara Bush, Marvin Harvey, Sharon Morris and John McDaniel

Sen. Pat Thomas and John – May 7, 1993

John in race benefitting youth ranches – May 30, 1994 – Boss Hogg
Speedway

John III, Carole and John IV at his son's wedding – April 1994

John and his mom Ruth – November 1996 Election Results

John with Governor Childs – December 14, 1998

John and Mellie's wedding – April 1999

Vacation with Mellie – Cherokee, NC – December 2000

Tara, Mellie and John – Vacation to Dollywood in 2000

Charlie Daniels, John and Mellie – 2005

John and Judge Woody Hatcher – March 2007

Celebrating the 4th of July with siblings – Cindy, John and Wayne

John feeding seagulls at beach with grandson Kaden – March 2015

John giving away Granddaughter Meghan - wedding
9/26/2009

Trip to the Last Frontier – Alaska 2015 – John
and Machelle

REFERENCES

Chapter 1
Interviews with John P. McDaniel III, 2013 - 2016
Jackson County Tax Books for 1936 – 1940, Jackson County Courthouse
Federal Census for Jackson County, Florida, 1936
State of Florida, County of Jackson, Central Bureau of Vital Statistics – Marriage License
State of Florida, County of Jackson, Central Bureau of Vital Statistics – Birth Certificate
Ibid
Individual pamphlets, books, photographs from the McDaniel Family Collection

Chapter 2
Interviews with John P. McDaniel III, 2013-2016
Weather Bureau, Washington, D.C. – The Weather of 1944 in the United States – January 1945
Interviews with John P. McDaniel III, 2013-2016
Jackson County Tax Books for 1945, Jackson County Courthouse
Federal Census for Jackson County, Florida, 1945

Chapter 3
Interviews with John P. McDaniel III, 2013-2016
Jackson County Tax Books for 1946, Jackson County Courthouse

Chapter 4
Interviews with John P. McDaniel III, 2013-2016
Marianna Jackson County Floridan, February 14, May 16, August 8, December 19, 1941 and January 22, 1943
Marianna Times, March 6, 1942

Marianna Jackson County Floridan, May 28, July 2, 1943, February 25, 1944
Jackson County Commissioners Minutes, December 30, 1942, March 26, 1943, April 9, May 28, 1943
Marianna Jackson County Floridan, December 25, 1942, October 13, 1944, September 28, 1945
Jackson County Commissioners Minutes, January 8, 1946
Marianna Jackson County Floridan, June 8, 1945

Chapter 5
Interviews with John P. McDaniel III, 2013-2016
Jackson County Tax Books for 1946-48, Jackson County Courthouse
Federal Census for Jackson County, Florida, 1946-48
State of Florida, County of Jackson, Central Bureau of Vital Statistics – Divorce Record

Chapter 6
Interviews with John P. McDaniel III, 2013-2016
Individual pamphlets, books, photographs from the McDaniel Family Collection
Federal Census for Jackson County, Florida, 1946-48
Jackson County Times, July 31, 2008 – Great Flood of 1947 Remembered

Chapter 7
Interviews with John P. McDaniel III, 2013-2016
Federal Census for Jackson County, Florida, 1946-48
Chapter 8
Interviews with John P. McDaniel III, 2013-2016

Chapter 9
Interviews with John P. McDaniel III, 2013-2016
Jackson County Tax Books for 1948-50, Jackson County Courthouse

445

State of Florida, County of Jackson, Central Bureau of Vital Statistics – Marriage License
State of Florida, County of Jackson, Central Bureau of Vital Statistics – Birth Certificate
State of Florida, County of Jackson, Central Bureau of Vital Statistics – Divorce Record

Chapter 10
Interviews with John P. McDaniel III, 2013-2016

Chapter 11
Interviews with John P. McDaniel III, 2013-2016

Chapter 12
Interviews with John P. McDaniel III, 2013-2016
National Aviation Flight Safety Organization Report Occurrence # 156276 Jackson County
Jackson County Floridan, July 25, 1952
Jackson County Floridan, November 2, 2015 – Campaign Begins for B47 Crash Marker

Chapter 13
Interviews with John P. McDaniel III, 2013-2016
Individual pamphlets, books, photographs from the McDaniel Family Collection

Chapter 14
Interviews with John P. McDaniel III, 2013-2016

Chapter 15
Interviews with John P. McDaniel III, 2013-2016
State of Florida, County of Jackson, Central Bureau of Vital Statistics – Marriage License
Jackson County Florida, May 26, 1958

Chapter 16

Interviews with John P. McDaniel III, 2013-2016
United States Navy Department of Defense, June 1958 –
Enlistment Roster

Chapter 17
Interviews with John P. McDaniel III, 2013-2016

Chapter 18
Interviews with John P. McDaniel III, 2013-2016
State of Florida, County of Jackson, Central Bureau of Vital
Statistics – Marriage License
Jackson County Floridan, July 30, 1961
Jackson County Chamber of Commerce, Life in Jackson
County – 1965

Chapter 19
Interviews with John P. McDaniel III, 2013-2016
World History Project – 1962
Jackson County Floridan, April 23, 1963
Jackson County Floridan, May 4, 1963
Jackson County Floridan, October 15, 1965
Jackson County Floridan, August 17, 1968
Jackson County Floridan, April 21, 1969
Jackson County Floridan, February 17, 1972
Jackson County Floridan, October, 5, 1972

Chapter 20
Interviews with John P. McDaniel III, 2013-2016
Jackson County Tax Books for 1973, Jackson County
Courthouse
Jackson County Commissioners Minutes, January 9, 1973

Chapter 21
Interviews with John P. McDaniel III, 2013-2016
Jackson County Commissioners Minutes, February 13, April
10, July 10, 1973

Chapter 22
Interviews with John P. McDaniel III, 2013-2016

Chapter 23
Interviews with John P. McDaniel III, 2013-2016

Chapter 24
Interviews with John P. McDaniel III, 2013-2016
Jackson County Supervisor of Elections Official Records –
September 1976
State of Florida, County of Jackson, Central Bureau of Vital
Statistics – Divorce Record
Interview with then Deputy John Dennis
Jackson County Tax Books for 1976-78, Jackson County
Courthouse
Jackson County 14th Judicial Circuit Trial Records of Jimmy
Lee Smith
Florida US Court of Appeals for the 11th Circuit – Jimmy
Lee Smith case findings
Supreme Court of Florida – Jimmy Lee Smith v Richard L.
Dugger, etc., et al.,
Jackson County Floridan, October 29, 2006 – Parole
Hearing
State of Florida, County of Jackson, Central Bureau of Vital
Statistics – Marriage License
Jackson County Floridan, April 6, 1980

Chapter 25
Interviews with John P. McDaniel III, 2013-2016
Individual pamphlets, books, photographs from the
McDaniel Family Collection
Jackson County Floridan, June 8, 1980
Jackson County Floridan, July 2, 1980
Jackson County Floridan, September 2, 3, 7, 10, 1980

Jackson County Supervisor of Elections Official Records of First Primary – September 9, 1980
Jackson County Floridan, October 5, 1980
Jackson County Supervisor of Elections Official Records Second Primary and Special Election – October 7, 1980
Jackson County Floridan, October 8, 12, 1980
Jackson County Floridan, November 6, 1980

Chapter 26
Interviews with John P. McDaniel III, 2013-2016
Individual pamphlets, books, photographs from the McDaniel Family Collection
Interviews with then Deputy John Dennis, 2014-2016
Interviews with then Deputy Donnie Branch, 2016
Jackson County Sheriff's Department Investigative File 80-12-01
Jackson County 14th Judicial Circuit Court Case 89-435
Florida Department of Law Enforcement Case Number 522-01-0135 and 801211839
Graceville Police Department Case 80-12-28
Jackson County Floridan, December 16, 17, 1980
Jackson County Floridan, January 1, 21, 23, 1981
Jackson County Floridan, May 4, 1989

Chapter 27
Interviews with John P. McDaniel III, 2013-2016
Individual pamphlets, books, photographs from the McDaniel Family Collection
Jackson County Floridan, January 7, 15, 1981

Chapter 28
Interviews with John P. McDaniel III, 2013-2016
Jackson County Floridan, February 22, 25, 1981
Jackson County Commissioners Minutes, February 24, March 10, March 24, 1981

Jackson County Floridan, March 11, 19, 21, April 15, 16, 29, May 7, 17, June 3, 1981

D.O.C. Inspection Report of Jackson County Jail – March 24, April 21, 1981

Jackson County Tax Books for 1981-82, Jackson County Courthouse

Chapter 29
Interviews with John P. McDaniel III, 2013-2016
Jackson County Floridan, June 23, July 11, 15, August 11, 1981
Panama City News Herald, June 28, July 11, 1981

Chapter 30
Interviews with John P. McDaniel III, 2013-2016
Individual pamphlets, books, photographs from the McDaniel Family Collection
Memorial – Marvin Chapel Freewill Baptist Church, Marianna

Chapter 31
Interviews with John P. McDaniel III, 2013-2016

Chapter 32
Interviews with John P. McDaniel III, 2013-2016
Jackson County Floridan, October 18, 21, November 5, 15, 11, 17, 22, 25, December 3, 9, 16, 27, 31, 1981

Chapter 33
Interviews with John P. McDaniel III, 2013-2016
State of Florida, County of Jackson, Central Bureau of Vital Statistics – Divorce Record

Chapter 34
Interviews with John P. McDaniel III, 2013-2016
Interviews with then Inv. John Dennis, 2014-2016

Jackson County Floridan, March 5, 1985
Washington County Sheriff's Office – Investigative File 85-03-0032
United States District Court – Northern District of Florida – Panama City Division – Case No. MCA 86-2002-RV – Thomas "Jack" Fitzgerald vs. John P. McDaniel and Wayne "Cowboy" Morris as Sheriff and Deputy Sheriff of Jackson County, Florida, respectively
United States Court of Appeals Eleventh Circuit – Case No. 87-3135 – John P. McDaniel and Wayne "Cowboy" Morris vs. Thomas "Jack" Fitzgerald.

Chapter 40
Interviews with John P. McDaniel III, 2013-2016

Chapter 41
Interviews with John P. McDaniel III, 2013-2016
Jackson County Commissioners Minutes, March 12, 1985
Jackson County Floridan, March 13, 21, 1985

Chapter 42
Interviews with John P. McDaniel III, 2013-2016
Interviews with then Inv. John Dennis, 2014-2016
Interview with then dispatcher Hayes Baggett, 2014
Jackson County Sheriff's Department Investigative File Documents
Jackson County Clerk of Court – Case File and Trial Documents
Jackson County Floridan, April 5, 7, 9, 1985

Chapter 43
Interviews with John P. McDaniel III, 2013-2016
Interviews with Officer Quinton Hollis, 2014-2016
Jackson County Floridan, June 18, 19, 1985
Jackson County Clerk of Court – Case File and Trial Documents

Chapter 44
Interviews with John P. McDaniel III, 2013-2016
Interviews with then Chief Deputy John Dennis, 2014-2016
Jackson County Tax Books for 1985-86, Jackson County
Courthouse

Chapter 45
Interviews with John P. McDaniel III, 2013-2016
Interview with then Commissioner Ernie Padgett, 2016
Interview with then County Manager Leon Foster, 2016
Interview with Machelle McDaniel Campbell, 2013-2016

Chapter 46
Interviews with John P. McDaniel III, 2013-2016

Chapter 47
Interviews with John P. McDaniel III, 2013-2016
Jackson County Supervisor of Elections Office – Official
Records of Jackson County Presidential Preference Primary
- March 8, 1988
Interview with then County Manager Leon Foster, 2016
Interview with then Administrative Director of Jackson
County Sheriff's Office Jim Williams, 2016
Interview with then County Administrator Ernie Padgett,
2016
Interview with then Jail Warden Sammy Efurd, 2014

Chapter 48
Interviews with John P. McDaniel III, 2013-2016
Individual pamphlets, books, photographs from the
McDaniel Family Collection
Interviews with then Chief Deputy John Dennis, 2014-2016
Interviews with then FDLE Special Agent Donnie Branch,
2016

Jackson County Sheriff's Department Investigative File 80-12-01

Jackson County 14th Judicial Circuit Court Case 89-435

Florida Department of Law Enforcement Case Number 522-01-0135 and 801211839

Graceville Police Department Case 80-12-28

Jackson County Floridan, May 4, 1989, December 16, 1990, September 22, 1991

Chapter 49
Interviews with John P. McDaniel III, 2013-2016
Interviews with then Chief Deputy John Dennis, 2014-2016
Jackson County Floridan, August 7, 9, 1988
Jackson County – The Monitor, August 11, 1988
Jackson County Clerk of Court – Case File and Trial Documents

Chapter 50
Interviews with John P. McDaniel III, 2013-2016
Jackson County Floridan, August 16, 17, 1988

Chapter 51
Interviews with John P. McDaniel III, 2013-2016
Jackson County Supervisor of Elections Official Records of First Primary – September 6, 1988
Jackson County Floridan, September 7, 1988

Chapter 52
Interviews with John P. McDaniel III, 2013-2016
State of Florida, County of Jackson, Central Bureau of Vital Statistics – Marriage License

Chapter 53
Interviews with John P. McDaniel III, 2013-2016
Interviews with then Chief Deputy John Dennis, 2014-2016

Jackson County Floridan, January 22, 31, February 1, 2, 1989
Tuscaloosa News, October 16, 2002
Robert A. Waters, Writer of Blog Kidnapping, Murder and Mayhem, January 28,2013

Chapter 54
Interviews with John P. McDaniel III, 2013-2016
Interviews with then Chief Deputy John Dennis, 2014-2016
Jackson County Floridan, March 14, October 1, 1989

Chapter 55
Interviews with John P. McDaniel III, 2013-2016
Interviews with Carole McDaniel Barnes, 2013-2014
Geneva County Sheriff's Department Records
Hartford Police Department Records
Alabama State Troopers Records
Interview with retired Alabama State Trooper Earnest Tyson
Interview with Director of Bottoms Funeral Home
Meadowlawn Funeral Home in Hartford
Pondtown United Methodist Church Cemetery Records
Interview with Carrie Elizabeth Justice Family Member
Dothan Eagle, December 17, 1990

Chapter 56
Interviews with John P. McDaniel III, 2013-2016
State of Florida, County of Leon, Central Bureau of Vital Statistics – Divorce Record

Chapter 57
Interviews with John P. McDaniel III, 2013-2016
Interviews with then Chief Deputy John Dennis, 2014-2016
Interviews with then FDLE Special Agent Donnie Branch, 2015-2016
Jackson County Floridan, December 10, 11, 12, 13, 17, 20, 1991

WTVY – Channel 4 – Headline News, December 24, 2008
Jackson County Floridan, May 3, 2009
Jackson County Tax Books for 1991, Jackson County Courthouse
Cypress Baptist Church Cemetery Records
WJHG – News Channel 7 – Headline News, May 4, 2009
WJHG – News Channel 7 – Headline News, December 10, 2012

Chapter 58
Interviews with John P. McDaniel III, 2013-2016
Interview with Leon Foster, 2016
Interview with then Jail Warden, Sammy Efurd, 2016
Interviews with then County Administrator Ernie Padgett, 2016-2017
Jackson County Tax Books for 1990-1994, Jackson County Courthouse
Interview with then Administrative Director of Jackson County Sheriff's Office Jim Williams, 2016
Jackson County Commissioners Minutes, May 30, 1991
Jackson County Commissioners Minutes, February 2, April 17, 1992
Memorial – Marvin Chapel Freewill Baptist Church, Marianna
State of Florida, County of Jackson, Central Bureau of Vital Statistics – Marriage License

Chapter 59
Interviews with John P. McDaniel III, 2013-2016
Jackson County Floridan, September 4, November 6, 1996
Jackson County Supervisor of Elections Office – Official Records of Jackson County – 1996

Chapter 60
Interviews with John P. McDaniel III, 2013-2016

Individual pamphlets, books, photographs from the McDaniel Family Collection
Jackson County Commissioners Minutes, January 27, March 24, April 14, June 9, July 30, December 17, 1998
State of Florida, County of Jackson, Central Bureau of Vital Statistics – Marriage License
Jackson County Commissioners Minutes, March 9, 23, April 13, May 25, June 8, August 10, 24, September 28, October 8, November 9, 23, 1999

Chapter 61
Interviews with John P. McDaniel III, 2013-2016
Jackson County Commissioners Minutes, February 22, May 23, October 10, 2000
Jackson County Floridan, September 5, 6, 7, 2000
Jackson County Supervisor of Elections Office – Official Records of Jackson County – 2000
Interview with then Deputy Billy Dozier, July 2015

Chapter 62
Interviews with John P. McDaniel III, 2013-2016
Interview with Carole McDaniel Barnes, 2014
Individual pamphlets, books, photographs from the McDaniel Family Collection
Jackson County Floridan, June 10, 11, 2001, June 24, 2004
Cottondale First Baptist Church Cemetery Records

Chapter 63
Interviews with John P. McDaniel III, 2013-2016
Jackson County Commissioners Minutes, August 24, 2004
Jackson County Floridan, August 31, September 1, 2, 3, 4, 2004

Chapter 64
Interviews with John P. McDaniel III, 2013-2016

457

Individual pamphlets, books, photographs from the McDaniel Family Collection
Marvin Chapel Freewill Baptist Church Cemetery Records
Interviews with then Chief Deputy John Dennis, 2014-2016
Jackson County Commissioners Minutes, June 13, 2006
Jackson County Floridan, June 27, 28, 29, 2006
Ocala Star Banner, June 30, 2006

Chapter 65
Interviews with John P. McDaniel III, 2013-2016
Individual pamphlets, books, photographs from the McDaniel Family Collection
Interview with CPL Billy Dozier, July 29, 2015
Interviews with then Chief Deputy John Dennis, 2014-2016
Florida Department of Law Enforcement Case Number: PC-27-008
Interview with FDLE Special Agent Jimmy Gilbert, 2015
Jackson County Floridan, January 31, February 1, 2, 4, 2007
Panama City News Herald, January 31, 2007
Dothan Eagle, February 4, 2007

Chapter 66
Interviews with John P. McDaniel III, 2013-2016
Individual pamphlets, books, photographs from the McDaniel Family Collection
Interview with Rev. Jack Hollis
Memorial James & Sikes Funeral Home

Chapter 67
Interviews with John P. McDaniel III, 2013-2016
Interviews with Machelle McDaniel Campbell, 2013-2016
Jackson County Times, July 19, August 30, 2007, March 27, October 30, November 6, 2008
Alford City Cemetery Records

Jackson County Supervisor of Elections Official Records – 2008
Jackson County Floridan, November 5, 2008

Chapter 68
Interviews with John P. McDaniel III, 2013-2016
Jackson County Times, November 13, 2008
Jackson County Tax Books for 2007-2008, Jackson County Courthouse

Chapter 69
Interviews with John P. McDaniel III, 2013-2016
Individual pamphlets, books, photographs from the McDaniel Family Collection

Chapter 70
Interviews with John P. McDaniel III, 2013-2016
Individual pamphlets, books, photographs from the McDaniel Family Collection

Chapter 71
Interviews with John P. McDaniel III, 2013-2016
Individual pamphlets, books, photographs from the McDaniel Family Collection

ACKNOWLEDGEMENTS

I would like to personally thank all who made this book possible. Almost four years ago, I set about to complete a book about the life of John P. McDaniel III. The further down the road I went, the more my fear rose. How could mere words on paper depict such a great man's life?

I originally did so because I considered the events which made the McDaniel administration a long-standing success to be of historical significance to Jackson County, Florida. I came to realize that tucked away in Johnny Mac's recollections, reminiscences, and remembrances are not only the unique and intriguing stories of his life but a living anecdotal history of Jackson County, Florida, during a period of rapid growth and turbulent times. I also discovered a man whose faith in God led him through every event in his life.

I hope through the pages contained in this book you have come to know and appreciate Johnny Mac as I do. He is an unforgettable character from the child, son, father, husband, friend, and survivor, to the man behind the badge. He is a throwback to the days when a handshake was all that was needed to finalize a deal—a self-made, God fearing man of courage. I am proud to call him my friend.

Thank you, Johnny Mac, for opening up your whole life in the many interviews and enduring repeated brain-picking sessions and phone-calls. I love you dearly.

Many thanks to John Dennis for the numerous interviews and hours you provided, reviewing dates and cases which helped me better capture accurate timelines.

Thanks Sgt. Quinton Hollis for believing in this endeavor and providing photos and much needed details when I became stumped.

Thanks to Sue Tindel. Your assistance from the archives at the Jackson County Courthouse was invaluable.

Professor Dean DeBolt, university librarian university archivist at University Archives and West Florida History Center. I don't know what I would have done without the massive contributions from your archives.

Thanks to Dale Guthrie for your assistance and guidance with old cases and records at the Jackson County Courthouse.

Thanks to the Jackson County Sheriff's Office Records Division.

Thanks to FDLE – Florida Department of Law Enforcement Records Division and Special Agent Jimmy Gilbert for your tremendous insight.

A very special thanks to all the contributors for the commemorative section. Your reminiscences and remembrances added an extra breath of life to a man that is truly "Everything to Everybody."

ABOUT THE AUTHOR

R. L. Dodson grew up in Southern Alabama and holds a B.S. in History and Criminal Justice. She spent twenty years working in the Criminal Justice arena in the northern panhandle of Florida, where she now resides. From an early age, she loved to read and later wrote poetry.

She enjoys writing, spending time with her daughter, Jade; granddaughters, DeLayne, JaLynne, and Benzley; and her four-footed baby, Belladonna.

She also enjoys visits to her mom; sister, Deb; brother-in-law, Mark; and nephews, Matt (Ana) and Brewer. And she can't leave out their four-footed babies, Colt and Chambers.

She has published two fiction novels in the justice series: *Heart of Jaded Justice* and *Eternal Justice*.

The High Sheriff: John P. McDaniel III is her first non-fiction book. She hopes you enjoy taking this journey with her.

ABOUT THE EDITOR

Jeff LaFerney taught English/language arts for thirty years in Davison, Michigan. He was an English major with a master's degree in educational leadership. Jeff has written five novels of his own, two of which were award winners. For the past seven years, he has also been using his knowledge to edit books. Visit his blog, "The Red Pen," to learn more about his editing. http://jefflaferney.blogspot.com/

73177707R00262

Made in the USA
Columbia, SC
06 July 2017